ATTORNEYS
From Charles Town to Charleston

ATTORNEYS

From Charles Town to Charleston

RUTH W. CUPP

ASSOCIATION PUBLISHING COMPANY
Birmingham, Alabama

ATTORNEYS

From Charles Town to Charleston

Published By
ASSOCIATION PUBLISHING COMPANY
100 Oxmoor Road, Suite 110, Birmingham, Alabama 35209
(205) 941-4623

JOHN COMPTON, Publisher

Published with the cooperation and assistance of
THE CHARLESTON COUNTY BAR ASSOCIATION
JOSEPH McGEE, Project Chairman

Written By
RUTH W. CUPP

Consultant and Special Advisor to the Author
ALEXANDER MOORE, PH.D.

Law Firm History Writer
HUNTER H. KERRISON

Design By
ROBIN McDONALD

Editor
ALISON GLASCOCK

Photo Editor
MIKE COKER

Index Editor
JIM SUMMERVILLE

Published 2006

Printed in the United States of America by
TAYLOR PUBLISHING COMPANY
DALLAS, TEXAS

FIRST EDITION

ISBN 0-966-8380-6-8

Library of Congress Catalog Card Number 2005 936 760

Title spread: St. Michael's Church, representing religious law, and the U.S. Courthouse, representing federal law, are two of Charleston's famous Four Corners of Law.

TABLE OF CONTENTS

FOREWORD

Ladies and Gentleman of the Charleston County Bar,

In 1699, Nicholas Trott stepped off an English ship at the small settlement called Charles Town. He landed on a peninsula, Oyster Point, between the Ashley and Cooper rivers and found before him a small walled city with few inhabitants.

Trott had studied law at the Inner Temple of London. As Charleston's first practicing lawyer, he introduced the English legal system to colonial South Carolina.

After more than 300 years and with almost 2,000 members of the South Carolina Bar residing in Charleston County, it was clearly time that an authoritative history of the bar be prepared and presented to its members and to the general public.

Drawing on her own deep knowledge of local history and after thorough and extensive research over the past four years, Ruth Cupp has produced a wonderful history of the Charleston County Bar Association. Clearly, this book is a gift to future generations of lawyers and the present members of the Charleston County Bar. As you will see, the history of the bar is intrinsically entwined with the culture, politics, and everyday affairs of the people of this great American city.

We are well aware of the pride that members of the bar in Charleston County share with each other. There is a well-deserved reputation of cordiality, honesty, and diligence in the practice of law. Charleston is a unique place. Its history, well-documented and varied in this fine book, joins together with the history of our profession for all to enjoy. Thank you, Ruth, for your wonderful book and for sharing it with all of us in the Charleston County Bar.

Sincerely,

Francis X. McCann
President, Charleston County Bar Association

October 17, 2005

The Grand Courtroom is the centerpiece of the historic Charleston County Courthouse. The restored courtroom reopened on March 19, 2002, with a session of the South Carolina Supreme Court.

CHAPTER I

IN THE BEGINNING

THE SETTLEMENT OF CAROLINA AND its metropolis, Charles Town, by the English during the great European migration of the 1600s brought with it the enduring legacy of the "rights of Englishmen" created by the Magna Carta of 1215, centuries of Parliamentary statutes, and English common law. The Carolina settlers brought with them to the New World a tradition which sought to limit the discretionary power of judges, ecclesiastical courts, and lawyers. They were the constitutional heirs of Henry II, Edward Coke, and Oliver Cromwell. The 1670 Carolina settlers arrived under the immediate sponsorship of eight British dukes, earls, and knights, and the authority these Lords Proprietors of Carolina wielded was based upon a grant from King Charles II.

King Charles I had asserted England's rights to North America by virtue of the 1497 discoveries of John Cabot, the first European explorer to reach the North American mainland. Cabot's expeditions carried letters patent from King Henry VII of England and the mariner was hence a royal employee. In 1629, Charles I granted to his attorney general, Sir Robert Heath, all the lands of North America between 31° and 36° latitude north under the name of Carolana. A few attempts were made to settle the southern part of the continent under the Heath Charter but all failed. When Charles II recovered the British throne in 1660, he declared Heath's charter forfeited and in 1663 granted the land to eight friends who had aided greatly in his restoration. The eight Proprietors were Edward Hyde, Earl of Clarendon; George Monck, Duke of Albemarle; Lord William Craven; Sir John Berkeley; Sir Anthony Ashley Cooper; Sir George Carteret; Sir William Berkeley; and Sir John Colleton. For these Lords Proprietors, the settlement of Carolina was a commercial enterprise. Heath's heirs demanded compensation for the loss of their charter and were given 100,000 acres in the interior of New York. The Lords Proprietors secured a second charter, dated June 30, 1665, and added the Bahama Islands to their empire. The King's grant gave the Lords Proprietors certain royal privileges to exercise in their own right but, despite this grant of powers, Carolina remained an English colony. The Proprietors' privileges included the right to create a distinctive structure of government and to pardon felons. Criminal indictments were to read that offenses were committed against the Lords' peace, rather than against the King's peace.

Before he earned fame as a political philosopher and proponent of religious and political tolerance, John Locke was secretary and physician to Lord Ashley Cooper, the Palatine, or chief Proprietor. Together, the two men crafted a written document, the *Fundamental Constitutions of Carolina*, in July 1669. The *Constitutions* contained specific

ABOVE: *When Charles II recovered the British throne in 1660, he declared the Heath Charter forfeited and in 1663 granted the land to eight friends who had aided greatly in his restoration. These eight were the Lords Proprietors. For these Lords Proprietors, the settlement of Carolina was a commercial enterprise.* OPPOSITE PAGE: *The seal of the Lords Proprietors of South Carolina.*

articles covering legal practice in Carolina and one of those articles prohibited attorneys from practicing their profession, saying "It shall be a base and vile thing to Plead for money or Reward..." The origins of this principle and some others in the *Fundamental Constitutions* were in the writings of James Harrington, a contemporary of the political philosopher, Thomas Hobbes, and author of the utopian political tract, *Oceana.* The *Constitutions* also guaranteed religious freedom to all faiths, including non-Christians.

The first ships with about 130 people left England in August 1669 and arrived on the Carolina coast in March 1670. The settlers founded Charles Town and quickly took control of the coastal regions surrounding their settlement. They were entrepreneurs and ruthless exploiters of the Native Americans and of their environment. But, they survived and eventually began to thrive in their unusual proprietary colony. It is important to record that they never adopted any of the five versions of the *Fundamental Constitutions* that the Proprietors offered them. The settlers did, however, uphold and support limited concepts of religious freedom. The Anglican Church was established as the state church in 1706 and received public funds, but, unlike some of the New England colonies, no nonconformist church member's basic freedom of worship was prohibited or persecuted in any way. Of course, Roman Catholicism was proscribed but that restriction was so universal in the English colonies as to be unremarkable.

ABOVE: *Lord Ashley Cooper, the Palatine, or chief Proprietor, and his secretary and physician John Locke (left), crafted a written document, the* Fundamental Constitutions of Carolina, *in July 1669.* OPPOSITE PAGE, ABOVE: *Charles Towne Landing is a reconstruction of the original settlement on Albemarle Point.* OPPOSITE PAGE, BELOW: *This illustration imagines the moving of Charles Town away from its original location on Albemarle Point.*

The surviving records of the colony identify 684 names of people who arrived in the first decade of settlement (1670-1680), none of whom were practicing attorneys. The first settlers planted Charles Town on a rise of land on the south bank of the Ashley River, called Albemarle Point.

The functions of colonial government were vested in a governor and Grand Council, both of whom were appointed by the Lords Proprietors, and a Commons House of Assembly, whose delegates were elected by the settlers. The General Assembly was the joint Council and Commons House. As laymen, the members of the Grand Council roughly administered justice in the first decades of the colony. Despite the absence of lawyers or courts, litigation began as early as 1671. English common law arrived in Carolina with the first settlers, who tenaciously claimed it as their birthright. The *Fundamental Constitutions* and the two Carolina Charters recognized the authority of common law. (Common laws are those rules which do not rest for their authority upon any expressed statute, but rather upon precedents and statements of principles found in the decisions of the courts.)

The court system included the Court of Common Pleas (civil actions), the King's Bench (criminal actions), Chancery (an equity court), and the Vice-Admiralty Court

(maritime torts, some contracts, and some special causes). The actions of this last court would later be a source of conflict between the Crown and the Proprietors. All of the judges were lay people prior to 1700. Historian and attorney Edward McCrady found evidence of the Court of Common Pleas in operation as early as 1693 and he described it as a "…scene of altercation and confusion; that bold and seditious speeches were made from the bar in contempt of the proprietors and their government."

An English barrister, Stephen Bull, arrived with the first fleet aboard the *Carolina* but he did not come to practice law. He came as a deputy of one of the Lords Proprietors. James Colleton, Esquire, third son of Proprietor Sir John Colleton, was another attorney who came to Carolina but did not practice law. He was in the colony before 1672, served a two-year term as governor beginning in 1686, and was later forced by a legal *coup d'etat* to abandon the province in 1690.

By 1680, the settlers had relocated Charles Town to the peninsula called Oyster Point, between the Ashley and Cooper rivers, and constructed a walled city on the Cooper River side of the peninsula. On three sides they built walls of logs covered by earth with an outer moat. A substantial brick wall defended the fourth side, along the waterfront, and a drawbridge across the moat was

constructed on Broad Street, just west of present-day Meeting Street.

The British Parliament enacted a series of Navigation Acts in 1696 which the Crown used as a basis for establishing a chain of colonial vice-admiralty courts. The constitutional issue of proprietary versus royal authority over this court created friction during the whole Proprietary period. The Navigation Act of 1696 was a part of the

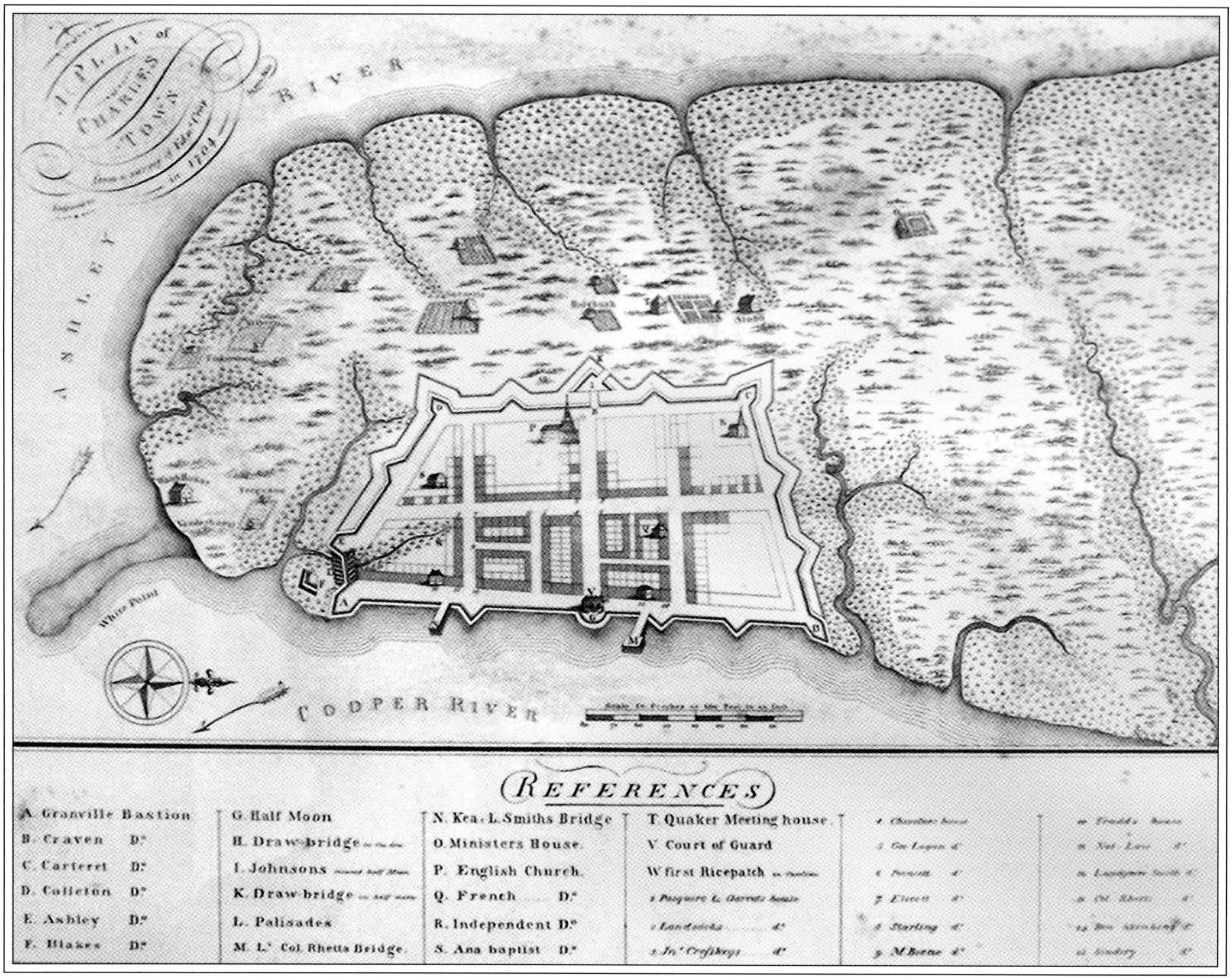

Crown's reorganization of its revenue machinery and the Vice-Admiralty Court in Charles Town generated more revenue from customs and ship condemnations than any other court in the English colonies.

Historian George C. Rogers described South Carolina before 1700 as "a rude frontier society." Edward McCrady dated the beginning of the legal profession from the arrival in 1699 of Nicholas Trott, political veteran, seasoned advocate, and legal scholar. His rise to power in Charles Town certainly signaled the introduction of English legal training into the colonial judicial system. Trott had been schooled at the Inner Temple of London and was a man of considerable erudition. Abel Ketleby, another attorney, also arrived that year. He had studied law in the Middle Temple and at Oxford, but Ketleby did not open a law practice or secure appointment to the bench.

Trott arrived with a commission from the Lords Proprietors to be Attorney General, Advocate General, and Naval Officer in the Vice-Admiralty Court. He promptly

The 1704 Crisp map is one of the earliest maps of Charles Town, showing its second location on Oyster Point, a peninsula located between the Ashley and Cooper rivers.

became directly involved in the operation of this court and in conflict with the presiding judge, who had been appointed by the Crown. Conveniently for Trott, the Crown's appointee to the Advocate General post died in the summer of 1699, the year Trott arrived. Disagreements between Trott and Admiralty Judge Joseph Morton led Morton to prevail upon the Council to suspend Trott's commission. This issue of dual responsibility in the Vice Admiralty Court was never solved during the Proprietary period. After he was suspended, Trott was elected to the Commons House of Assembly and became its speaker. In this capacity, he engineered an admiralty law change and secured a repeal of his suspension. In 1703, the Proprietors appointed Trott to be the first Chief Justice of South Carolina who was schooled in the law. Sometime between 1708 and 1714, Trott convinced the Proprietors to appoint him to the Council.

Then, in 1716, the Proprietors appointed him to be Vice-Admiralty Court judge. As his fortunes improved, Trott lost interest in the tug-of-war between the Crown and the Proprietors over the Vice-Admiralty Court. However, the more his rapport with the Proprietors increased, the more he lost influence with local attorneys and other settlers, who had begun to actively oppose the Proprietors' government.

Throughout this period, immigrants were arriving daily, swelling the population of the settlement and pressing their way into the Carolina hinterland but there were still no courts established outside of Charles Town. The first trial records date from 1703 and they continue in near complete succession to the present. Since the beginning of the twentieth century, these priceless documents have been kept in the South Carolina Department of Archives and History in Columbia.

Between 1703 and 1720, court records reveal that 16 lawyers were admitted to the practice of law in Charles Town. In 1712, the General Assembly enacted a broad "reception" statute and with it adopted or "received" into South Carolina certain English statutes and Parliamentary decrees by name that were to be in force and effect henceforth in the colony. Among them were the Magna Carta of 1215, the Petition of Rights of 1628, the Habeas Corpus Act of 1670, and the Bill of Rights of 1689.

In October 1718, Charles Town was the scene of the most celebrated trials of the Proprietary era. These were a series of piracy trials and Nicholas Trott, Vice Admiralty judge, presided over them. Major Stede Bonnet, the "gentleman pirate," and 33 of his crew members were captured off the coast of Cape Fear on October 3, 1718, by Colonel William Rhett and his experienced seamen. Rhett brought his captives to Charles Town for trial. The seamen were locked in the watch tower at the southwest corner of Meeting and Broad streets while Bonnet was put under house arrest at the home of the Provost Marshall.

Trott appointed ten assistant judges, all laymen, to assist him with the trials. Under the English law of that time, defendants were denied counsel as it was the judge's duty to see that the accused had a fair trial. One of Bonnet's crewmen turned state's evidence and the trials against the pirates commenced. Bonnet came before the court on November 10, 1718, and, arraigned on an indictment of piracy, pleaded "not guilty." Trott brought into Bonnet's case testimony taken in the previous trials against the seamen at which Bonnet was not present. Upon such inadmissible testimony, Trott found him guilty. Trott's conduct on the bench was overbearing and self-aggrandizing. He availed himself of the practice of the times by interrogating the defendant. The next day Bonnet was arraigned on a second charge. On the third day, November 12, Trott delivered one of his remarkable charges to the jury, described by Edward McCrady as "...a most learned one, exhibiting erudition, quoting from many authors in Latin and Greek, and though it would be regarded to-day as pedantic, was a most able exposition of the law of the case." Bonnet changed his plea to guilty and was sentenced to death. He was hanged at White Point, the spit of land at the confluence of the Ashley and Cooper rivers, probably on December 10.

The definition of piracy which Trott framed for this trial was cited by legal scholars throughout the eighteenth and nineteenth centuries. He published a transcript of the trial

Pirates and their gold were welcome in early Charles Town until the town became the target of their attacks.

in London and it was used as a primary source of information by the famous British writer, Daniel Defoe, in his *General History of Pirates*.

Trott's aggregation of nearly all of the province's legal power unto himself set the stage for all of the other members of the bar to turn against him and sign a petition to have him removed from his offices. Charles Town's bar had nine members and each signed the 1719 petition, which contained 31 articles condemning Chief Justice Trott's corruption and tyranny. Among other malfeasances, it stated that he was guilty of partial judgments; that he contrived many ways to multiply and increase his fees contrary to the Acts of Assembly, and to the great grievance of the subjects; that he assessed a fee for continuing cases from one term to another, then put off the hearings for several years; that he took upon himself to give advice on cases pending in his court; that he had shown partiality in court-contested matters involving documents he had drawn; and that the whole judicial powers of the province were lodged in his hands alone of which he made very ill use, he being the sole judge of the Pleas, the King's Bench, the Vice Admiralty, and "one of the council and of consequence" in the court of chancery. The Assembly endorsed these allegations but Trott retorted that he was answerable only to the Proprietors. The Assembly sent the petition with the endorsement by courier to England, where the Proprietors ignored it.

Colonel William Rhett (above) led the capture of Major Stede Bonnet, the "gentleman pirate," and 33 of his crew members in 1718.

Trott's alleged malfeasances and the condoning of them by the Proprietors were two of several grievances the colonists had against the Proprietors by the year 1719. The Proprietors had failed to provide assistance and even obstructed the Crown's attempt to send assistance during the devastating Yemassee War. The Proprietors refused because they thought the Crown would charge the Proprietors for the cost and they vetoed several acts of Assembly that were cornerstones of Carolina's government.

By the fall of 1719, the colonists determined to overthrow the Proprietors' government and seek Crown protection. Several Charles Town attorneys, including Thomas Hepworth, Benjamin Whitaker, and Robert Hume, were among the conspirators. On December 16, 1719, rebellious Commons House members constituted themselves a convention of "Representatives of the People" and drafted a document, "Resolutions of the Convention of the People of South Carolina," that spelled out the grievances against the Proprietors. The Convention requested Governor Robert Johnson to continue in office in the King's name but he refused. They then named one of their own, James Moore, temporary governor and sent representatives to London to petition the Crown for protection.

This was a *coup d'etat* but one that was punctilious in following precedents established by the Convention of 1689 that had ousted James II and offered the British Crown to William of Orange and his wife, Mary Stuart. The Carolina Convention's "Resolutions" were closely modeled in form and constitutional argument upon the Glorious Revolution's Declaration of Rights. If ever there was a colonial American revolt led by lawyers, the South Carolina Revolution of 1719 was one.

The transition of South Carolina from a Proprietary province to a royal colony began with the Revolution of 1719 and was complete by 1729, when the Crown bought out the Proprietors. But, the first royally appointed governor, Sir Francis Nicholson, an attorney and experienced colonial administrator, arrived in 1720. The rise to power of a stable, established merchant class stimulated the growth of the bar, and the creation of extensive rice plantations created markets for surveyors, clerks, and experts in real estate. By the 1720s, the walls and moats that confined the walled city were torn down. The colony was expanding and on a path to a remarkable level of prosperity. South Carolina was the land of opportunity for its white residents.

Between 1721 and 1728, ten new lawyers were admitted to the South Carolina Bar, one of whom was a native Carolinian, Charles Pinckney. In his practice, he represented many London merchants in the colony. Between the date of his admission to the bar in the 1720s and 1750, he tried 224 cases. After a long and distinguished career, he was appointed chief justice of the South Carolina Supreme Court.

NICHOLAS TROTT

Man of Letters, Man of Law

DR. NICHOLAS TROTT was a judge, a justice, an advocate, and a Hebrew and legal scholar. In addition to his energetic judicial activities, he compiled and published two early editions of colonial American laws. His reputation as a Hebrew scholar was based on a lexicon of the Psalms that he wrote and on a famous lifetime research project to explicate the Hebrew Old Testament. Trott is best known as a legal editor and publisher though such knowledge is generally limited to specialists in Colonial statutes and judicial administration. Trott's 1736 publication of the South Carolina colonial laws is regarded as his most celebrated work. This book covered the laws up to 1719 and was titled *The Laws of the Province of South Carolina.*

Nicholas Trott presided over the trial of Major Stede Bonnet, sentencing him to be hanged.

Among the manuscript treasures of the Charleston Library Society is a bound manuscript volume, in Trott's handwriting, of eight grand jury charges that he made as judge of the general sessions in Charles Town between 1703 and 1708. These charges constitute sophisticated explications of English legal history and practice as well as an examination of common and statute laws that relate to duties and oaths and grand juries. One of his charges is a discourse on the crime of witchcraft. He examined the secular laws relating to the crime and recounted histories of witchcraft and prosecutions in England and the New England colonies.

Trott was admiralty judge in Charles Town, and presided over the famous trials of Stede Bonnet and 48 other pirates in late 1718. He published the proceedings of the trials in 1718 and his explications on British piracy laws became useful legal citations in successive centuries. His *Trial of Major Stede Bonnet and Other Pirates* was an important source of information to Daniel Defoe when that writer published *A General History of the Pirates* under the name Captain Charles Johnson. Trott also preserved the minutes of the South Carolina Vice Admiralty court, some of which entries are in his own handwriting. Also, the South Carolina Historical Society has some writs and court orders Trott issued before 1720.

The Revolution of 1719 ousted the Lords Proprietors' governance in Charles Town and brought an end to Trott's judicial career. Shortly after he left the bench, he sailed for England hoping to solicit support for yet another publication. While in Great Britain he was awarded an honorary Doctor of Civil Laws degree from Oxford. He returned to South Carolina in 1722 where he continued his legal practice and his scholarship. In 1726, the University of Aberdeen awarded him a Doctor of Civil Laws degree. The remainder of his life was devoted to completing his work on the Old Testament. He was unable to get support for publishing this book and no trace of it has survived. Late in life he married Sarah Rhett, widow of William Rhett. Nicholas Trott died in 1740 and was buried in Saint Philip's churchyard.

In the rare book collection of the Library Society there are Trott's writings on pirates: *Manuscript of the speech of Vice Admiralty Judge Nicholas Trott at the handing down of the verdict in the case of Stede Bonnet and others* and *A Complete Collection of State-Trials and Proceedings upon High-Treason and other Crimes and Misdemeanours from the Reign of King Richard II to the End of the Reign of King George I.*

The practice of appointing non-lawyers as judges persisted. Historian Robert M. Weir found that the lawyers ridiculed non-lawyer judges and some of the lay judges saw the lawyers as a "junta, manipulating public affairs to palm immense sums." By the 1740s, Charles Town was commonly called Charlestown. Its society and culture rapidly matured but before 1750 there were never more than a dozen attorneys practicing law in any single year.

Free blacks and African-American slaves did not have access to the judicial system but they were rigidly subject to its decrees. The slaves could not testify in court, but free blacks—and there were a handful in the earliest years—could testify in court. In keeping with English practice, a woman needed a guardian to transact business and when a man and woman married, the woman became a *femme couvert,* whose legal existence was submerged with the person of her husband.

The colony grew rapidly and its population reached 6,800 by 1743. Between 1728 and 1760, 42 new attorneys were admitted to the practice of law. Admission to one of the four courts—Equity, Admiralty, Common Pleas, and General Sessions—did not guarantee admission to any of the other courts. An attorney had to apply to each court separately for admission. An aspiring law student could qualify for the bar by matriculating at one of London's Inns of Court or at the University of Dublin. Of 73 Charlestown colonial lawyers who studied at the Inns of Court, 43 were students at the Middle Temple. Charlestown sent more young men to study at the Inns of Court than any other American colony, including Virginia. An alternative method was to be an apprentice to a member of the local bar for four years, which was an accepted method to enter the profession until the mid-twentieth century,

Apprentices could read law books that were available in the collections of the Charlestown Library Society af-

Following the Revolution of 1719 to overthrow the rule of the Lords Proprietors, the Carolina Convention requested Governor Robert Johnson to continue in office in the King's name but he refused. This illustration show the welcome he received upon his return to Charles Town as Royal Governor in 1729.

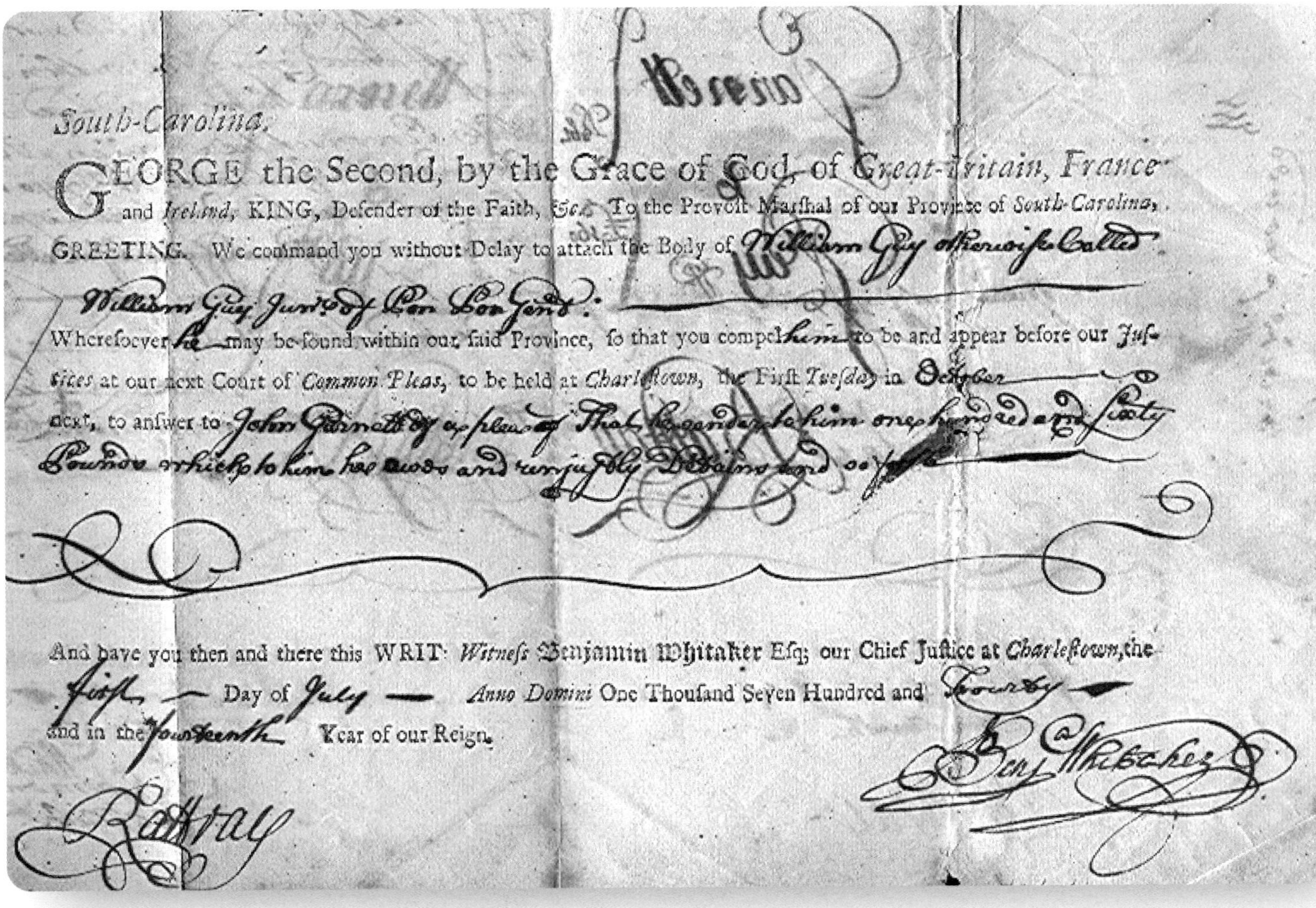

South-Carolina.

GEORGE the Second, by the Grace of God, of Great-Britain, France and Ireland, KING, Defender of the Faith, &c. To the Provost Marshal of our Province of South-Carolina, GREETING. We command you without Delay to attach the Body of William Guy otherwise Called William Guy Junr of Pon Pon Gent:

Wheresoever he may be found within our said Province, so that you compel him to be and appear before our Justices at our next Court of Common Pleas, to be held at Charlestown, the First Tuesday in October next, to answer to John Garnett of a plea of That he render to him one hundred and Sixty Pounds which to him he owes and unjustly Detains

And have you then and there this WRIT: Witness Benjamin Whitaker Esq; our Chief Justice at Charlestown, the first Day of July Anno Domini One Thousand Seven Hundred and Fourty and in the Fourteenth Year of our Reign.

Rattray

Benj Whitaker

This 1740 summons orders the Provost Marshall of South Carolina to "attach the Body of William Guy . . . so that you may compel him to appear before our Justices at our next Court of Common Pleas, to be held in Charlestown, the First Tuesday in October next, . . ."

ter its establishment in 1748. Two attorneys, James Grindlay and William Burrows, were among its founders. Inventories of some attorneys' estates recorded large libraries that contained law books. At Grindlay's death, five law books were in his library of 312 volumes. They were: *Coke's Institutes*, Spellman's *Larger Treatise Concerning Title* (1647), Thomas Wood's *Institutes of the Laws of England* (a precursor to Blackstone's volumes), and Sir William Blackstone's *Commentaries*. Among the law books ordered from London by the Library Society were Cunningham's *Laws of Bills of Exchange, Promissory Notes, Bank Notes and Insurances* (London, 1760); *Instructions for a Code of Laws for the Empire of Russia; Laws of Evidence, Laws of Nature;* Cunningham's *Law Dictionary; Laws of Several Provinces of America;* Nicholas Trott's *Laws of the Province of South Carolina;* and *Laws of Trade*. In 1768, attorney John Rutledge offered to make a compilation of the laws of the colony, but too few subscribers agreed to purchase the collection and he dropped the project.

The only way to gauge the practice of law in colonial days was by the number of cases a lawyer had in the courts. Between 1703 and 1750, James Wright was the lawyer most often in court with 471 cases and Robert Hume was second to Wright with 454 trials. The colonial period was not a time when individuals pursued a single career. Many combined the practice of law with other occupations and some men who became planters or merchants had been trained in the law but never practiced. A judge assigned each lawyer one pro bono case per year.

Andrew Rutledge tried 124 cases from the date of his arrival in 1730 to 1750. Before he emigrated from Ireland, Rutledge had been a member of the bars of Dublin and London. In his first position in Charles Town, he shared office space with Nicholas Trott. Governor Robert Johnson referred to Andrew Rutledge as "a lawyer of very good repute in this place." Rutledge was the uncle of three Charleston attorneys of the next generation. After the 1750s, new lawyers were predominantly native born. The increase in litigation in the 1750s was another indication of the colony's commercial success.

CHAPTER II

THE AMERICAN REVOLUTION

In 1751, the Commons House of Assembly authorized construction of a statehouse or colonial capitol at the northwest corner of Broad and Meeting streets. Earlier, this site had been reserved "for the place where judges sit to hear and try cases. For the courts to share space with the General Assembly in a new building was a decided improvement of facilities. In the 1680 Grand Modell plan of Charles Town, this location was described as a, "square of two ackers of land upon which the four great streets of 60 foot wide doe center." Royal Governor James Glen laid the cornerstone for the statehouse, which was sufficiently complete for use by 1756. The magnificent colonial statehouse was two stories tall and made of brick, plastered over, and scored to resemble stone. The building also housed a law library. When the Charleston County Courthouse was restored at the end of the twentieth century, a modern copy of an early portrait of Governor Glen, a London barrister as well as governor, was placed in a prominent spot to memorialize his contributions to the city and to the colony.

Another place that lawyers gathered late in the day was Shepheard's Tavern, on the northeast corner of Broad and Church streets. The late afternoon "punch hour" was the time to arrive. The tavern was the place where such matters as lawsuits were settled and where delegates were elected in 1774 to the First Continental Congress in Philadelphia. Another place of resort for attorneys was a small park on the southeast corner of Broad and Church streets. Several wooden benches were shaded by two enormous trees, a live oak, and a magnolia. The vacant lot was known simply as "The Corner." Women and African Americans never went there. The Corner passed for the town's stock exchange, bar association, gentlemen's club, and public forum. All of the city's law offices were within three blocks of The Corner.

The first generation and some members of the second generation of lawyers wore robes in the courtroom. This tradition soon fell from use but judges continued to wear robes. The custom of wearing wigs seems never to have been adopted in Charles Town. When young John Rutledge, one of Andrew Rutledge's three nephews, returned in 1761 from his studies at the Middle Temple, he brought home with him the regalia of a proper London barrister he had tailor-made for him on Regent's Street. Rutledge "appeared for his admission to the bar wearing a new wig, deeply powdered in dead white. He wore a white muslin ruching around his neck and had delicate cuffs of French lace under his brocaded silk gown. He just swore to the oath, no questions were asked about his education."

When John Rutledge made his professional debut, his oratory was irresistible. His legal arguments and oratory gave him a reputation for eloquence, which was not surpassed in his lifetime. From the age of 12, John studied law books in the office of his uncle Andrew and in the library of James Parsons. When John returned from the Inns of Court, he married and built his home and office at 116 Broad Street, a house he called "The Palace." His office was in the basement and it opened onto the street.

Lawyers and judges conducted their legal proceedings with an informality that might have shocked English barristers. Rutledge observed that, "though lawyers were better trained, many of them confused in practice such basic distinctions of English jurisprudence as the difference between law and equity. It was not surprising that few lawyers or judges bothered to cite statutes and precedents in most cases. The chief justice regularly signed blank writs and allowed the lawyers to fill them out. Such lax legal conduct made appeals on procedural points virtually impossible."

Colonial Charles Town was a litigious place. The Court of Common Pleas maintained an annual caseload of 350 actions throughout the decades between 1751 and 1780 and, during those years, 61 new attorneys were admitted to the bar. The three leading attorneys of that day were the "triumvirate" of John Rutledge, James Parsons, and Charles Pinckney II. Between 1750 and 1780, Parsons tried 1,073 cases; Rutledge tried 985 cases; and Pinckney tried 960 cases. In 1764, when Rutledge was 25 years of age, he was appointed attorney general as a ploy by the

OPPOSITE PAGE: *One of the oldest known depictions of the Charleston courthouse appeared on a piece of 1767 currency.* BELOW: *This 1780 view of the Charles Town waterfront shows the Old Exchange Building prominently featured in the background.*

As a lawyer, John Rutledge tried 985 cases between 1750 and 1780. In 1776, the South Carolina Provincial Congress elected him as the state's president. In 1779, Rutledge was the first chief executive to be elected under the state constitution that changed the title of the office from president to governor.

royal governor to break up the "triumvirate." He accepted the post but never served as attorney general. Within a few months, he resigned and returned to his practice.

Rutledge's income from his practice was believed to have been twenty-five percent more than any other professional income in the colony. Later in his career, Rutledge served as Chief Justice and Associate Justice of the United States Supreme Court, Chief Justice of the South Carolina Supreme Court, and president and governor of the state. His two younger brothers, Edward and Hugh, also practiced law. Donald T. Rutledge, a 2006 member of the Charleston Bar, is a direct descendent of the grandchildren of both John and Edward Rutledge.

James Parsons was a successful businessman and an attorney. He had immigrated to South Carolina from Ireland and practiced from 1751 to 1774, when his health failed. Parsons' name appears as notary on more than one hundred deeds of lease and release in the real estate records of that period. He died in 1779 at his home on Church Street and the value of his estate exceeded that of any other active attorney in the city.

Charles Pinckney II (1757-1824), nephew of the former chief justice of the same name, was described as an "urbane leader" of the bar and credited with being a principal architect of the United States constitution. Later, he served two terms as governor of the state, as United States senator, and as ambassador to Spain, and then retired to continue an active life. Two Pinckney cousins, Thomas and Charles Cotesworth Pinckney, also practiced law during that remarkable era. They, too, had prepared for the law at the Middle Temple. Thomas gave up the practice of law to manage his rice plantations on the Santee River. At a meeting held at Shepheard's Tavern, Charles Cotesworth Pinckney was elected to represent the colony at the First Continental Congress in Philadelphia in 1774. After the British evacuated Charles Town in 1782, he set about retrieving his law practice when President George Washington offered him a position as Associate Justice of the United States Supreme Court. He rejected the offer, but later accepted Washington's appointment to be ambassador to France. The Pinckneys are especially noted in history for their contributions to ambassadorial service.

William Henry Drayton, whose legal education took place at Oxford and Westminster, was admitted to the bar in the 1760s. Writer and historian of the South Carolina Bar, Judge John Belton O'Neall said of Drayton, "his father's large estate saved him from the necessity of pursuing any business as a means of living." The Crown ap-

HUGH RUTLEDGE

(1745-1811)

"HUGH RUTLEDGE WAS A LAWYER'S LAWYER, THAT is why he is my favorite Rutledge ancestor," says attorney B. Alston Moore, Jr., who is generally known as "Ben" to the Charleston Bar of the twentieth and twenty-first centuries. He was so well regarded by the lawyers of the time that the gentlemen of the bar resolved to "wear a crape on the left arm for thirty days" regretting the death of the late Honorable Hugh Rutledge.

Hugh was the middle brother, between John and Edward, all three of whom played a leadership role here in the eighteenth century. Hugh studied law in the office of his brother, John, then at the Middle Temple in London's Inns of Court and was admitted to the bar of this state on January 20, 1768. He began his practice by compiling a collection of all the laws of this province, fulfilling an agreement John had made with the General Assembly in 1775. In that same year, Hugh was elected judge of the Court of the Admiralty, a part-time position. Very early in his practice he became one of the busiest lawyers in the Court of Common Pleas.

Five years later he had a large practice in the Court of Chancery and resigned his position as judge of the Court of Admiralty. He was a justice of the peace, vestryman of his church, and a Trustee of the College of Charleston. Thomas S. Grimke, Esquire, is quoted as saying he "is rated as among the very best common-law lawyers of the day."

In 1791, Hugh Rutledge was elected by the General Assembly to be the judge of the Court of Equity where he served until his death. By statute, three judges were to serve on this court, but Rutledge alone served on that court for two years. Hearings were held twice a year in three South Carolina cities, Charleston being one of them, of course.

An example of a decision made by Chancellor Rutledge which has been considered the law ever since it was rendered is that of *Charles Lining v. R.H. Peyton and others, 2 DeSaussure's Equity Reports 376.* The facts of the case centered around a *cestui que* trust, which had the power to sell land out of the trust with the proviso that the trustee shall hold the purchase money subject to the uses set forth in the trust. The purchaser asked the court if he was bound to see that the trustee held the money subject to the said uses. Chancellor Rutledge held that the purchaser is not required to see that the trustee fulfills his duties to the trust.

---

pointed Drayton to be a privy counselor in the colony, but because Drayton favored the revolution, he resigned. In March 1776, Drayton was elected chief justice of the state. Historian George C. Rogers, Jr. has stated that this eighteenth-century bar represented the greatest generation of lawyers in South Carolina history and John Rutledge was the foremost legal figure of them all.

A major legal crisis occurred in Charles Town when the British Parliament passed the Stamp Act. It was to take effect November 1, 1765, and required that a tax be paid and a stamp affixed on a variety of papers, including all legal documents. A ship bringing the stamps from Britain arrived in Charles Town Harbor on October 18th. Overnight, a gallows appeared at the corner of Broad and Meeting streets and an effigy of the local stamp distributor dangled from it. A crowd of about two thousand people carried the effigy down Broad Street to the bay where it was buried in a coffin labeled "American Liberty." Acting Governor William Bull secretly had the stamps transferred to another ship to protect them from destruction and refused to distribute them. The Commons House appointed three delegates—John Rutledge, attorney; Thomas Lynch; and Christopher Gadsden, merchant—to a Stamp Act Congress of all the colonies.

British officials in Charles Town shut down all business because they feared violence if they tried to enforce use of the tax stamps. The shutdown itself greatly disrupted life in the city. The courts closed because, to be made official, all legal papers except those of the general sessions court required stamps. The lawyers made their first efforts to test the closing of the courts when seven attorneys demanded that the clerk of court, Dougal Campbell, give them a process form. Campbell refused, stating that he would not affix his seal to any papers with-

Above: *Wealthy Charles Town merchant Christopher Gadsden was one of three South Carolina delegates to the Stamp Act Congress. Later he served as a delegate to the First and Second Continental Congress.* Right: *An example of the stamps required by the Stamp Act of 1765.* Below right: *William Pitt spoke out on behalf of the colonists during the stamp crisis with the British.*

out permission of the chief justice. Attorney Robert Williams then produced a 40-shilling note and demanded a writ and other attorneys present did likewise. Campbell said he had no writs in his office. The attorneys then approached the chief justice.

Chief Justice Charles Shinner met with the members of the bar on November 12th. Their request to open the courts placed him in a quandary because "that closing posed serious economic and social problems (and) human law must give way to emergencies." Eventually, Justice Shinner decided that he would not be a party to any violation of the Stamp Act and clung to his decision with monumental stubbornness. Governor William Bull tried to circumvent Shinner by appointing three new assistant judges. When court opened for the spring term, attorney Rawlins Lowndes spoke for the bar. He asked rhetorically, "Was the Stamp Act intended to unhinge the Constitution of the Colonies, to unloose the hand of violence and oppression, to introduce anarchy and confusion amongst us, and reduce us to a state of outlawry? Thus the act should not be construed to require the suspension of all legal business merely because stamped paper was unavailable."

The present situation was much attributed to an act of God, as if the ship that brought them had been cast away in a storm. Shinner was unimpressed by such reasoning and refused to proceed with business. Lowndes went on to become Chief Justice of the South Carolina Supreme Court. One of his descendants, Thomas P. Lowndes, is a 2006 member of the Charleston Bar.

The Commons House and the bar then turned their attention to removing Shinner and the governor. But this course of action was deemed trivial politics compared to the joy they felt at the repeal of the Stamp Act in March 1766. To celebrate the event, the Commons House commissioned the creation of a statue of William Pitt in gratitude for his assistance in Parliament in repealing the act and ordered a full-length portrait of each of the Stamp Act Congress representatives. The statue of Pitt, in Roman toga, was erected in the middle of the intersection of Meeting and Broad streets. It now stands in the large entrance hall of the Charleston County Courthouse.

The people who lived in the South Carolina Upcountry far from Charles Town had long been neglected. They had

CAUSES AT ISSUE, NOVEMBER TERM, 1768.

No. of Causes at Issue.	No. of Terms at Issue.	PARTIES' NAMES.		CAUSE OF ACTION.	PL'FF'S ATT'Y.	DEF'T'S ATT'Y.	PLEAS.	VERDICTS.
1	5	Thomas Edmanson	vs. Francis Lamon,	Case.	Rutledge.	Pinckney.	Non Culpa's.	Pl'ff £150 and Costs.
2	2	James Simpson	vs. James Stobo, Jr.,	Case.	Simpson.	Rutledge.	Non Assum't.	Pl'ff £23 and Costs.
3	2	John Graham	vs. John Caldwell,	Debt.	Pinckney.	Parsons.	Non est Factum.	Ended.
4	2	Brewton & Smith	vs. John Hume,	Debt.	Pinckney.	Rutledge.	Non est Factum.	Plea withdrawn.
5	2	Philip Hart	vs. Griffith & Cape,	Case.	Rutledge.	Parsons.	Non Ass't et disc.	Pl'ff non-suited.
6	2	Rawlins Lawndes	vs. Thomas Adam,	Debt.	Rutledge.	Pinckney.	Non est Factum.	Plea withdrawn.
7	2	Idem	vs. Michael Kalhison,	Debt.	Rutledge.	Pinckney.	Non est Factum.	Plea withdrawn.
8	2	John Swint	vs. Roger Pinkney,	Case.	Rutledge.	Pinckney.	Non Assum't.	Stands over by consent.
9	2	Executors Waties	vs. Micajah Williams,	Case.	Rutledge.	Pinckney.	Non Assum't.	Ended.
10	1	Thomas Moggs	vs. James Stobo.	Case.	O'Brien.	Rutledge.	Non Assum't.	Pl'ff £93 and Cost.
11	1	Jacob Valk	vs. Tonans et al.,	Case.	Ward.	Pars. & St. Leger	Non Assum't.	Ended.
12	1	Logan et als. Sur's.	vs. John McDougal,	Debt.	Ward.	Pinckney.	Non est Factum.	Stands over.
13	1	Thomas Kirton	vs. Jonathan Avant,	Case.	Leigh.	Rutledge.	Non Assum't.	Stands over.
14	1	Robert Weaver	vs. Godwin & Hamn,	Case.	Pinckney.	Parsons.	Non Assum't.	Stands over.
15	1	Brewton & Smith	vs. Adm'r Shinner,	Debt.	Pinckney.	Rutledge.	Non est Factum.	Plea withdrawn.
16	1	Sarah Wood	vs. James McClenachan,	Trover.	Pinckney.	Leigh.	Non Culpa's.	Pl'ff £370 Damages and Costs.
17	1	Thomas Kirton	vs. Jonathan Avant et al.	Case.	Leigh.	Pinckney.	Non Assum't.	Stands over.
18	1	Lessor of Kesson et ux.	vs. Cath. Wigfall,	Ejectment.	Rutledge.	Parsons.	Non Culpa's.	Pl'ff non-suited.
19	1	Richard Proctor	vs. Sarah Purry,	Case.	Rutledge.	Parsons.	Non Culpa's.	Pl'ff £900-Damages with Costs.
20	1	John McCall	vs. John Gordon,	Trespass.	Rutledge.	Parsons.	Non Culpa's.	Stands over.
21	1	Joseph Dobbins	vs. Samuel Singleton,	Trespass.	Rutledge.	Pinckney.	Non Culpa's.	Ended.
22	1	Joseph Huggins	vs. Joseph Brown,	Trespass.	Rutledge.	Pinckney.	Non Culpa's.	Pl'ff £900 and Costs.
23	1	Adm'rs Weatherly	vs. Jacob Cowen,	Case.	Rutledge.	Leigh.	Non Culpa's.	Stands over.
24	1	Moses Dayguiere	vs. John Davis,	Case.	Williams.	Mason.	Non Assum't.	Pl'ff.
25	1	Thomas Spencer	vs. Robert Gibb,	Case.	Leigh.	Parsons.	Non Culpa's.	Stands over.
26	1	Adm'rs Tankard	vs. Neh'a Rivers et al.,	Case.	Rutledge.	Leigh & Bee.	Non Culpa's.	Stands over.
27	1	Joshua Lockwood	vs. Paty Holmes,	Case.	Leigh.	Dwight.	Non Assum't.	Settled.
28	1	Lazarus Brown	vs. John Davis,	Debt.	Parsons.	Pinckney.	Solvit post diem.	Stands over.
29	1	James Oneal	vs. Wm. Whitaker,	False imprisonm't.	Parsons.	Leigh.	Non Culpa's.	Stands over.
30	1	Thomas Cowen	vs. Isaac Fendin,	Debt.	Parsons.	Leigh.	Non est Factum.	Stands over.
31	1	John Jones	vs. Wm. Holliday,	Case.	Parsons.	Leigh.	Non Assum't.	Pl'ff £52 6s. Damages and Costs.
32	1	Cornelius McCarty	vs. Executor Weatherly,	Case.	Parsons.	Leigh.	Non Assum't.	Plea withdrawn.
33	1	Adm'rs Newington	vs. Thomas Humphreys,	Case.	Parsons.	Rutledge.	Non Culpa's.	
34	1	Ex'rix Moffatt	vs. Robert Dearington,	Trover.	Parsons.	Rutledge.	Non Culpa's.	Stands over.
35	1	William Logan	vs. William Fitch,	Case.	Parsons.	Pinckney.	Non Culpa's.	Pl'ff non-suited
36	1	Robert Martin	vs. Thomas Hervey,	Case.	Parsons.	Pinckney.	Non Assum't.	Pl'ff.
37	1	Adm'r Hunter	vs. And. Mar. White,	Case.	H. Rutledge.	Leigh.	Non Assum't.	Pl'ff.
38	1	Rapor Adm'r	vs. Wm. Allston,	Case.	H. Rutledge.	Pinckney.	Non Assum't.	Pl'ff.
39	1	McLeod & Co.	vs. Joseph Dopson,	Debt.	H. Rutledge.	Pinckney.	Non est Factum.	Pl'ff.
40	1	John Davis	vs. Lazarus Brown,	Debt.	H. Rutledge.	Parsons.	Def't in duress.	Stands over.
41	3	Thomas Harvey	vs. Will Guess,	Trespass.	Mason.	Simpson.	Non Culpa's.	Discontinued.
42	1	Thomas O'Brien	vs. Jacob Wirth,	Replevin.	Parsons.	Mason.	Non Culpa's.	Stands over.
43		James Clitherall	vs. John Paul Grimke,	Case.	H. Rutledge.	Burrows.	Non Assum't.	Stands over.
44		Ogilvie, Forbes et al.	vs. Cunningham Sur's,	Case.	Parsons.	Leigh.	Non Assum't.	Plea withdrawn.

MR. JUSTICE ROBERT PRINGLE.

The bench docket of Judge Robert Pringle for the November term of 1768 includes many well-known names among the attorneys listed.

no local courts, jails, or convenient meeting sites. Their anger against Lowcountry lawyers and Charlestown's monopoly of power reached a peak in 1767. They organized a protest movement called the Regulation that was part vigilante law enforcement and part insurrection. The Regulators declared that they were ready to "pull down all the Houses of the Lawyers about their Ears." The Circuit Court Act of 1769 diffused much of the Upcountrymen's anger by providing for six circuits and courts, jails, and judges for each circuit. The judges of these courts did not come from the Charles Town Bar, but were sent from London.

The American Revolution began in Massachusetts in April 1775 and by June 28, 1776, warfare had reached Charles Town. The General Assembly elected four delegates to the Philadelphia meeting of the colonies where they signed the Declaration of Independence. All four were Charles Town lawyers: Thomas Heyward, Jr., Thomas Lynch, Jr., Arthur Middleton, and Edward Rutledge.

After a failed attempt to capture Charles Town in 1779, the British army and navy conducted a skilled, determined campaign the next year to capture the southern metropolis. On February 11, 1780, the British landed 5,000 British troops on Johns Island. A week earlier, Charles Town residents knew the invasion was coming and were fearful. The Commons House was in session that day. It hastily took an extraordinary legislative step when it voted its President, John Rutledge, dictatorial powers as if to say, "you take care of it" and quickly adjourned.

As he was copying a conveyance of "one Hundred and seventy two acres in St. Andrews Parish, be the same more or less…unto the said Thomas Tucker…and further," the Registrar of Deeds learned the alarming news of the British landing and put his quill down. He closed Deed Book C-5 at page 172 and left without recording the rest of the title. All this fast action was necessary because the citizens

LEGAL EXPERTISE PROVED VALUABLE TO THE DECLARATION OF INDEPENDENCE

In the summer of 1776, there were about 20 lawyers in Charles Town. The state's four delegates to the Continental Congress were members of this bar and were all under 35 years of age.

The Declaration of Independence first arrived in Charles Town on Friday, August 2, 1776. The most prominent attorney at the bar, John Rutledge, was then also president of the state. Over the weekend of August 2-4, Rutledge arranged for the first public readings of the Declaration to take place on Monday, August 5. At noon that day, the local militia were drawn up under arms on Broad Street and Rutledge led a parade of the privy council and lower house members from the courthouse to face the militia. At that time, the Declaration was read aloud to the public for the first time.

Forty-five minutes later, this parade proceeded east on Broad Street to the Exchange building where the Declaration was read again, this time to cheering crowds and sounds of cannon fire. South Carolina was no longer a colony; it was a state.

Following its first reading (left), the Declaration was read again to a cheering crowd in front of the Old Exchange Building (below).

Above: *This famous image shows Sergeant William Jasper raising the flag of South Carolina over the fort on Sullivan's Island during the first, unsuccessful, British assault on Charles Town on June 28, 1776. The British were defeated when their cannonballs failed to penetrate the palmetto log fortifications. Following the battle, the fort was renamed Fort Moultrie in honor of its commander and a palmetto tree was added to the flag.*
Right: *Henry Laurens, vice president of South Carolina, served as president of the Second Continental Congress.*

of Charles Town wanted to evacuate all the sick, elderly, and children before the city was encircled.

In the months following their landing on Johns Island, Sir Henry Clinton's army moved northward and cast a large noose around the Charles Town peninsula. By the end of March, they had cut off the city by land and sea, constructing extensive siege lines across the Charles Town peninsula. Once the British began to bombard the city in early May, General Benjamin Lincoln was forced to surrender his army of 5,000 troops and hand over Charles Town to the invaders. The British restored Crown authority in the city and carried out retribution against

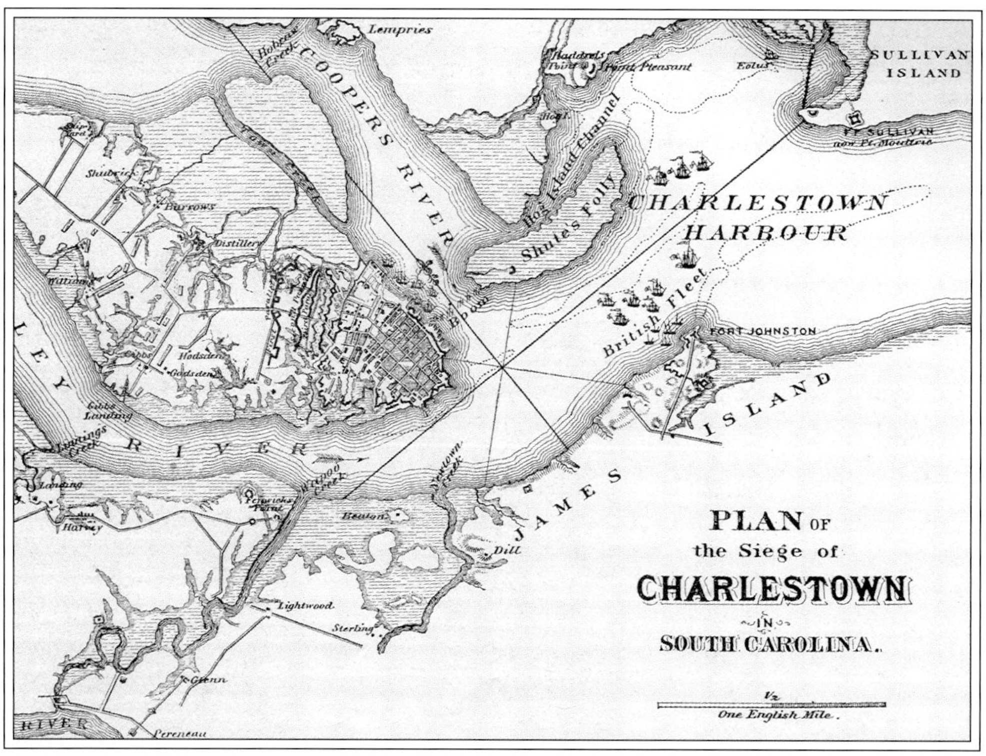

ABOVE AND LEFT: *The British finally captured Charles Town in May 1780 following a three-month siege led by Sir Henry Clinton. Charles Town was occupied until December 14, 1782, when the British evacuated the city following a series of military defeats.* OPPOSITE PAGE, BELOW: *Dr. David Ramsey was among the forty Charles Town patriots imprisoned by the British at St. Augustine.* OPPOSITE PAGE, ABOVE: *The citizens of Charles Town joyfully welcome the return of the patriots following the British evacuation in 1782.*

former patriots of all classes. Their occupation created much bitterness and thirst for revenge.

Two and a half years of bitter fighting throughout the length and breath of the state were required to turn the tide of war and to liberate the state. Pushed back into Charles Town by a series of defeats, the British evacuated the city on December 14, 1782, carrying with them the church bells of Saint Michael's Anglican Church, 3,000 Loyalists, who dared not remain behind, and 5,000 slaves, who had been released from bondage by declaring allegiance to the Crown. The state had won its independence through great sacrifices of blood and property.

After the American Revolution, the state legislature adopted an act which continued the recognition of common law in full force and effect provided that it was not in conflict with or inconsistent with the state code or with the laws and the new state constitution. In 1783, the city of Charleston was incorporated and obtained its first municipal charter from the new state government. Three of the four men elected delegates to the Confederation Congress,

the new national government, were members of the Charleston Bar—John Mathews, William Henry Drayton, and Thomas Heyward, Jr. A few years later, three of the five delegates to the Constitutional Convention in Philadelphia in 1787 were Charleston lawyers: Charles Cotesworth Pinckney, John Rutledge, and Charles Pinckney. In 1785, the General Assembly voted to move the state capital and the functions of the state government to a new city at the confluence of the Broad and Saluda rivers. The new city was called Columbia.

Thirty-eight members of the local bar began to reestablish the unity of the profession that had been shattered by war and revolution. On March 24, 1791, each member signed an agreement setting certain minimum fees for designated professional services. This agreement is preserved in the first volume of John Belton O'Neall's *Biographical Sketches of the Bench and Bar*. Edward Rutledge had signed his full name to the Declaration of Independence, but on this agreement he used his familiar name, "Ed Rutledge," because he was among friends. The Lowndes member of the bar in 2006 detected that the signatures of the two Lowndes attorney brothers who attested to the fee agreement were actually written by one of the brothers. Another member of the 2006 bar, Charlton DeSaussure, Jr., is a direct descendent of Henry William DeSaussure, who also signed the minimum fee schedule of 1791.

A fire in 1788 gutted the old statehouse that was then home to the Charleston District Court. In the early 1790s, the building was renovated. A third floor was added and some of the fenestrations (windows) were altered. In July 1795, while John Rutledge was Chief Justice of the South Carolina Supreme Court, President George Washington appointed him Chief Justice of the United States Supreme Court. Rutledge took his seat on the court on August 12 in Philadelphia. The court had already been in session for a week and the justices had continued four cases until the next term. Rutledge filed decisions in two cases heard in that term and the court adjourned on August 24.

TOP: *A signer of the Declaration of Independence, Edward Rutledge was elected governor in 1799.* ABOVE: *Charleston lawyer Thomas Heyward, Jr. was also a signer of the Declaration.*

At the time, these federal justices rode circuit and held court in company with a local federal district judge. On the southern circuit, Rutledge and a local judge heard 15 cases which mostly dealt with ship seizures. On the way to Raleigh, North Carolina, for a circuit court term, Rutledge became ill and returned to Charleston. His appointment to the Court had been made between Congressional sessions and when the Senate next convened, it refused to consent to his appointment, perhaps because of his poor health or because he had strongly opposed adoption of the Jay Treaty with Great Britain.

By an act of Assembly dated December 19, 1796, the qualifications necessary to seek admission to the bar were changed to provide that a graduate of a college or university only had to read law in the office of a practicing attorney for three years. Without a college degree, the student had to read law for four years.

To the last day of the eighteenth century, John Rutledge kept his office in the same place at 116 Broad Street. He spent his mornings there, his afternoons at The Corner, and his evenings at the Exchange. In 1798, Edward Rutledge was elected governor but in the first year of the new century, both Edward and John died. Their deaths brought down the final curtain on this golden period of the Charleston Bar.

The prominent attorneys among the state's Founding Fathers were succeeded by a new generation of lawyers, many of them the sons of illustrious fathers. These new men, most of whom bore familiar surnames, dominated the intellectual life of the state through the antebellum period. The man who would have the greatest influence on the profession during this new era was James Louis Petigru.

ORIGINAL FEE BILL, 1791

WE, THE SUBSCRIBERS, from a conviction of the Justice and Reasonableness of the undermentioned Table of Charges for Conveyancing, &c, in order to make the practice of the Bar as uniform as may be, consent and agree not to take less than the sum therein allowed for each particular: the propriety of Receiving more being left entirely to the discretion of each judicial and the peculiar circumstances of the case:–

"For every common Letter of Attorney, General Release, Bill of Sale and the like printed instrument, not requiring attendance from home, 10s. 10-½d.

Query. Special Bond, Letter of Attorney, General Release, Bill of Sale and the like instrument in Writing, £1 1s. 9d.

Drawing and Engrossing common Conveyance by Lease or Release, £3 5s. 3d.

Filling up printed ditto, £1 17s. 4d.

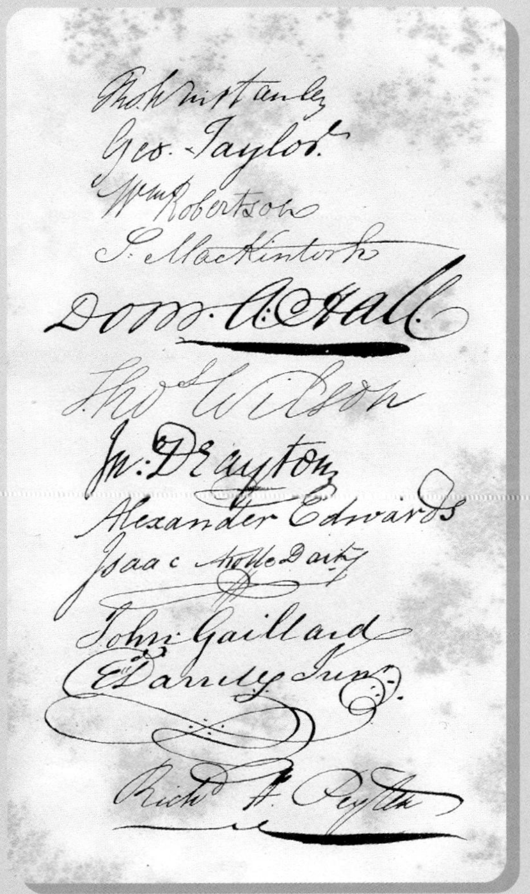

On March 24, 1791, 38 Charles Town lawyers signed an agreement setting minimum fees.

Each Dedimus Posteatamus, for taking do., including clerk's fees, £1 1s. 9d.

For proving and signing away Release of Inheritance, or Renunciation of Dower, when prepared by gentlemen, and who are not attorneys of the Courts of Law and Equity in this State, £2 3s. 6d.

Drawing and Engrossing two parts of articles of Co-partnership, being usually special and always different, £5 8s. 9d.

Drawing and Engrossing Common Wills, £3 5s. 3d.

Each Lease of a Plantation and House, or Lot of Land, and Counterpart, with the usual covenants for Payment of Rent, Repairing the Premises, and quiet Enjoyment, £3 5s. 3d.

Each opinion on a question of Law and Equity, £3 5s. 3d.

Drawing and Engrossing Conveyance, by Lease or Release, with special Recitals, £4 7s. -d.

Drawing and Engrossing Mortgages, the same as for Conveyances, adding a charge for the Bond for payment of the money.

Marriage Settlements of Real Estate, by Lease and Release, and counterpart with Special Limitations, £7 12s. 3d.

For ditto, by assignment of Negroes, or other personal property, £5 8s. 9d.

Each Release of Inheritance, or Renunciation of Dower, including clerk's fees, £2 3s. 6d.

For each Letter previous to an action brought, £- 10s. –d.

For Retaining Fee in every contested cause at Common Law, £3 5s. 3d.

Counsel Fee in every Chancery Cause (15 guineas.) £16 6s. 3d.

The cases under the Summary Jurisdiction to be left to the option of each gentleman who may receive what he pleases."

Note: Each of the 30 members of the bar signed this fee agreement. Abstracted from Biographical Sketches of the Bench and Bar *by John Belton O'Neall, Vol. 1, page XXIX (1849)*

CHAPTER III

THE ANTEBELLUM PERIOD

In 1800, Charleston had 33 practicing lawyers. The names of some of them hark back to the colonial era and endure to the present generation because one of the most notable features of the Charleston Bar is that most of its members did not move away and successive generations of their progeny chose to remain in Charleston.

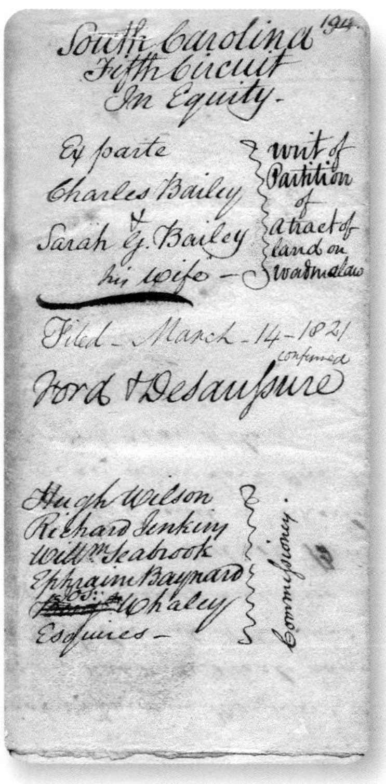
South Carolina
Fifth Circuit
In Equity.
Ex parte
Charles Bailey
&
Sarah G. Bailey
his wife —
Writ of Partition of a tract of land on Wadmalaw
Filed — March 14 — 1821
Ford & Desaussure
Hugh Wilson
Richard Jenkins
Willm Seabrook
Ephraim Baynard
Whaley
Esquires —
Commissioners

In the 60 years before the Civil War, the bar saw a period of growth, consolidation, and maturation, beginning with significant changes in legal education. There was no state law school, so young aspirants to the profession apprenticed themselves to members of the bar. Certain attorneys enjoyed good reputations as teachers and students gravitated to their offices. But since these mentors had to endorse the applications of those who sought admission to practice, the names of the best teachers may have made their reputations. In any case, the colonial tradition of studying law at London's Inns of Court collapsed with the American Revolution and the creation of the new nation. Judge Theodore Gaillard, who died in 1829, was the last Charleston lawyer who had received an English legal education.

What was it like to "read law?" Members of William Alston Pringle's family recalled an experience in 1843. Pringle's sister, Susan, noted that he was "thrown into ecstasy" by obtaining a place as a clerk to the esteemed attorney, William Ford DeSaussure, and that his elderly grandfather, John Julius Pringle, had given him a copy of Sir William Blackstone's *Commentaries on the Laws of England,* the foundation for British and America legal practice for a century after its publication in 1760. Young Pringle had shown little energy or enterprise in earlier studies but he committed himself wholeheartedly to the law. His mother wrote to grandfather Julius, "he goes to Mr. deSaussure's office, and devotes himself to Blackstone, in his own chamber, until 11 o'clock at night, and is up at 6 in the morning."

ABOVE: *This engraving shows the harbor of Charleston in the mid-1800s. Much of Charleston's wealth was due to its maritime shipping.* OPPOSITE PAGE: *A "writ of partition of a tract of land" filed in 1821 by Ford & DeSaussure.*

The study of law was not cheap. Even after attending the famous Litchfield Law School in Connecticut, John C. Calhoun paid $485 tuition to study in the Charleston office of Timothy Ford and Henry William DeSaussure. Local traditions of apprenticeship dominated the education of lawyers as the bonds of kinship, friendship, and mentoring linked one generation to another and made each new class of law students a fraternity of peers. William Johnson read law under Charles Cotesworth Pinckney. President Thomas Jefferson appointed Johnson to the United States Supreme Court in 1804 and he served for 30 years. Edward McCrady, Jr. studied under Johnson and tutored his son and namesake, Edward McCrady, an historian and leader of the bar after the Civil War. Even when teacher and student were unrelated, the relationship often became filial. Langdon Cheves taught law to young Robert Young Hayne and passed his practice on to him.

But position, favor, or success at the bar was not guaranteed. Charles Fraser was one of Charleston's most famous artists but he was also an attorney. He recorded in his *Reminiscences of Charleston* (1859) that the city's four leading attorneys earned between $10,000 and $12,000 a year. They were at the apex of the legal profession while many attorneys more often struggled. William Alston Pringle "presented an upper middle-class façade" but, by 1857, he depended heavily on his annual salary of $2,000 as Recorder for Charleston. One of his brothers wrote, "it is more than most of his contemporaries are making at the bar."

At least one woman, Sarah Grimke, expressed interest in becoming a lawyer. She was the daughter of the distinguished Charleston jurist, Judge John Faucheraud Grimke. When her brother Thomas was apprenticed to Langdon Cheves, she asked to study law as well. Her father and brother crushed her hopes but Judge Grimke was reported to have said that, "If Sarah had only been a boy, she would have made the greatest jurist in the country." She and her sister Angelina left the South and became nationally known for their public lectures against slavery and for the rights of women.

While decades passed before lawyers organized themselves to take control of legal education in antebellum Charleston, they were strongly entrenched among the intellectual and cultural aristocracy. Charles Fraser, admitted to practice in 1807, helped organize one of the early

ABOVE: *William Johnson served on the U.S. Supreme Court from 1804 until his death in 1834.* RIGHT: *Sarah Grimke was the daughter of a judge and the sister of a lawyer. Frustrated in her desire to study the law, she and her sister Angelina left the South and went on to become nationally known as abolitionists and early proponents of the rights of women.*

debating societies, the Philomathean, where law students practiced their forensic skills. Timothy Ford and Robert J. Turnbull were noted newspaper polemicists of the day. Ford was the epitome of a Federalist while Turnbull's "Crisis" essays of 1827 were a full explication of states' rights and the doctrine of nullification.

Hugh Swinton Legare wrote *belle lettres*, an old term for light, occasional literature distinguished by elegant style and social content. His more intellectual studies appeared in the *Carolina Law Journal* and *The Southern Review*, the foremost quarterly journal in the antebellum South. Legare served in the United States House of Representatives from 1837 to 1839 and was Attorney General during John Quincy Adams's presidency. William Crafts, Jr. was a poet, essayist, and attorney.

For several years in the mid-1820s, members of the Charleston Bar and some law students began to meet to improve their forensic skills and the study of law. Three of these lawyers—George Buist, Richard Yeadon, Jr., and Charles C. Strohecker—petitioned the General Assembly and, on December 20, 1825, received a charter of incorporation for their organization. Their plan was to raise money to begin "a regular Law Institute" in the city. Hugh S. Legare is presumed to have been the leader of the group.

On October 10, 1826, the first statewide organization of lawyers was founded, with Charleston attorneys taking the lead. Among them were Joseph Clarke, Henry Cruger, Edward Frost, John Gadsden, Thomas S. Grimke, Mitchell King, and Christopher G. Memminger. Sixty attorneys attended the first meeting in City Hall, at the corner of Meeting and Broad streets. The group established a public law library in 1829. Attorney Grimke spoke in favor of publishing the state's laws. Five years before, Governor Thomas Bennett, a Charleston native, had proposed such an undertaking, but nothing had been done. But, with the backing of the lawyers' organization, the legislature appropriated funds for the president of South Carolina College, Thomas Cooper, to undertake the task. By the time of his death in 1839, Cooper had compiled and pub-

"...EMPLOYING THE BEST CHARLESTON LAWYERS..."

THE ONLY QUESTION IN THE MARLBORO COUNTY case of *Heirs at law of Mason Lee v. Ex. Of Mason Lee, 4 McCord 182 (1824)* was whether at the time of making his Last Will and Testament, Mason Lee was of sound and disposing mind. The beneficiaries of his assets were the states of South Carolina and Tennessee and his will excluded all his heirs. Hence, he expected litigation. He was convinced, and so stated in his will, that his kinfolks "squibbed and darted and summered him."

To be tough in fighting his family, his will further provided, "...no part or parcel of my estate shall be enjoyed or in anywise inherited by either or any of my relations, while wood grows and water runs. And my executors are enjoined to contend with them either in law or equity to enforce this my will, by employing the best Charleston lawyers, at the expense of my estate, or in any way, again, again, and again."

Mason Lee claimed that, one day in the woods, he made an agreement with God. If the Almighty would let him get rich, he would live poor. At his death, his estate was worth $50,000.00.

To show that Lee's thoughts were a morbid disease of the brain and not any ordinary belief in witchcraft, the following facts were asserted: "He believed that all women were witches, and would not sleep in a bed made by a woman. He believed that persons at a distance could exercise an influence over his body and mind. He believed that the Wiggins were in his teeth, and to dislodge them he had 14 sound teeth extracted, evincing no suffering from the operation. He believed that spells were laid on him, and that he could be spelled if he made water on the ground. He had the quarters of his shoes cut off, saying that if the devil got into his feet he could drive him out easier. He had holes cut in both sides of his hat, so that if the devil came in one side, he could drive him out the other. His daily dress was an Oostburg shirt, a Negro cloth, a short coat, breeches, and leggings. He always shaved his head close, as he said that in the contest with the witches they might not get hold of his hair, and to make his wits glib. He had innumerable swords of all sizes and shapes, 15 or 20 in the course of a year, which he was continually altering. One of his swords was four feet long, with two edges; another eleven inches wide by fourteen inches long, with a handle. They were made by a neighboring blacksmith to enable him to fight the devil and witches with success. In the daytime, while neglecting his business, he dozed in a bed made from a hollow gum in his miserable hovel; and at night he kept awake by contending with the devil and the witches with success...(H)e suffered no bull or boar to be castrated; he cut off the tails of hogs and cattle to the roots...(H)e once purchased a horse, then cut off his ears and mounted him while bleeding. He hoed his corn after frost and said it would come out green again. He assigned various reasons for making his will, and not providing for his illegitimate sons or relations. His reason for not providing for one son was that, although he was the twin brother of the other, he was the father of only one of them...."

This case is taught in law school as an example of a definition of a person who is mentally competent to sign a will. Lee's reference to the "best lawyers in Charleston" was not raised as an issue in an effort to prove his incompetence. A Marlboro County jury found that the deceased had been competent when he made his will and this judgment was confirmed by the South Carolina Supreme Court. Did the best Charleston lawyers win this case? No. Lee's executor was a Marlboro county attorney who put the trial in the hands of a Columbia attorney, William Campbell Preston.

THE GREAT ORGAN CONTROVERSY

By Ben Goldberg

When the great fire of 1838 destroyed Charleston's Kahal Kadosh Beth Elohim (KKBE, Holy Congregational House of God) synagogue, the flames ignited a controversy that led to a famous lawsuit that ultimately was heard in the Supreme Court of South Carolina.

Charted in 1749, KKBE was the first organized Jewish congregation in the city. The founders were strict in their adherence to rituals that they had learned in the Sephardic tradition, that is, traditions that were established in Spain and Portugal prior to 1492. The synagogue that burned in 1838 had been built on Hasell Street in 1794 and, from the outside, appeared much like the Protestant churches of the city. Inside, conservative Jewish practices held sway, with severe restrictions that forbade religious gatherings outside the synagogue and levied fines on members who missed meetings.

Beth Elohim Reform Temple on Hassell Street was built in 1840 after the original building was destroyed in the great fire of 1838. A controversy between reform and orthodox members of the temple was eventually resolved in the South Carolina Supreme Court.

Early in the 1700s, Charleston had the largest population of Jews in any city in North America. For years, all shadings of Jewish opinion in the community made KKBE their place of worship because it was the only congregation in the city. However, in the early 1820s, dissenting voices arose among some members, complaining of the lack of decorum at services and expressing a wish for sermons in English.

A group of reformers led by Isaac Harby (1788-1828) petitioned the synagogue leaders to liberalize the congregation's governance and modernize some of its rituals. Harby was a prominent young Charleston intellectual, a poet, journalist, lawyer, and playwright, who was influenced by American republican values. He composed an English language prayer book and was the founder of the Reform Society of Israelites. One of Harby's plays was performed in the twentieth century at Charleston's Footlight Theatre and his likeness appears in the panoramic mural depicting the city's theatrical history which hangs in the theatre. The Reform Society disbanded in 1833 and its members returned to KKBE. Upon their return, and together with others, changes began to be made in the services. At the dedication of the new synagogue in 1841, the rabbi commented: "This synagogue is our temple, this city is our *Jerusalem*, and this happy land our Palestine." His statement is often quoted by members of the Reform movement in America.

Prominent Charleston attorney Christopher G. Memminger represented the orthodox congregation in the "Great Organ Controversy." Later he served as Secretary of the Treasury in the first Confederate cabinet.

Unfortunately, this 'happy land' was not reached. During the construction of the synagogue, a decision was made that had momentous results. On July 26, 1840, the congregation voted to install an organ. This time, the orthodox members abandoned KKBE, leaving the congregation in the hands of the Reform Society. The seceders formed a new synagogue, Sherith Israel, meaning Remnant of Israel. The reform element, KKBE, mocked them as "Remnants."

Sherith Israel established a cemetery on Coming Street and erected a brick wall to separate their burying ground from the adjoining KKBE cemetery. Soon the group decided that KKBE belonged to them, not to the reformers, and both sides claimed possession of the property. Physical confrontations occurred and each side changed the locks to the synagogue doors. Cooler heads tried to prevail but the controversy headed for court. On October 4, 1846, the reform membership sued the orthodox congregation. The case was styled *ex rel. Ottolengui v. Ancker, et al. 2 Richardson 245 (1846)* but was better known in the Jewish community as "The Great Organ Controversy."

James L. Petigru represented the reformers and Christopher G. Memminger was the attorney for the orthodox. Both of these attorneys were leaders of the antebellum bar. The reformers claimed the orthodox were trespassers. The orthodox insisted that they were members of KKBE and that the reformers had improperly changed the synagogue ritual when they installed the organ. A jury found for the reform side, but attorney Memminger and the orthodox appealed to the state Supreme Court. The court declined to become involved in what amounted to a matter of religion. Instead, the justices decided the case on two basic issues. How many congregants in good standing voted for the organ? Of those in good standing, who had voted, how many of these were reform and how many orthodox? The court found that the reform contingent was the larger and ruled in their favor.

After the Civil War, the remnants again returned to KKBE because the war had left Charleston's Jews too impoverished to sustain two synagogues. Few physical reminders of the bitter controversy survived. The wall that once divided the two cemeteries was torn down and acrimony gave way to peace and tranquility. The imposing reminder of the litigation is the majestic temple of KKBE on Hasell Street. Inside this house of God is the original instrument that led to the 'Great Organ Controversy.'

lished five volumes and left five more in manuscript form. David J. McCord, a non-lawyer but respected editor, completed the project. The ten volumes, containing the laws of the state from its beginning in 1836, were called *The Statutes At Large of the State of South Carolina* and known ever since as *Cooper and McCord.*

ABOVE: *In 1826, the first statewide organization of lawyers was founded. Sixty attorneys attended the first meeting at the Charleston City Hall.* LEFT: *Charleston lawyer James L. Petigru was a candidate for state senator on the State Rights and Union ticket, a South Carolina political party founded in 1830 which was opposed to the doctrine of nullification.*

Of all the lawyers of his era, James Louis Petigru had the greatest influence on the development of the Charleston legal profession. He has been called the "last South Carolina Federalist" for his deep and profoundly felt personal loyalty to the preservation of the Union. He saw the Founding Fathers as heroes who had created a nation capable of glory and greatness. Petigru understood the Constitution as a contract perpetually binding to all the states who were parties to it. Like those of Daniel Webster, his pleas for the Union were emotional and they did not aim to rebut the constitutional argument and historical reasoning of John C. Calhoun, the great champion of states' rights.

Petigru practiced law for a total of 43 years. In 1848, he built a new office building on St. Michael's Alley. The building is a notable landmark of the city's culture. He was a famous litigator and an equally famous teacher of the law. Among his students were several distinguished post-Civil War leaders of the bar. For all the respect accorded him, Petigru was a voice crying in the wilderness. By 1860, most South Carolinians supported states' rights and free trade doctrines and were willing to dissolve the Union to preserve their way of life, which included black slavery and state sovereignty.

JAMES LOUIS PETIGRU

(1789-1863)

On May 11, 1863, a long funeral procession followed the coffin of James Louis Petigru into the sanctuary of St. Michael's Episcopal Church. In the ranks of the procession marched most of the city's bankers and merchants, city and state officials, judges, former governors and United States senators, the Confederate military commanding general, and all of the military officers who were in Charleston. Onlookers lined the streets to show their respect to the city's most principled and prominent man. The funeral procession proceeded with Union troops a mere twelve miles away. Never mind that Petigru had been loyal to the Union, the Constitution, and the country.

Late in his life, Petigru wryly observed that his success as an attorney really came from overcoming the fact that "I had no vocation for it.' This bookish man had been born in Abbeville, educated at South Carolina College, and read law while teaching in Beaufort County. Petigru was admitted to the bar in 1812 and opened his first office in Coosawatchie in Beaufort District. In his first practice he was not overburdened with clients and actually made more money by teaching law than he made in legal fees. When he moved to Charleston as junior partner of the powerful politician James Hamilton his fortunes improved. By 1855, the R.G. Dunn Company of New York, which rated the value and creditworthiness of American businessmen, reported of Petigru, "...his law partnership grossed between $26,000 and $30,000 a year" and advised businessmen that only "cases of great importance should be placed in their hands, when they will warrant the payment of a big fee. Their largest fee was $10,000 for appearing in the United States Supreme Court."

James Louis Petigru was considered to be "a lawyer's lawyer, respected for his knowledge and logic." He remained loyal to the Union and the Constitution until his death in 1863.

One of Petigru's biographers said that his courtroom presentation, "came straight to the point. He was a lawyer's lawyer, respected for his knowledge and logic. He was also a suburb performer whose sudden changes of mood and outbursts of humor brought witnesses up short and carried juries before him. Just as he would score a point, he would whip out his gold snuffbox with a dramatic flourish, sneeze and abruptly conclude."

He became a legend at the South Carolina Bar because he never hid his scorn for those who led the state into the nullification crisis of the 1830s. He stood alone in Charleston against his passionately committed warlike friends. He embodied an idealism that rose above the emotions on both sides. Petigru was eulogized and "praised for his legal mind, his love of truth and justice, loyalty to community" and was called "the greatest moral hero of the age."

His name continued to invoke American patriotism into the twentieth century. The first two law school buildings on the campus of the University of South Carolina were named after him and an important part of the restoration of the old Charleston County Courthouse was the creation of the James L. Petigru Law Library on the second floor of the building. Law students who thought of themselves as libertarians in the early 1970s formed a Petigru Society at the University and three members of the Charleston Bar, Gedney M. Howe, III, Robert Rosen, and Ann M. Stirling, were the leaders. When attorney Natalie P. Bluestein was a student there in the early 1980s, she too attended meetings of the Petigru Society. The law students and members of the bar continue to recognize Petigru as a major figure in our history.

In 1819, the first serious financial panic occurred in American history, and the South and West were hit particularly hard. Although the causes were complex, Southerners blamed the tariff policies of Congress. Southern planters exported cotton to Europe and bought manufactured goods there, paying higher prices for them because of import duties that protected industrial markets in the North. Congress enacted these tariffs periodically to encourage American industry but Southerners paid the tariff costs. For example, in 1816, the U.S. Congress imposed an import duty of 25 cents per yard on cheap cotton cloth, which made it too expensive for British cotton manufacturers to compete in the American market. This and later tariffs struck the South a double blow. Southerners were the chief consumers of this fabric, which they bought to clothe their slaves. But, even worse, the South produced the cotton, which they shipped to England to make the cloth. When British producers could not easily sell the cloth, they bought less cotton. These one-two punches of import tariffs extended to other products that Southerners either imported from abroad and paid high tariffs on or paid premium prices on to their Northern brothers. In 1828, members of Congress, intent on embarrassing the likely Democratic candidate for President, Andrew Jackson, passed a bill raising tariff rates even higher. The South Carolina legislature passed numerous resolutions declaring the duties unconstitutional, oppressive, and unjust. Vice President John C. Calhoun, who had been educated at Yale College and studied law in Charleston, penned the *Exposition and Protest*, which declared that, in extreme situations, individual states had the constitutional power to decide for themselves if an act of the federal government was constitutional, a doctrine known as nullification.

Charleston attorney and U.S. Senator Robert Y. Hayne joined Calhoun in defense of state sovereignty. In January 1830, Hayne and Daniel Webster of Massachusetts engaged in a lengthy debate that became one of the most famous arguments ever held in the United States Senate. Hayne made the case that the tariffs weighed down the economic interest of South Carolina and argued that the

In 1830, Senator Robert Y. Hayne (left), a Charleston attorney, and Daniel Webster (below) engaged in a famous debate in the U.S. Senate on the subject of nullification, foreshadowing some of the issues that would lead to secession. In May 1847, Webster was a guest of the Charleston Bar.

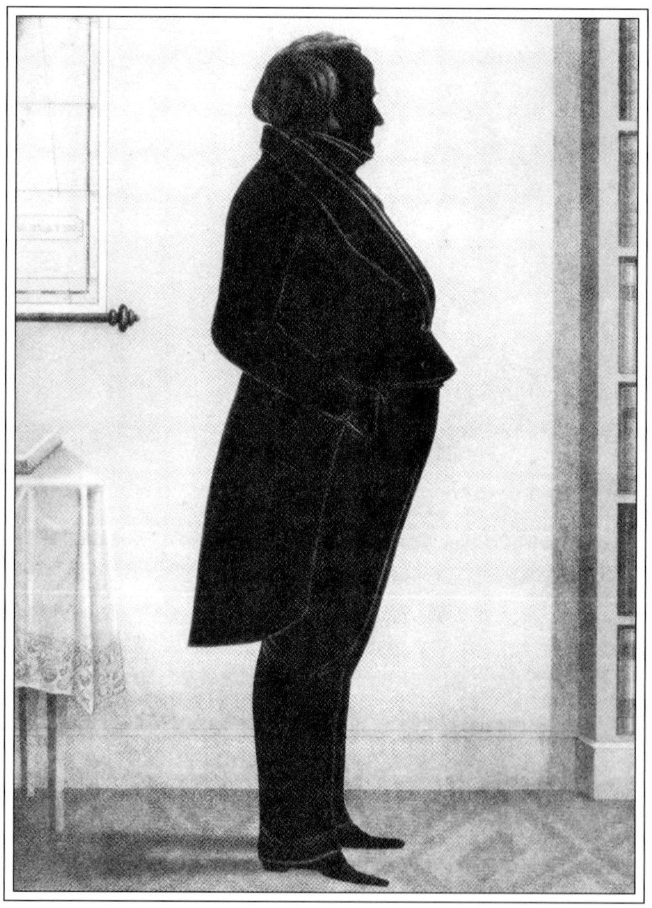

Constitution was a compact of states which could be altered by the sovereign states. Webster, a powerful voice for Northern industry, argued that the union was inseparable. This showdown between federal and state governments was averted when Congress passed legislation for a gradual cutback in the tariffs, but at the same time gave the President the power to enforce other tariff laws. The prelude to secession and Civil War had begun.

A graduate of Yale University, John C. Calhoun studied law in Charleston. Author of the doctrine of nullification, and the leading spokesman for states' rights, Calhoun served in the U.S. Senate, and was elected to two terms as vice president during the presidency of Andrew Jackson. He controlled South Carolina politics until his death in 1850.

In an interesting sidelight, the Charleston Bar entertained Daniel Webster in May 1847. Henry A. DeSaussure, a son of Chancellor Henry W. DeSaussure, presided and Unionists James L. Petigru and John Belton O'Neall, Chief Justice of the South Carolina Supreme Court and later author of the classic *Biographical Sketches of the Bench and Bar of South Carolina* (1859), sat at the head table. Webster won the hearts of his hearers when he declared, "I love our common profession. I regard it as a great ornament and one of the chief defenses and securities of free institutions. It is indispensable to and conservative of public liberty. I honor it from the bottom of my heart. If I am anything, it is the law that has made me what I am." Later in the evening, the controversial issues in the famous 1830 debate were mentioned. With grace and kindness, Webster rose and proposed a toast to the memory of his late colleague and forensic opponent, Robert Y. Hayne.

Such comity did not last. In the years after the nullification crisis, an antislavery movement gained strength in the North. As the example of James Petigru demonstrated, there was a range of opinion in South Carolina about the morality of owning slaves and a minority of citizens were slaveholders. But, just as the abolitionists' voices grew loud in condemnation of the practice, so did the slaveholders' words and acts grow in its defense. The Civil War that had loomed like storm clouds on the horizon for 30 years would strike the nation like a September hurricane.

CHAPTER IV

MINDS SET ON WAR

ECONOMIC PROSPERITY smiled on Charleston's business and professional establishments during the 1850s. According to the 1852 city directory, 79 attorneys were in practice, more than double the number in 1800. In the 1850s alone, 41 new lawyers entered the field.

Most of those aspiring to the profession continued to receive their training by reading law in the office of a member of the bar. However, early in the 1850s, five Charlestonians made their ways to Gottingen and Berlin in Germany to broaden their education: Basil Lanneau Gildersleeve, brothers Gabriel Wesley and W. B. Dingle, David Ramsey, and Samuel Lord, Jr. Among these, Lord enjoyed the highest professional esteem.

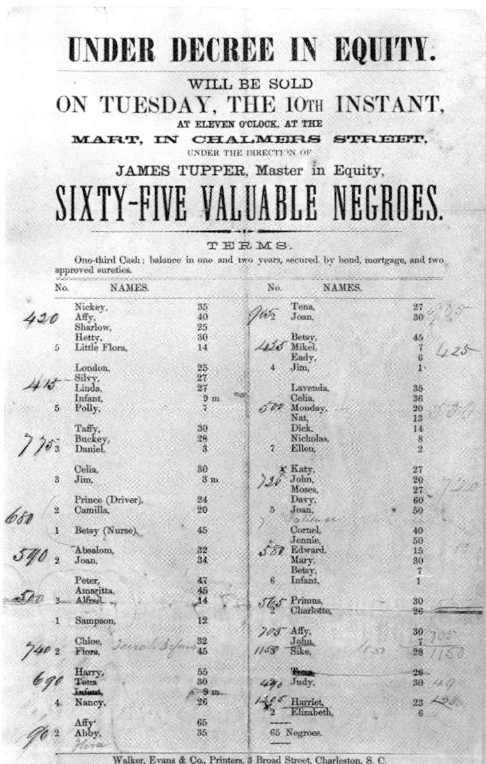

UNDER DECREE IN EQUITY.

WILL BE SOLD
ON TUESDAY, THE 10TH INSTANT,
AT ELEVEN O'CLOCK, AT THE
MART, IN CHALMERS STREET,
UNDER THE DIRECTION OF
JAMES TUPPER, Master in Equity,

SIXTY-FIVE VALUABLE NEGROES.

TERMS.

One-third Cash; balance in one and two years, secured by bond, mortgage, and two approved sureties.

No.	NAMES.	
	Nickey,	35
	Affy,	40
	Sharlow,	25
	Hetty,	30
5	Little Flora,	14
	London,	25
	Silvy,	27
	Linda,	27
	Infant,	9 m
5	Polly,	7
	Taffy,	30
	Buckey,	28
3	Daniel,	3
	Celia,	30
3	Jim,	3 m
	Prince (Driver),	24
2	Camilla,	20
1	Betsy (Nurse),	45
	Absalom,	32
2	Joan,	34
	Peter,	47
	Amaritta,	45
3	Alfred,	14
1	Sampson,	12
	Chloe,	32
2	Flora,	45
	Harry,	55
	~~Tena~~	30
	~~Infant,~~	9 m
4	Nancy,	26
	Affy,	65
2	Abby,	35

No.	NAMES.	
	Tena,	27
2	Joan,	30
	Betsy,	45
	Mikel,	7
	Eady,	6
4	Jim,	1
	Lavenda,	35
	Celia,	36
	Monday,	20
	Nat,	13
	Dick,	14
	Nicholas,	8
7	Ellen,	2
	Katy,	27
	John,	20
	Moses,	27
	Davy,	60
5	Joan,	50
	Cornel,	40
	Jennie,	50
	Edward,	15
	Mary,	30
	Betsy,	7
6	Infant,	1
	Primus,	30
2	Charlotte,	26
	Affy,	30
	John,	7
	Sike,	28
	~~Tena,~~	26
	Judy,	30
	Harriet,	23
2	Elizabeth,	6
65	Negroes.	

Walker, Evans & Co., Printers, 3 Broad Street, Charleston, S. C.

By 1859, however, Charleston's business directory listed only 23 lawyers in active practice. One reason for the decrease in practicing lawyers may have been because business and planting were more profitable. Twenty names in that roster—Brewster, Brown, Burnet, DeSaussure, DeTreville, Dingle, Dukes, Duncan, Flagg, Jervey, Lord, McCrady, Memminger, Porter, Raymond, Rivers, Rutledge, Simons, Whaley, and Wilkinson—have continued to appear on court dockets down to the present day.

In 1859, the Chief Justice of the State Supreme Court, John Belton O'Neall, published a two-volume work of original research and historical significance, *Biographical Sketches of the Bench and Bar of South Carolina*. In it, he identified 1,787 attorneys who had qualified before the courts between 1783 and 1859 and he published original biographies of the chief judges and attorneys of the colony and state. A Newberry native, O'Neall was one of the legal luminaries of antebellum South Carolina. A strong Unionist, in *McCrady v. Hunt (1835)*, he and Judge David Johnson struck down as unconstitutional the state oath of allegiance imposed by the General Assembly during the nullification controversy. He was a nationally known temperance leader and advocate for women's education, a businessman, and

As a southern port, large numbers of slaves first entered Charleston before being sold on to other locations. Illustrated here are a broadside listing slaves for sale at a Charleston auction with prices marked in pencil in the margins (opposite page) and an engraving of a Charleston slave auction in the 1850s (above).

a planter. In addition to the *Biographical Sketches of the Bench and Bar of South Carolina*, O'Neall wrote *Annals of Newberry* (1859), and codified the state's laws on slaves and free blacks in *Negro Law of South Carolina* (1846). He was a supporter of slavery but fought all his life to ameliorate the lives of the state's slave and free black population.

In the late 1850s, interest in the codification of laws and statutes revived across the state and nation. In May 1859, the General Assembly commissioned James Louis Petigru to codify the state's code of laws and offered him a salary larger than any other state official. He was given authority to use his judgment to delete conflicting or duplicate laws. This assignment was a tribute to him and a measure of the state's confidence in his preeminent legal expertise. He worked during the turmoil of the Civil War and compiled a three-volume manuscript but died before the work could be published. His codification was not adopted but sections were included in the state's constitution of 1868.

States' rights lost their foremost champion when Senator John C. Calhoun died on March 31, 1850. Historian David D. Wallace wrote in his 1961 history of the state, "Thus passed the most powerful mind, the most impressive personality, the most talented, though by no means the wisest, leader in South Carolina history." At the unveiling of Calhoun's statue in the national Capitol in 1910, Senator Henry Cabot Lodge of Massachusetts said of him, "He was the greatest man South Carolina has given to the nation. That in itself is no slight praise, for from the days of the Laurenses, the Pinckneys, the Rutledges, from the time of Moultrie and Sumter and Marion to the present day, South Carolina has always been conspicuous in peace and war for the force, the ability, and the character of the men who have served her and given her name its high distinction in history." Calhoun was buried in Charleston's Saint Philip's churchyard in a massive sarcophagus. His attainments in life would speak for

themselves, rather than any epitaph; only the name CALHOUN was chiseled into the marble. He died intestate, with his financial affairs in disarray.

Publication of Harriet Beecher Stowe's novel *Uncle Tom's Cabin* in 1852 incensed much of Charleston, even as it stoked the fires of abolitionism in the North. Stowe gave the odious plantation owner the name "Legree," and many South Carolinians believed this was a calculated insult to the city's respected Legare family.

Four years later, in 1857, one of the most important cases in American history was heard by the U.S. Supreme Court. The court's decision in *Scott v. Sanford, (60 US 393, 1856)*, the Dred Scott Case, pushed the nation fast and far down the road to disunion and civil war. Dred Scott, a slave, had been taken out of the South to live in the Wisconsin Territory, a free territory by virtue of the 1820 Missouri Compromise. When his master died, Scott sued for his freedom in 1846. The case moved through the lower courts and made its way to the Supreme Court in 1857. Chief Justice Roger B. Taney, a Maryland slaveholder, wrote in his majority opinion that, because he was a slave, Scott had no legal rights to sue in the U.S. courts and that the Missouri Compromise was unconstitutional because it abolished slaveholders' rights to their slave property. The decision struck down all barriers to slave ownership and all previous constitutional agreements that had regulated slavery. Taney's decision outraged northern abolitionists and set up the conditions for "Bleeding Kansas" and other violent battles over slavery.

For many in South Carolina, the question was becoming this: Would the state secede alone, or take that action only if other southern states did likewise? Robert Barnwell Rhett, a Lowcountry attorney and plantation owner, has been called the "father of secession" because of his persistent advocacy of disunion. Rhett read law in the office of Thomas Grimke. After three years of study, he was admitted to practice and formed a partnership with a cousin, Robert W. Barnwell. In the 1830s, Rhett served in the General Assembly and was state attorney general. He succeeded John C. Calhoun in the U.S. Senate and, once the Confederate States of America was created, hoped in vain to become its president.

LEFT: *Former slave Dred Scott gave his name to one of the most notorious decisions of the U.S. Supreme Court.* BELOW: *Judge Andrew McGrath left the bench the day after the election of Abraham Lincoln. He served as governor from 1864 to 1866.*

This newspaper illustration shows "a warlike demonstration in Charleston, S.C." with Palmetto troops marching on Meeting Street.

The Rhett family owned the daily newspaper *The Charleston Mercury*, and Rhett's son, Robert Barnwell Rhett, Jr. edited it for ten years, beginning in 1858. An editor's pen reached far and wide in those times and often exercised more influence over public issues than an officeholder. Rhett lived amid controversy and acrimony, wielding the *Mercury*, before and during the Civil War, as a personal weapon. The names Rhett and Barnwell have regularly appeared on the rosters of the Charleston Bar ever since.

News of Abraham Lincoln's election as President of the United States on November 6, 1860, rang out across Charleston like a fire alarm. In his campaign, Lincoln had muted his views attacking slavery, but for the first time in American history, the United States had a president whose Republican Party platform declared that "the normal condition of all the territory of the United States is that of freedom." Within days, leaders across the South declaimed from street corners, podiums, benches, and pulpits arguing the necessity and inevitability of secession.

The day after the ballots were cast, the United States District Court was in session at 23 Chalmers Street with Judge Andrew Magrath presiding. Rankled by the election result, the grand jury refused to carry out its duties. Judge Magrath rose from the bench, took off his robe, and threw it on the dais. In a bold and formal voice he addressed the lawyers, jurors, and spectators:

"For the last time, as a judge, I have administered the laws of the United States...So far as I am concerned, the temple of justice, raised under the Constitution of the United States, is now closed. If it shall never again be opened, I thank God that it has been closed before its altar has been desecrated with sacrifices to tyranny." Along with Magrath, U.S. Attorney James Conner resigned. This was one of the first public acts of secession in the state and in the future Confederacy. On December 20, 1860, South Carolina, in a convention held in Charleston, solemnly and unanimously passed its Ordinance of Secession.

In his inaugural address on March 4, 1861, President Lincoln declared, "I have no purpose...to interfere with the institution of slavery." At the same time, he warned, "No state, on its own mere action, can get out of the Union." If a war was to come, he seemed to say, it would be over secession, not slavery. By then, Alabama, Georgia, Louisiana, Mississippi, and South Carolina had declared their independence from the United States and formed the provisional government of the Confederate States of America. A week after Lincoln's inauguration, the Confederacy adopted a constitution based on that of the U.S. constitution but stressing states' rights and protecting slavery.

Learning that President Lincoln had ordered the provisioning of the federal garrison at Fort Sumter, Governor Francis W. Pickens demanded, on April 11, 1861, that the fort surrender. When its commander, Colonel Robert Anderson, refused, General Pierre G. T. Beauregard's Confederate forces in Charleston Harbor fired the first shot at Fort Sumter at 3:30 a.m. on April 12. These were the first shots of a war that most expected to be short but which lasted for four years.

At the Charleston Bar no legal papers were filed that day. At last, the die had been cast, and holiday hilarity swept the city. The author has found only one reference to a reaction by a Charleston slave, who referred to the U.S. president as "Uncle Abe," a clear expression of a close personal feeling. Within a year of that first shot, a thousand free blacks left Charleston.

A little more than six months after the capture of Fort Sumter, a new Confederate court convened at 23 Chalmers Street under the laws of the new confederation with Judge Andrew G. Magrath again presiding. The transition between the United States' and the Confederate civil and criminal courts appears to have gone smoothly. Existing indictments by U.S. courts were tried by Confederate juries and judgments of the former courts were executed by Confederate marshals. There was no Confederate State Supreme Court.

On December 11, 1861, the most destructive fire in the city's history burned a swath across the peninsula from the Cooper River to the Ashley River. It seemed to many a miracle that the Confederate courthouse at 23 Chalmers Street and the state court building at the corner of Broad and Meeting streets were untouched. The fire was caused by men cooking near the corner of East Bay and Hasell streets and did not have any connection to the war.

Some Confederate court rules were printed by Evans and Cogswell, a Broad Street printing company that later in the war printed currency. Under the Confederacy, legal fees, court costs, and jury verdicts were payable in Confederate dollars. The few Confederate coins were minted in silver only at the beginning of the war. The bills were called "dollars" and in the same denominations as those of the Union. Legal documents filed at the courthouse, such as deeds and mortgages, recited the consideration in dollars. At least one merchant would not transact business in Confederate dollars but would do business only in silver coins. The author recalls hearing an attorney, Mary S. Allan, express anger because her Civil War ancestors had to accept, by order of a court, worthless Confederate dollars to satisfy a note and mortgage her family had taken in 1862. Both of the families continue to have descendents who live in Charleston. Civil War diarist Mary Chesnut "sold eggs and butter that brought $85 a month. But in what 'In Confederate money.'"

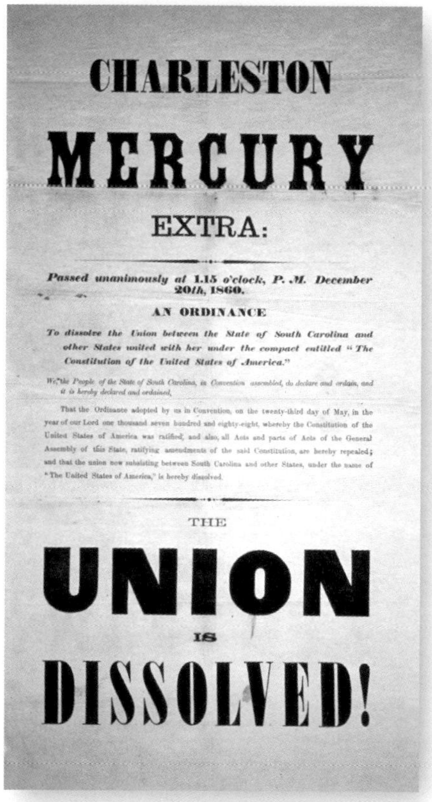

CHARLESTON

MERCURY

EXTRA:

Passed unanimously at 1.15 o'clock, P. M. December 20th, 1860.

AN ORDINANCE

To dissolve the Union between the State of South Carolina and other States united with her under the compact entitled "The Constitution of the United States of America."

We, the People of the State of South Carolina, in Convention assembled, do declare and ordain, and it is hereby declared and ordained,

That the Ordinance adopted by us in Convention, on the twenty-third day of May, in the year of our Lord one thousand seven hundred and eighty-eight, whereby the Constitution of the United States of America was ratified, and also, all Acts and parts of Acts of the General Assembly of this State, ratifying amendments of the said Constitution, are hereby repealed; and that the union now subsisting between South Carolina and other States, under the name of "The United States of America," is hereby dissolved.

THE

UNION

IS

DISSOLVED!

TOP: *Robert Barnwell Rhett, a Lowcountry attorney and plantation owner, has been called the "father of secession."* ABOVE: *Rhett's family owned the daily newspaper* The Charleston Mercury, *edited by Robert Barnwell Rhett, Jr., which published this special edition to announce the dissolution of the Union.*

ABOVE: *The first shots of the Civil War were fired on April 12, 1861, when Confederate artillery under the command of General P. G. T. Beauregard opened fire on Fort Sumter in Charleston Harbor.* LEFT: *This engraving shows the bombardment of Fort Sumter as a Union side-wheeler looks on helplessly. The attack was ordered after Governor Pickens learned that President Lincoln had ordered the provisioning of the federal fort. Pickens demanded the surrender of the fort and the fort's commander, Colonel Robert Anderson, refused. The bombardment lasted for thirty-four hours.*

Confederate States District Attorney pro tempore, Charles Richardson Miles, and Samuel Lord, Jr. prosecuted cases for the new government under instructions from the Confederacy's Department of Justice in Richmond. One case the grand jury had to consider was an alleged treason, wherein some Confederate sailors had tried to persuade their officers to surrender their ship to the United States. A few ships were captured and sold as prizes by the court. Some northern businesses were confiscated as required by the Confederate States Congressional Sequestration Act. These court sales provided revenue for the South's war effort.

The sequestration acts required all citizens to tell Receivers where contraband property was located. Some lawyers refused to comply with the duty to report their client's assets. The bar believed that the law violated the attorney-client privilege of confidentiality. Prominent attorneys James L. Petigru, Edward McCrady, Nelson Mitchell, William Whaley, and James W. Wilkerson were ordered before the court at 23 Chalmers Street as a test case. In the end, Judge Magrath ruled that only Wilkerson could avoid the disclosure of a client's secrets. The Charleston grand jury then asked the Confederate Congress to reconsider the act in view of these potential problems.

THE CONFEDERACY'S DEPARTMENT OF JUSTICE

by Warren Moise, Attorney

Jefferson Davis's first Confederate cabinet included Attorney General Judah P. Benjamin (seated left) and Secretary of the Treasury Christopher G. Memminger (standing left).

On February 21, 1861, the Confederate congress created the first department of justice of any Anglo Saxon nation, predating that of the United States by nine years. The chief officer of that department was the Attorney General of the Confederate States. Among its numerous duties, the Department of Justice was to prosecute all suits relating to the government, advise the president and department heads on legal matters, handle claims against Confederate states, supervise the court officials (including the clerks of court and marshals), and also monitor court officials' financial accounts.

The first attorney general appointed by President Jefferson Davis was former United States Senator Judah Philip Benjamin, who organized the new department. After the Confederate federal government moved to Richmond, the Department of Justice was located in the Virginia Mechanics' Institute on Ninth Street. An amazing man, Benjamin, by the outbreak of war had already refused a nomination to the United States Supreme Court from President Millard Fillmore, as well as an appointment to be Minister of Spain. (He was a member of the Charleston Bar.)

The Department of Justice continued to function throughout the war as a vital organ of the Confederate government. As Union armies approached Richmond, the last attorney general fled south with the fugitive Confederate government. Attorney General George Davis of North Carolina gave a final opinion on constitutional issues regarding surrender to President Davis, then left Charlotte to join his family in the war-ravaged state, and the Confederate States Department of Justice thus faded into history.

Two years later after the war, the United States Congress began addressing the possibility of creating a similar department. On July 1, 1870, a United States Department of Justice was born, but it did not equal the status of the Confederacy department until about 50 years later.

This story was taken from Chapter 2 of Rebellion in the Temple of Justice, The Federal and State Courts in South Carolina During the War Between the States *by Warren Moise (Universe, Inc., New York, Lincoln, Shanghai, 2003.)*

ABOVE: *Ironically, the greatest destruction to Charleston during the Civil War was caused by a fire on December 11, 1861. The cause of the fire did not have any connection to the war.*
LEFT: *Governor Francis W. Pickens led South Carolina into secession, and for the first year of the war.*

When President Jefferson Davis declared martial law in Charleston on May 12, 1862, the city became an armed camp. The declaration was the first of many to come. Martial law is a directive that, during wartime, the army, instead of civil authority, governs because of a perceived need for military security and public safety. During this time, Judge Magrath transferred all the court's cases to Columbia.

In May 1863, the Confederate Congress declared that black men bearing arms against the Confederacy would be subject to the criminal laws of the state where they were captured. That meant that an African-American citizen of the Northern states fighting for the Union could be captured in the South and be subject to the laws of the Confederacy. In response, President Lincoln signed an order that, for any United States soldier executed in violation of United States laws, a rebel would be executed in retaliation. The issue first reached trial in 1863 when two soldiers of the famous 54th Massachusetts Regiment were captured and jailed in Charleston. Two Charleston attorneys, Nelson Mitchell and Edward McCrady, were appointed to defend them pro bono. Mitchell and McCrady won their case. They went to the jail at midnight and called to their clients, "All of you can rejoice. You are recognized as United States soldiers."

As part of the Union strategy, the Union Navy established a naval blockade of Charleston Harbor to stop all imports and exports. A new enterprise of blockade-running was created and never stopped until the war ended, but the cost of groceries and other such items skyrocketed. In late summer 1863, Federal troops on the islands south of the city began an eighteen-month bombardment of the city, and the action just about halted the practice of law at the Charleston Bar. The cannons were trained

For eighteen months, starting in late summer 1863, the citizens of Charleston suffered through a bombardment inflicted by Federal artillery located on the islands to the south of the city, aimed mainly on the area to the south of Calhoun Street where the courthouse and all the law offices were located.

One of the most important strategies devised by the North to defeat the Confederacy was a naval blockade of southern ports. This engraving illustrates an incident in Charleston harbor in 1863. Two Confederate iron-clads attacked ships of the blockade in an attempt to recapture the Princess Royal, *a blockade runner captured while attempting to deliver an important cargo of military supplies, including engines for iron-clads, guns, ammunition, and medical supplies.*

on the city south of Calhoun Street, including all of the city's law offices and the courthouse. Business that had to be transacted took place north of Calhoun Street. The only members of the bar still in Charleston were those physically unable to fight in the war. This writer suggests that only emergency legal matters were handled, such as deathbed wills. Although President Abraham Lincoln entered the Civil War for the stated purpose of preserving the Union, he changed his mind, and on January 1, 1863, emancipated by proclamation all slaves residing in those states in rebellion against the Union.

District courthouses were closed in most of the Lowcountry. The answer to where and how records were stored is not found in any standard history books. It is possible that those valuable records were stored in the Fireproof Building, the majestic edifice designed by Robert Mills and built in the 1820s to serve as a repository for the records of the Charleston District. Today, the building on the corner of Meeting and Chalmers streets is the home of the South Carolina Historical Society, with its library and vast collections of manuscripts of South Carolina history. During the nineteenth century, the building housed a variety of district, county, and state agencies. Historian Warren Ripley has suggested that courthouse officers probably personally hid the records to preserve them. Several Lowcountry districts, including Beaufort, Colleton, and Georgetown, sent their records to Columbia for safekeeping, but more of them were destroyed by the fires that ravaged Columbia on February 16 and 17, 1865, as General William T. Sherman's Federal troops occupied the city. General Sherman's troops systematically burned courthouses and other public buildings as they cut their path of destruction through the state.

Charleston surrendered in February and the war was over in April 1865. The war had brought the practice of law to a grinding halt and the legal profession, like every other element of southern society, had to begin again almost from nothing.

CHAPTER V

RECONSTRUCTION AND A NEW CENTURY

UNION FORCES OCCUPIED Charleston on February 17, 1865, as the Confederates evacuated the city. General Robert E. Lee, commander of the Army of Northern Virginia, surrendered to Union General Ulysses S. Grant at the Appomattox Court House, Virginia, on April 9, 1865. Later surrenders at Durham Station, North Carolina, and in Alabama and Florida brought an end to all hostilities. "Exhaustion and defeat" is how South Carolina historian David D. Wallace described 1865, the year the war was lost.

The city of Charleston was a mournful spectacle in ruins, virtually a ghost town. The waterfront was in shambles, the wharves were rotten, and weeds grew in the streets around the courthouse. The Federal Freedmen's Bureau saved city dwellers from starvation when it distributed food rations in June 1865 to 20,000 black and white residents. Fortunes that had been invested in slaves and plantations evaporated as the slaves were liberated and some plantation lands were seized by the U.S. military as forfeited or abandoned property. Seized real estate was redistributed to freedmen to establish them as independent farmers. Black citizens also struggled for the first time in American history to build independent lives, but they also celebrated their freedom throughout the year with big parades and parties. Everyone was free and Charleston had at least escaped the destruction of cities like Atlanta and Columbia.

President Lincoln mandated a reconstruction plan which began on June 30, 1865, with the appointment of a Greenville lawyer, Benjamin F. Perry, as provisional governor. He had instructions to organize the state and prepare it for readmission to the Union. The Freedmen's Bureau managed by Federal officers was given jurisdiction to protect the civil rights and the safety of the new black citizens until reorganized state courts recovered their authority. How were Charleston lawyers to make a living? They did not do this by practicing law. The state was a military district governed first by General Quincy Gillmore and then by General Daniel Sickles.

There seems to be neither a directory of lawyers nor record of any law practice in Charleston for the year 1865. There are no deeds or other real estate records registered between December 16, 1864, and May 1866. No Charleston County court records at all exist for 1865. The *Mercury*, the only newspaper of general circulation, suspended publication on February 12, 1865, and did not resume until November 15, 1866.

In September 1865, Governor Perry called a constitutional convention which abolished chattel slavery but did not give blacks the right to vote. In December, the legislature passed what became known as the "Black Codes," because the governor believed that freedmen needed some

OPPOSITE PAGE: *Edward McCrady was an historian and leader of the Charleston Bar after the Civil War. He had studied law under his father Edward McCrady, Jr., one of the prominent lawyers in Charleston during the antebellum period.* BELOW: *Charleston was a city in ruins in the immediate aftermath of the Civil War.* RIGHT: *William Perry, a Greenville lawyer, was appointed provisional governor of South Carolina by President Abraham Lincoln in 1865.*

limited legal protection to permit the state to rejoin the Union. The black codes guaranteed freedmen's property rights but severely restricted their civil liberties. They defined who was a person of color—an individual having one-eighth African-American blood. Prior to these laws, issues of race had been questions for juries to decide. The following year, military governor General Daniel Sickles voided the black codes for their lack of civil rights guarantees.

The General Assembly repealed the state's usury laws in an attempt to increase the amount of capital available for loan with the result that interest on some loans reached extortionate rates as high as 30 percent. In a weak economy, collection on any kind of debt was difficult for lawyers.

There were three large real estate developments in the Charleston area that offered lots for sale to freedmen and lawyers probably prepared all the deeds. One large tract on old Meeting Street Road was divided into 100 lots which were sold to freedmen for $20 each. This subdivision was named Petigru for the Unionist lawyer, James Louis Petigru. Small farms were subdivided and sold out of another tract called Liberty Hill and owned by a group of freedmen. Freedmen also had the opportunity to purchase 132 lots in Lincoln Village near Summerville. The incorporated town of Lincolnville, in Charleston County, preserves the memory of this real estate venture.

In 1867, the mining of phosphate rock began to rejuvenate the economy of Charleston County. This industry became a major economic factor in the local economy, and, by 1877, the county had 16 phosphate mines that employed 3,000 workers.

In antebellum days, agriculture dominated the state. As the state began to recover from the war, phosphate entrepreneurs, bankers, merchants, railroad men, and in the following decade, industrialists, created wealth and therefore had great influence. The practice of corporate

In the years following the Civil War, a new industry—the mining of phosphates—had a major impact on the recovery of the economy of Charleston County. Phosphate entreprenuers and other commercial and industrial clients such as banks, merchants, and railroads added a new and lucrative field of practice to the traditional areas of real estate, trust, and criminal law.

THE WHIRLPOOL OF CONFEDERATE MONEY LITIGATION

AFTER THE CIVIL WAR NUMEROUS LAWSUITS WERE filed throughout the former Confederacy grounded upon the devaluation of Confederate money. Many people tried to pay off their mortgages on their homes, plantations, and businesses with worthless Confederate money. Those who succeeded had incurred their mortgages during the life of the Confederacy.

An example of litigation that grew out of the Confederate experience was the case of *Rachel M. Mayer v. Benjamin Mordecai and others*. This lawsuit was first tried by the Charleston Equity Court in March of 1868. The question in this legal action centered on the issue of whether or not Mordecai, as Trustee, was liable to the beneficiary for her trust funds which he had invested in Confederate bonds.

The Charleston County Equity Court held for the Trustee, Mordecai, but upon appeal the case was remanded by the South Carolina Supreme Court with instructions for an order directing Trustee Mordecai to account for the monies to the Mayer beneficiary. Mrs. Mayer, by deed dated May 1860, assigned to Mordecai certain bonds and mortgages to be held in trust to invest the proceeds as soon as received and in such manner as Mordecai may think proper on consultation with the beneficiary. He was then to permit her to receive the income from investments. Shortly thereafter, Rachel Mayer moved to New York and remained there during the Confederate War.

The bonds were paid to Mordecai in the years 1862 and 1863 in Confederate paper money. Mordecai in turn invested those proceeds in Confederate States of America bonds but at that time it was impractical to communicate with Mayer in New York. Commenting on this period of time, the Supreme Court took judicial notice, in a decision written by Chief Justice Franklin Moses, Sr., that, "It should be borne in mind that, in 1862 and 1863, the doors of the court were practically closed against creditors, and there was no means of enforcing the payment of either principal or interest....that he sold, during the war, his own residence, in Charleston, and invested largely in Confederate bonds, while it exhibits great faith in the ultimate establishment of the Government whose currency he so much favored, may be accepted as the evidence of patriotism so controlling as to absorb every selfish and interest motive. He could do as he pleased with his money, but he had not the right to take a risk, to the chances of the whirlpool, with the means of others entrusted in his care and protection."

law joined Charleston's traditional legal fields of real estate, trust, and criminal practice.

Amid the changing character of the legal profession, a new development improved the bar and legal profession in Charleston. African-American attorneys began to open offices and to practice their profession. A pioneer black lawyer Jonathan J. Wright of Pennsylvania, came to South Carolina in 1865 and was the first African American to join the South Carolina Bar. He was also the first black judge on the state Supreme Court, a state senator, and founder of a large practice in Charleston. Wright had a role in the creation of a law school at Claflin College in Orangeburg, South Carolina, and trained young men for the bar in his office.

Another African-American attorney, William J. Whipper of Philadelphia, also moved to South Carolina in 1865. A Beaufort-area politician and attorney, he established Charleston's first African-American law firm. Whipper, Robert Brown Elliott, and Macon B. Allen practiced law together in an office at 91 Broad Street. Elliott was also one of the foremost black statesmen of his age.

The first post-Civil War listing of all the lawyers of the Charleston Bar was published in the *City Directory* for 1867-1868. In addition to listing the familiar family names of

JONATHAN JASPER WRIGHT

(1840-1885)

Jonathan J. Wright was a justice of the South Carolina Supreme Court during the tumultuous years of Reconstruction. A man of judicious reasoning and broad education, he helped to maintain the rule of law at a time when African-American South Carolinians first joined and then dominated the state government and white South Carolinians chafed under the rule of United States troops and then freed the slaves. By virtue of his position on the South Carolina bench, Wright became the first African American to serve on a state Supreme Court in the nation. His career as an attorney and jurist was evidence of the revolutionary transformation that took place in South Carolina in the years after 1865. When Wright was born and a young man, South Carolina and its neighbors owned African Americans as personal property.

The son of a runaway slave, Wright was born February 11, 1840, in Luzerne County, Pennsylvania. At the age of 13, he was the only member of his family of eight to present himself to join the local all-white Presbyterian church. Wright's schooling began in the local common school, followed by three years as a private pupil of a church elder and then he studied two years at Lancasterian Academy in New York. While working as a schoolteacher, he read law in the chambers of a local judge. In the same year, Wright made an informal application for admission

Jonathan Jasper Wright was the first African American to serve as a justice on any state Supreme Court in the nation.

Charleston's prewar legal profession, it contained the names of a new generation of lawyers. Their names are today as familiar in Charleston as the older names of Rutledge, Young, and Simons.

The 1867-1868 *City Directory* described some of the legal turmoil of that day:

> *Owing to the disturbed condition of our local government, arising from the military control of the Municipality, some difficulty has occurred in procuring a proper register of the names and addresses of the citizens (but) an earnest energetic canvas has, we trust, enabled us to present a work unequalled for accuracy and mechanical execution, by any former Directory of the City of Charleston.*

Sixty-seven attorneys were listed but another roster of members of the bar recorded that a large number of attorneys had abandoned the practice of law and taken up more profitable pursuits. For example, young W.L. Lawton left Broad Street to join his family's cotton factor business. Some new names in the 1867-1868 directory were: Clancy, Cohen, Decatur, Ficken, Hanckel, Kirk, Lawton, Lining, Lockwood, Mikell, Muckenfuss, Nathans, O'Connor, Phillips, Schroeder, Seigling, Smythe, Tennent, and Yeadon. Nearly all of these names have become familiar to members of the modern Charleston bar.

The name of Rutledge and Young reappeared in the 1869-1870 *City Directory*. This firm's history began in the 1830s when two men, Joseph Underwood Rutledge Young to the Pennsylvania Bar. Justice Mercur, of the Pennsylvania bench, advised him that the application would be rejected. Wright then accepted a position with the American Missionary Association to teach school to black federal troops in Beaufort, South Carolina. After a year in South Carolina, Wright received word that Pennsylvania Judge Mercur had left the bench. Consequently he successfully applied for admission to the state bar.

In 1864, he attended the first national black convention where he heard the famous orator and abolitionist, Frederick Douglass. At the convention he also became acquainted with Richard H. Cain and Francis L. Cordozo, two men with close ties to Charleston. The Freedmen's Bureau asked Wright to return to Beaufort as "an agent assisting free people in legal affairs." He arrived in time to be elected to the 1868 constitutional convention in Charleston. Upon the opening of this convention, the Bureau forced Wright to resign as its employee. As a private citizen, Wright was then elected to the state senate from Beaufort County.

Two years into his senate service, Wright saw an opportunity when a seat opened up on the three-member state Supreme Court. He and his senate seatmate, William J. Whipper, contested this election. Wright was elected with 72 votes to Whipper's 57. This singular event did not go without notice. *The Charleston News* reported that Wright held "the highest position held by a colored man in the United States." He wrote 90 decisions and never missed a day of court.

In 1876, white Democrats regained control of the government of the state. The election of Confederate General Wade Hampton to be governor and the resolution of a bitter controversy in the state House of Representatives in favor of the Democrats paved the way for the formal end of Reconstruction. In exchange for South Carolina's votes in the electoral college, the Republican Presidential candidate, Rutherford B. Hayes, agreed to remove federal troops from the state. Once the troops were withdrawn, whites began a systematic campaign to remove and exclude blacks from power.

As part of this campaign, Justice Wright was impeached for drunkenness. The Senate impeachment called upon Wright to resign quietly. He refused and, in the subsequent senate trial, was removed from office. Wright then moved to Charleston and opened an office at 84 Queen Street, where he practiced law and taught students for the rest of his life. Wright was also dean of the law school at Claflin College, Orangeburg.

The former justice developed tuberculosis at the age of 45. At that time, there was no known cure for the disease and on February 17, 1885, he signed his deathbed will. He bequeathed his law library to his first law student and named another to be his executor. The black members of the Charleston Bar called the court's attention to his death by conducting a ceremony in the Court of General Sessions. Wright was buried at Calvary Episcopal Church at 106 Line Street in Charleston. In January 2000, the South Carolina Supreme Court placed a granite marker in the churchyard to honor his service to his adopted state.

For comments on Wright's Supreme Court opinions and additional biographical material see *At Freedom's Door: African American Founding Fathers and Lawyers in Reconstruction South Carolina*, edited by James Lowell Underwood and W. Lewis Burke, University of South Carolina Press (2000).

and Benjamin Mordecai, shared an office at 28 Broad Street. This law partnership was also one between Jewish and Christian faiths. "Young took pleasure in knowing his initials spelled jury," explained J. Rutledge Young of today's bar. In 1850, Henry E. Young entered the firm and his son Arthur followed him in 1909. Then, Arthur Young joined with Benjamin A. Hagood and M. Rutledge Rivers in the practice of law. Joseph R. Young joined their firm in 1940, followed in later years by G.L. Buist Rivers, Jr., Robert L. Clement, and Thomas S. Tisdale and the firm became Young, Clement, Rivers and Tisdale, LLP. Despite the transformations, the firm's address is still 28 Broad Street, where it has been for more than 175 years, although it is now known as Young, Clement and Rivers.

The 1869-1870 *City Directory* listed the Buist and Buist firm, which is still in practice in the twentieth century under the name of Buist Moore Smythe McGee. Also listed was Whipper, Elliott, and Allen at 91 Broad Street. William Whipper's descendants are members of the Charleston Bar in the twenty-first century.

On January 23, 1867, the General Assembly provided for the first professors' chairs of law and of medicine at the University of South Carolina. The first law professor was appointed in June 1867, and the law school opened in October with a two-year program. The University of South Carolina was the first school in the South to provide legal training for freedmen and it was not long before both races were attending the school. The first African American to enroll in the University of South Carolina Law School was Walter Riley Jones of Charleston, son of Septima A. Jones. Student Jones had graduated from the Avery Normal Institute of Charleston and Oberlin College of Ohio. As a law student he was elected librarian of the Clariosophic Society, a debating and scholarly club of great traditions. Jones was admitted to the bar in 1874 but his life was tragically cut short by meningitis on November 29, 1876.

No law degrees were awarded in 1869, but degrees began to be awarded in 1870 when five students graduated. Between 1868 and 1876, the law school had 39 graduates and 11 of them were African Americans. The law school ceased to function in 1876 when the whole university closed.

President Lincoln's reconstruction plan ceased in March 1867 when the Radical Republicans in Congress took direct control of the defeated Southern states. Congress created military districts in South Carolina, declaring that the state governments of the former Confederate states had ceased to exist. A general was appointed commander of the state and a new constitution suspending that of 1865 was required before South Carolina could reenter the Union.

Another constitutional convention, the second in three years, was held in Charleston between January 14 and March 18, 1868, at 45 Meeting Street. The building was the home of the antebellum Charleston Club and was the Federal district courthouse after the war. The site is now a park adjacent to the south side of the United States Federal Court House. The majority of the delegates at the 1868 convention were black. The *Charleston Daily* newspaper reported on January 14, that,

"The convention is held by authority of the Reconstruction law of congress to frame a state constitution for South Carolina...

The Place of Meeting.
"...once celebrated as the Charleston Club...The classic edifice in times gone by...the handsome grounds and ornamental shrubbery alone remain of the honored association connected with this spot...The building itself has passed into other hands and is now owned by J. P. M. Epting the United States Marshall for the District of South Carolina by whom it was rented to military authorities for the use of the convention for one thousand dollars. To adapt to the exigencies of the occasion, the large hall on the second floor has been divided in twain by a wooden rail...inside the rail there are comfortable chairs for the accommodations of the delegates. The platform is a twelve-foot structure surmounted by a plain pine desk...

The Personnel of the Convention
W. G. Whipper (colored) from Beaufort, educated as a lawyer, is a clear sharp, forcible speaker, and has an abundance of common sense, is not rabid, and will give trouble to any man who in the convention crosses foils with him in debate. He is a Northern man, and has been in South Carolina since the war. Another funny man will be J. J. Wright, a colored lawyer, of Beaufort, nominally from the North actually...He has one of your high Philanthropio-shaped heads of the H. Greely-ous style and as an agent of the Bureau is said to have done much good in relieving the wants of his people. He is a ready, off-hand speaker and woe unto any delegate from the rural districts who gets into his hands. He talks on the high pressure principle, forty-pounds to the square inch and is a perfect elocutionary steam engine.

Most modern historians agree that the 1868 constitution went far to establish democratic government in the state. It certainly marked an end of dominance by the pre-Civil War class of planters, merchants, and professional men. While there was a contingent of Lowcountry lawyer-delegates, many were black and others were immigrants from the North. The convention roster held none of the names of the old Charleston Bar.

In March, 1867, President Lincoln's reconstruction plan was supplanted by the harsher reconstruction plan of the Radical Republicans in the U.S. Congress. South Carolina became part of the Second Military District, along with North Carolina, under the command of General Daniel E. Sickles (above).

TOP: *After the war, agriculture in general, and cotton in particular, continued to be crucial to the economy of South Carolina. The abolition of slavery led to the new system of sharecropping and many African Americans in rural areas found their working lives had changed very little.* ABOVE: *Cotton was also important to the commercial life of the port of Charleston where it was still the most important agricultural export.*

This constitution joined law and equity courts into a single court and abolished the chancery court. Judges were given tenure conditioned upon their good behavior instead of lifetime appointments. They were not allowed to charge the juries as to matters of fact, only as to matters of law. The power to grant a divorce was given to the Court of Common Pleas, which, in effect, made divorce legal and obtainable for the first time in the state's history. Solicitors were to be elected by the people rather than the legislature; the creation of a compulsory public school was mandated; and the constitution was ratified by the electorate not by the legislature. This constitution remained in place for 27 years. At that time, admission to the bar by the Circuit Court allowed an attorney to practice only there and in the Probate Court. Admission to the bar by the South Carolina Supreme Court permitted an attorney to practice in any state court.

Eight notable African-American attorneys of that era were connected with Charleston or a member of its bar. Jonathan Jasper Wright was the first African American to be elected to the Supreme Court of South Carolina. He subsequently opened a law practice at 84 Queen Street in Charleston.

A Philadelphia native, William J. Whipper, came from Michigan to South Carolina with the Union Army after receiving his legal education in Detroit. He was admitted to the South Carolina Bar in September 1868 and first opened his law practice in Beaufort. Whipper and Wright persuaded the general in command of the United States troops in Beaufort to prosecute a white man for assaulting a black man. This was the first recorded legal action filed by a black attorney in any South Carolina tribunal.

Whipper was elected to the state senate as a member of the Republican party's radical wing. He was in the running to be elected a justice of the South Carolina Supreme Court but was defeated by Jonathan J. Wright. At the time they were Senate seatmates. In 1874, Whipper was elected Judge of the First Circuit, which included Charleston, but Governor Daniel Chamberlain refused to issue him a commission. Whipper earned a great deal of money in the practice of law and one story told of him was that, in 1875, while a member of the legislature, he lost $30,000 at poker, half of that amount in a single hand. His four aces were defeated by a straight flush. Whipper served as a delegate to the 1868 state constitutional convention. He was elected Probate Judge of Beaufort County in 1885 but was defeated for reelection in 1888. On September 2, 1869, Whipper paid $6,000 for about 90 acres of land at Seven Mile in Charleston's north area. He called this land "Whipper Barony." Today, Whipper Barony is a well-established subdivision and Whipper descendants are members of the local bar.

A native of Aiken, South Carolina, Robert C. DeLarge was admitted to the bar in November 1871. Before then, he had been a delegate to the 1868 constitutional convention and member of the state General Assembly. DeLarge posted a bond on March 26, 1870, to serve as Charleston County treasurer and on April 7, 1873, he posted another bond to serve as a trial justice. DeLarge was a U.S. Congressman from 1871 to 1873. He owned several properties on Calhoun and Princess streets and in the north area of Charleston.

Daniel Straker received his legal education from Howard University and was admitted to the South Carolina Bar in July 1875. Straker was a native of Barbados and was appointed Inspector of Customs. From 1882 to 1887, he was the first dean of the Law School at Allen University in Columbia. At one time he had a law office in Orangeburg but he mostly practiced in Sumter. In 1895, long after Reconstruction, Straker had a successful law practice in Detroit and was known as D. Augustus Straker. He was president of the National Federation of Colored Men, a Detroit organization established in 1895.

Broad Street, seen here in an 1875 engraving, has been called the "Wall Street" of Charleston due to the large number of law offices and banks located there, many of which can still be found today.

John M. Freeman, Jr. entered the bar in December 1875 and stated that his home was in Charleston. Macon B. Allen joined William Whipper and Robert Brown Elliott at 91 Broad Street after he was admitted to the bar in December 1875. He was a native of Indiana and in 1844 was the first black American admitted to the United States bar. Additionally, he was the first African American in the United States to be a Justice of the Peace.

Henry Barton Johnson was probably born a free person of color around 1850. He graduated from the law school at the University of South Carolina in 1875 and was admitted to the bar in November 1877. Johnson served as Chief Clerk to the Secretary of State, Henry E. Hayne, his brother-in-law. After Reconstruction, Johnson and Hayne left the state.

Francis Lewis Cardozo, a free person of color, was the son of Lydia Williams and Isaac Nunez Cardozo, both of Charleston. Isaac Cardozo was a member of a prominent Jewish family that shared a lineage with United States Supreme Court Justice Benjamin Nathan Cardozo (1870-1938). Francis Lewis Cardozo received his undergraduate degree in 1850 from the University of Glasgow, Scotland, before becoming a Congregational minister in the North. He returned to South Carolina in 1865 with the American Missionary Association and became its director of educational activities in Charleston. Cardozo established Avery Normal Institute of Charleston to train black teachers and was its principal. He was a delegate to the 1868 constitutional convention, state treasurer, secretary of state, and director of the land commission. When he was elected secretary of state, he became the first African American in the nation's history to be elected to a statewide office. While secretary of state, Cardozo enrolled in the law school at the University of South Carolina, graduated, and was admitted to the bar but did not practice law as a profession. After Reconstruction, Cardozo moved to Washington, D.C., where he held a post in the United States Treasury Department. He then became a teacher and principal in the public schools of the District of Columbia until his death in 1903. A Cardozo descendent, Cassandra E. Maxwell, became South Carolina's first African-American woman attorney on December 11, 1941.

Governor Daniel Chamberlain was elected in 1874, the last Republican to be elected governor of South Carolina for a hundred years. In 1876, he was defeated in a bid for reelection by Democrat Wade Hampton III.

Reconstruction began to unravel in the 1872 governor's election when the Republicans nominated for a second term Franklin J. Moses, Jr., a man of notoriously bad character who was indicted for stealing while governor. White Democrats worked to overthrow the Republican regime but were held in check by the presence of federal garrisons. In 1874, Republican Daniel H. Chamberlain was elected governor and he ran for a second term in 1876. At that election, Democrats nominated former Confederate General Wade Hampton III, a Richland County attorney and one of the state's most respected war veterans, as their candidate for governor.

The 1876 gubernatorial campaign centered upon which race, black or white, would capture the reins of government. Hampton's supporters were called Redeemers because they claimed that they would redeem the government from black control. They were also called Red Shirts because many were war veterans and their campaign costume was a red hunting shirt. Hampton was elected by 1,134 votes, but the result was in dispute for four months. During that time the state had two competing governments, both of which claimed legitimacy. For example, there were two speakers of the House of Representatives who sat by side by side in the House chamber. Because of its uncertain authority, Chamberlain's administration was only able to collect about 1,000 dollars in state taxes, a situation that prevented many state agencies from functioning.

The presidential election of 1876 was even more disorderly and produced results as uncertain as those in South Carolina. So many state elections were disputed that there was no clear winner between the Democratic candidate Samuel J. Tilden and Republican Rutherford B. Hayes. In exchange for Southern support on a special electoral commission, Hayes pledged to remove Federal troops from South Carolina and other former Confederate states. The Hayes election and the near simultaneous certification of Wade Hampton as governor marked the formal end of Reconstruction and the return of white rule in the state. The day after Hampton took office, Daniel Chamberlain left the state and started a lucrative law practice in New York. One lasting result of Reconstruction was the political polarization of the state's black and white citizens. In later decades, the polarization led to social polarization and enactment of "Jim Crow" laws that mandated separation of the races. Physicians in Charleston and throughout the

Democrats returned to power in South Carolina with the election of Wade Hampton III as governor in 1876, signalling the end of Reconstruction. Hampton's supporters were called Redeemers because of their claim that they could redeem the government of the state from black control.

state had two waiting rooms, one for "whites" and one for "coloreds." This segregation was practiced by other professionals but not by lawyers, who stuck to their tradition of using single waiting rooms for black and white clients. Segregated waiting rooms and strict separation of races in public places were the law and custom of the state well into the twentieth century.

To assert that Reconstruction concluded with the withdrawal of federal troops in 1877 is an inadequate explanation. In fact, Reconstruction had been in retreat for several years. Charleston lawyer James Conner was attorney general and a leader of the bar. He played an important role in the legal profession during Reconstruction and the time of reorganization that followed.

Hampton's administration immediately began to remove black Republican judges. Faced with unsubstantiated allegations of malfeasance, Supreme Court Justice Wright resigned. Hampton then replaced the two other justices of the Supreme Court. A legal action challenged the voice vote election of the sitting circuit judges and the newly unreconstructed Court declared those judicial elections void because the state constitution mandated the election of judges by ballot. Another change tightened the rules for admission to the bar. The authority to admit attorneys was removed from the Circuit Courts and placed in the hands of the Supreme Court. In 1877-78, the year after Hampton's election, the Charleston bar had 75 members.

Dueling was part of the social system of the state and known as an "affair of Honor." Although duels were against the law, participants and survivors, if prosecuted, were customarily acquitted if the fight had been fair; that is, if the duelists were of the same class of gentlemen. Dueling was so common in the antebellum era that Governor John Lyde Wilson, an attorney, published a *Code of Honor* in 1838 on the "punctilious decorum" of duels to bring some order and method to the mayhem. In 1881, one of the last duels in the state occurred between Colonel Ellerbee B. C. Cash and Colonel William M. Shannon, a Camden attorney. The challenge arose because Cash was denounced for abusively hounding Shannon as he publicly represented a client's best interest. Shannon was killed with the first shot. As a result of this duel, the state constitution was amended to require all officers of the court, including all lawyers, to swear an oath that they had not engaged in a duel since January 1, 1881, and would not employ an "affair of Honor" to settle a dispute. This provision remained in the oath administered to new members of the bar until the mid-twentieth century.

Charleston attorney Henry E. Young was a founding member of the American Bar Association and was elected vice president at the association's first meeting in August 1878 in Saratoga Springs, New York. A year later, in 1879, there were 228 members throughout the nation and 15 of those members were from Charleston, South Carolina.

JAMES CONNER

(1829-1883)

By Ainsley Fisher Tillman, Attorney and descendent of James Conner

Born on September 1, 1829, James Conner was the son of Juliana Courtney and Henry Workman Conner. He enjoyed horseback riding, was fond of balls and parties, and was an excellent marksman. Before he began college, Conner worked for John Fraser & Co., a successful Charleston importing and exporting business. Although he learned a great deal about business, Conner wanted to study law and went to South Carolina College and graduated with distinction in 1849.

After earning a degree, Conner "read law" in an attorney's office, which was the practice of the time for entering the bar. He was fortunate to learn the law from James L. Petigru, the recognized leader of the Charleston Bar. Conner was admitted to the bar in 1851, and in the early days of his practice had an office in his parents' home on lower Meeting Street. While living with his parents, he began to write a *Digest of the Laws of South Carolina*. Unfortunately, he chose an unconventional place to jot down his notes: on the walls around his bed. Once, he returned from a brief absence to find the walls covered by a fresh coat of paint.

In 1855, James Conner was appointed United States District Attorney for South Carolina, an indication of his talent as a lawyer. The position was not an easy one to fill at that time, as all questions relating to slavery were greeted by a population quick to resent any criticism. In August 1858, the *Echo*, the last slave ship brought into Charleston, was captured off the coast of Cuba by the United States Navy. The vessel was taken to Charleston Harbor, where its officers and crew were marched through the streets in handcuffs. James Conner aggressively prosecuted the cases against the prisoners, but he was unable to get any convictions.

Conner was dedicated to states' rights and was sensitive to the impending conflict. He resigned his position as United States District Attorney in December 1860, when Lincoln's election was certified. Conner stated: "For all that has been done, I have neither apology to make, nor explanation to offer. The record is clear, and speaks for itself. What the future will bring forth, none can tell. The reasons which have governed me in the present step are satisfactory to my own judgment. It is neither necessary nor appropriate to allude to them within the walls of a Court of Justice."

James Conner entered Confederate service as Captain of the Montgomery Guards. He took the position seriously and avidly studied military tactics. Although he was appointed Confederate States Attorney for the District of South Carolina, Conner refused to leave the military field. He was at the bombardment of Fort Sumter on April 12, 1861, and participated in the battles of First Manassas, Yorktown, New Stone Point, West Point, Seven Pines, Mechanicsville, Chancellorsville, Riddle's Shop, Darby's Farm, Fussell's Mill, Petersburg, Jerusalem Plank Road, Reams' Station, Winchester, Port Republic, and Cedar Creek. He was seriously wounded in his leg, which had to be amputated. By the end of the war he had risen to the rank of major general.

After his return to Charleston, Conner resumed the practice of law. He married Sallie Enders of Richmond, Virginia, on October 10, 1866 and they lived in Charleston, where they raised four children. For many years, Conner was assistant counsel and then solicitor of the South Carolina Railroad and the Bank of Charleston. In 1876, he was elected state Attorney General. He died a distinguished attorney and respected military hero on June 26, 1883.

The earthquake of August 31, 1886 caused widespread destruction in Charleston, damaging over 2,000 buildings. This photograph shows the impact on Hayne Street.

At a December 11, 1884, meeting in the Richland County Courthouse, 102 lawyers reorganized the South Carolina Bar Association. Charles H. Simonton was temporary president and Andrew G. Magrath was the association's first permanent president. Both of these attorneys were members of the Charleston Bar, which first promoted the idea of organizing the profession statewide. Of the original 288 members, 42 were from Charleston. There were no African-American members and the association was closed to blacks until the last quarter of the twentieth century. One reason for revitalizing the organization was a feeling that the profession had declined in quality. This new South Carolina Bar was an attempt to raise the profession to its pre-Civil War distinction.

The University of South Carolina reopened in 1884 as a whites-only institution. The law school also reopened in 1884 and Joseph D. Pope was its only professor of law. In the 1890s, the law school became a separate department and another professor was added to the faculty.

In the 1880s, the Charleston Bar was known as the Charleston Law Society. The 1894 *City Directory* stated the Society met on the first Tuesday of each month at the courthouse. At that time, U.S. Fourth Circuit Court of Appeals Judge C. H. Simonton was president and J. B. Chisolm was secretary and treasurer.

Between 1877 and 1899, 15 African-American lawyers had Charleston connections. Robert L. Gaillard, a member of the bar in the twenty-first century, is a descendant of John A. Gaillard, one of five lawyers admitted to the bar in 1897.

Thomas McCants Stewart became a justice on the Supreme Court of Liberia. He was the son of Anna Morris Stewart and George Gilchrist Stewart, a blacksmith in Charleston. His parents had been free persons of color. Stewart graduated from Avery Normal Institute in Charleston. From 1869 to 1873, he attended Howard University and graduated from the law school at the University of South Carolina in the class of 1875. After the conservative victory of 1876-77, Stewart entered Princeton Theological Seminary. He then served a congregation in New York City after his ordination. Later, he took an academic position in Monrovia, Liberia. He was a globetrotter as he went from Liberia to Hawaii where he was the first African-American attorney in the islands. Stewart returned to Liberia to become Deputy Attorney General, whereupon he renounced his American citizenship. His duties in the Liberian Attorney General's office were to reform the judicial system. As a reward for his service, Stewart was appointed an Associate Justice of the Liberian Supreme Court. In 1921, he retired to the Virgin Islands and died there in 1923.

Charleston experienced the shock of a great earthquake on the night of August 31, 1886 that was so powerful it was felt as far away as Wisconsin. The quake damaged 2,000 buildings, including the police station and the jail at the southwest corner of Broad and Meeting streets. It damaged but did not destroy the historic courthouse across the street. The police station and jail were torn down, and, ten years later, the federal government built a United States Court House and post office on the site. This intersection has become known as the famous "Four Corners of Law." The federal courthouse was built on the southwest corner and the state courthouse was built on the northwest corner. Charleston's City Hall is on the northeast corner and Saint Michael's Episcopal Church, a colonial-era building, adorns the southeast corner.

The late 1880s gave rise to a nationwide agrarian and democratic movement called Populism. Hard times for farmers led them to organize to improve their economic and political conditions. Among the first Populist leaders in the state was "Pitchfork" Benjamin Ryan Tillman. An Edgefield County planter, he served two terms as governor (1890-1894). Tillman was a racial demagogue and implacable opponent of the old regime of Wade Hampton and the "Bourbons" who had run the state for 20 years. His staunchest opponents were among the Charleston Bar. In 1894, Tillman called for a state constitutional convention to replace the Reconstruction-era 1868 constitution. The agrarians tried to exclude the Bourbon delegates from the convention, but Tillman blocked them because he knew that the best legal minds in the state were Bourbons. The main focus of the convention was to create a constitution to disfranchise African Americans and roll back the progressive features of the earlier one. The 1895 constitution incorporated the provision that lawyers had to swear not to settle disputes by dueling, but it also prohibited divorce, destroyed home rule, and outlawed racially integrated schools. Much amended over the years, the 1895 constitution still governs South Carolina.

In the final decade of the nineteenth century, remarkable inventions brought progress to the legal profession. Clients could reach their lawyer's office by bicycle or by horse-drawn streetcars. Typewriters were available, and telephones came to Charleston. An 1899 local business directory lists 83 lawyers, including one with a telephone number. Arnoldus Vanderhorst placed an advertisement in the directory stating: "A Vander Horst Attorney and Counselor 53 Broad Tel. 383."

Populist Governor "Pitchfork" Ben Tillman opposed the Bourbon Democrats personified by Wade Hampton III. Tillman in turn had some of his strongest opponents in the Charleston Bar.

William Haynsworth Lyles, a Columbia lawyer, recalled that, in this decade, lawyers did not appear in the courtroom unless clad in old-fashioned, double-breasted Prince Albert coats and were never seen on the street without their Prince Alberts and silk hats. Vests were very much in evidence but were made from a fabric that contrasted with the suit. Four-in-hand neckties were the center of attention because of their excessive bulk. Men's slacks had creases for the first time in history.

The twentieth century arrived in Charleston with much millennial fanfare. Some local preachers predicted that the world would come to an end on the stroke of midnight on New Year's Eve. The following day, the *Evening Post* reported that Charleston had experienced a "record snow" but, other than that event, the city and state left behind in the previous century the Civil War, the greatest crisis the nation has ever endured.

CHAPTER VI

FROM PROGRESSIVISM TO DEPRESSION

As the twentieth century began, lawyers hustled in and out of the old 1792 courthouse at the corner of Broad and Meeting streets. Business was often conducted by telephone rather than face to face. Clients traveled to Broad Street by streetcar and pleadings were written under electric lights rather than gas lamps. The more prosperous practices employed clerks, who assumed some of the routine labors of preparing forms and filing documents in court.

The lawyer's professional image was stained during these years by lynchings in which mobs flouted due process, murdering suspects and convicted criminals indiscriminately. Sheriffs and jailers often colluded with the lynch mobs and were influenced into failing to fulfill their duties. John Hammond Moore, historian and author, has discovered that most of the state's lynchings occurred in the northern and western parts of the state.

Charles A. Woods, president of the South Carolina Bar Association, reported in 1903 that there had been 45 lynchings in the state since 1893. In his annual speech to the state bar, Woods said, "...the rule of the mob and the pocket pistol must end...For a free people who makes its own laws, not to be able under all circumstances to give an accused man a fair trial before execution, is a condition not only evil in itself but ominous of greater evils; and it aught to be fairly faced and candidly considered." Woods asserted that mob lawlessness had been spawned by the defeat of the Confederacy and postwar chaos. "The triumph of the union was regarded as the triumph of democracy, and democracy went mad."

There were only two lynchings in Charleston County. Jim Black was hanged in Ravenel on June 2, 1902, for allegedly raping and killing a white woman and, on February 12, 1903, Jake Haynes was lynched by a mob after being accused of theft. Both men were African Americans.

The rule of unreason provoked the state bar to take a stand for due process under the law. Woods' successors asked their colleagues, "Could not law overcome the spirit of the lynch mob? Did lawyers themselves have any responsibility for conditions of lawlessness in this state?" The bar's courage did not hinder demagogues, some of whom sought and won the highest political offices within the gift of the people. Indeed, lawyers and their profession soon felt the wrath of politicians who used popular prejudices to inflame poor whites and blacks against the so-called "aristocrats" and "Bourbons."

"Whenever the Constitution comes between me and the virtue of white women of South Carolina," exclaimed Governor Coleman L. Blease, "I say, the hell with the Constitution." Pandering to the "common man," Blease of Newberry County won the governorship in 1910 and

1912. A former Tillman supporter, Blease was an unvarnished demagogue and racist. His rabble-rousing found little support among Charleston's civic leaders and members of the bar. Nevertheless, a young Charleston lawyer, John Patrick Grace, a populist believer in the rights, wisdom, and virtues of the common people, was elected mayor in 1913 and 1919. Defeated in 1923, Grace used his political pals and business and legal connections to lead the city to construct the first great Cooper River Bridge. Dedicated in 1929 and named for him, the bridge became a famous Charleston landmark.

The number of Charleston lawyers declined between 1900 and 1910 but new names still appeared on the roster. Among the newcomers were Altman, Cogswell, Finger, Fromberg, Grimball, Huger, Kroeg, Sinkler, and Wilbur. Some of these new men likely arrived in Charleston on the steamship *Wittekind* in a voyage sponsored by the South Carolina Immigration Bureau, a state agency charged with the "inducing of desirable settlers" to make the state their home. The *Wittekind* made a single trip across the Atlantic with "desirable settlers" and arrived at Charleston one Sunday morning in November 1906, bearing 476 passengers. Ominously, each passenger had a free return ticket to Bremen, Germany, in his or her pocket.

The *Wittekind* voyage was part of the state's slow evolution towards industrialization and the creation of a white blue-collar working class. The state was looking for skilled white industrial workers to help it find a place in the twentieth century. Most of the immigrants were put on trains bound for mill towns but within six weeks, 200 of them had drifted back to make homes in Charleston. Columbia attorney, R. Beverly Herbert, interviewed the immigrants and remarked that "they were over educated and over skilled."

On the whole, however, the optimism of the legal profession was growing. Historians have called the decades from the mid-1890s to the First World War the Progres-

This view of Charleston in the early 1900s shows a group of children posed in front of the statue of William Pitt in Washington Square park. The steeple of St. Philip's Church is visible in the distance.

STATE V. SCHIADARESSI

By William B. Regan and Frances Cantwell

IN CHARLESTON, DURING THE ADMINISTRATION OF Mayor John P. Grace, Ted Schiadaressi was charged in 1913 with selling Falstaff beer in violation of the State Dispensary Act. He was arrested by Officer Jimmy Cantwell, prosecuted by City Attorney Turner Logan, Mayor Grace's law partner, and convicted.

In his charge to the jury, the trial judge explained "I cannot, either, admit to you that we, the people of Charleston, are law-abiding. I cannot say that. I don't think there is any particular class or particular people to blame. (A)s much as I think of and love the people of Charleston, I think they are the most lawless set there ever was."

That same year Bishop William A. Guerry, in a powerful sermon at St. Philip's Episcopal Church, thundered that, "our most respectable citizens are aiding and abetting the spirit of lawlessness in our midst (as) 'their hands are tied' through their own failure to keep the law."

Charleston lawyer and historian Robert Rosen writes that the State Dispensary Act of 1893, which created a state monopoly on selling alcohol, was never really enforced in Charleston. Charlestonians ignored the state's liquor laws and continued to drink at illegal saloons called "blind tigers." At a U.S. congressional hearing over his challenge to the congressional election of political foe Richard S. Whaley, Grace discussed openly the realities of Charleston's behavior.

> MR. FREAR. *How many blind tigers are run in Charleston?*
>
> MR. GRACE. *Probably 250. But in doing what I did I only followed custom. Mr. Whaley's brother-in-law (R.Goodwyn Rhett) preceded me as Mayor, and Mr. Whaley's brother-in-law established this custom under which these men were in business. When I came in office that was the custom, namely, of every three months fining them $50, which was practically licensing them to sell. They do not have the right to exist at all.*

The fines were an important source of revenue for the city, but more importantly, both mayors Rhett and Grace believed that the blind tigers "'were too much a part of the web of life' in Charleston to close them down." The state's operation proved oddly useful and although

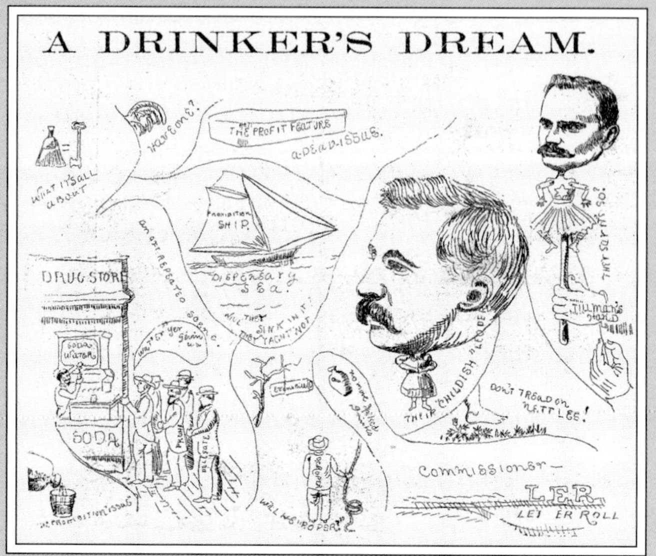

This Anti-Dispensary political cartoon from 1899 depicts the Dispensary as "A Drinker's Dream."

"Charlestonians did not patronize the official dispensaries…(they) became the wholesale suppliers for the blind tigers in the city. Fifteen dispensaries or blind tigers were located around City Hall and nineteen operated near St. Philip's Church."

Under state pressure, Charleston's mayors reluctantly began to enforce the law "just for the record.' Vincent Chicco, "the state's most notorious liquor dealer," was a close friend of Mayor Grace, served on the City Council for four consecutive terms, and even sat on a grand jury investigating local liquor violations. Another prosperous bootlegger was W. J. Cantwell, a brother of Grace's chief of police. Grace was surprisingly frank on the role of politics in the informal management of blind tigers. At the Congressional hearing, he commented on the truthfulness of one of his witnesses, "Rumpty Rattles" Hogan.

> MR. GRACE. *Yes, sir; and Mr. Whaley has always trusted him, but in this campaign there was a reason why he was with me and not with Whaley, for the first time in his life.*
>
> MR. ELDER. *What were his reasons?*
>
> MR. GRACE. *When I made my campaign for mayor he bitterly*

fought…, (H)e was on Whaley's side but when I was elected mayor I was in a position to drive him to the wall, absolutely… if I had shown the disposition to do so, to absolutely drive him to the wall.

MR. ELDER. *That is, the liquor business?*

MR. GRACE. *Yes, sir…but I treated, so far as the administration of the law was concerned—and I think everybody will agree with me in Charleston—everybody absolutely alike. I could have driven him to the wall, as I stated, but I gave everybody an absolutely square deal.*

Schiadaressi was not a Grace supporter. He even gave an affidavit against Grace at the Congregational hearing. Was, then, the Schiadaressi bust an effort to "drive him to the wall?" It was unsuccessful; for, during the federal prohibition era, he operated one of Charleston's speakeasies, the Occidental, on Market Street.

Some time after his arrest, Schiadaressi asked for the hand in marriage of Maybelle Bennett, the daughter of Charleston County jailer William J. Bennett. Permission to marry was granted on one condition—that Schiadaressi go straight, and he did so. In 1931, he opened the Folly Pier and Atlantic Pavilion, which became one of the most popular oceanfront venues in South Carolina for the next 25 years. Harry James, Guy Lombardo, the Inkspots, and other entertainers who rode the summer circuit from New York to Miami made frequent appearances at the Pavilion.

It took much longer for other Charlestonians to "go straight." The sale of illegal spirits continued in Charleston well into the 1960s, until the passage of the mini-bottle law, a more efficient, easily regulated system of beverage control.

As for Schiadaressi, neither conviction nor politics could compel him to "go straight" but he was willing to mend his ways for the sake of love.

ABOVE: *The Dispensary Law was sponsored by Governor Ben Tillman, but was very unpopular with the populace. To enforce the system, Tillman created a special liquor constabulary. Much of the resistance to the system was caused by the sometimes violent and high-handed tactics used by the constabulary. In Darlington, a riot broke out following a fatal shooting by the constables. This illustration shows militia troops guarding the Darlington Dispensary after the riot, under orders from Tillman.*

This photograph of King Street shows Charleston at the turn of the twentieth century, just before the advent of the age of the automobile.

sive Era. Progressivism in the South sought to bring the region into the modern world of science, technology, and humanistic reforms while preserving long-held values and traditions.

Industry, the growth of cities, the rise of the professional classes (including lawyers), and an emergent sense of responsibility for the social welfare of its citizens shaped Southern Progressivism. As the region recovered from the depression that followed the Civil War, uncertainty how blacks and whites would live together—the so-called racial question—was settled by disfranchisement, segregation, and the oppression of South Carolina's black population. Other political issues came to the fore, chiefly the development of railroads, textile mills, and large corporations, but all these issues were tinged by the "racial question."

South Carolina's progressives succeeded in passing legislation forbidding the employment of children under the age of ten years in factories, mines, or mills. The state's textile industry lobbied intensely against restrictions on child labor but the reform measure passed, largely due to a group of Columbia women progressives. Reform accomplished by legislation and regulation encouraged attorneys to specialize in such fields as workers' compensation, tort law for occupational injuries, and railroad law practice.

Two key slogans of Progressivism were "efficiency" and "sanitation." A 1913 state law permitted cities to assess abutting property owners one half of the cost of civic improvements. Suddenly, Charleston began to spend a great deal of money on paving, new sidewalks, curbs, and drainage. Commercial dairies were banned from the city but individuals continued to keep their own cows. A city health department was established and restaurant inspection was inaugurated. The city pest house was closed in 1915, and Mayor Grace commissioned the Medical College of Charleston to provide health care for the poor at Roper Hospital. Richard I. Manning was governor from 1914 to 1916. Many measures he recommended opened government to new ideas and he called for the state to enact legislation "hitherto unknown to us." Manning's administrations were bulwarks of progressivism in the state.

By 1910, women could practice law in 40 states, but Alabama was the only Deep South state that had enacted legislation to open the profession to females. South Carolina was one of the states that did not admit women to the bar but state authorities had been lax in their vigilance. Through inattention, the administrators of the University of South Carolina law school had admitted three women to the school. They were already enrolled and taking classes when someone realized that they lacked the franchise and did not enjoy full citizenship, much less the fact that, by law, they could not be admitted to the bar. A senior in her final law school semester, Claudia James Sullivan, faced the dilemma head on and convinced her local senator to introduce legislation permitting women to practice law. The bill was introduced on January 22, 1918, and moved quickly through the General Assembly. Governor Manning signed the act on February 14 of that year but no Charleston women took the bar examination until 1931.

Women's suffrage was a national issue before World War I. The movement to secure the right to vote united nearly all women, North and South, black and white. On August 18, 1920, the state of Tennessee became the thirty-sixth state to ratify the Nineteenth Amendment. Eight days later, the amendment became the law of the land and women prepared to vote in the November presidential election. South Carolina did not ratify the Nineteenth Amendment until 1969. Instead of recognizing the federal law, the General Assembly enacted its own statute granting South Carolina women the right to vote, but, because of the thicket of Jim Crow laws, the right was, for all practical purposes, restricted to white women.

This state suffrage law was followed by another act that excluded women from jury service. In his *South Carolina, A History*, Walter Edgar observed that "supporters of this latter legislation believed 'respectable women' had no real desire to be jurors" and it was the duty of elected officials to "protect the weaker sex from the unpleasantness of jury duty."

In another sphere of progressivism, Charleston's branch of the National Association for the Advancement of Colored People (NAACP) was established on February 23, 1917. Two founding members, F. E. Smith and T. St. T. Sasportas, were attorneys.

The reformist zeal lasted until the United States joined the Great War in April 1917. Locally, the war was a powerful economic stimulus. It brought enormous expansion to the Navy Yard, an enlarged military presence, and a boom to the economy. During March 1917, the War Department designated Charleston as the headquarters of the Southeastern Military District and the Navy Yard went on "war footing." Soon, there were 335 officers and 7,000

Natural disasters continued to take their toll on Charleston. A major hurricane in 1911 caused widespread flooding and property damage.

enlisted men supervising the training of 25,000 recruits at the Navy Base. By the end of the war, the city's annual military and civilian payroll exceeded nine million dollars. Surely a portion of those funds passed across many a lawyer's desk.

The city's tolerance for lawlessness drew notice during the war when federal agents were dispatched to close down a thriving red-light district that had grown up in response to the military presence. During 1917, local police and federal agents arrested 54 "fornicators" and closed eight brothels but, with its laissez-faire attitude toward vice, Charleston generally ignored federal and state prohibition laws.

The first decade of the twentieth century closed with 73 members of the bar practicing in Charleston. Fifty-five of this number had offices on Broad Street and all 73 worked within walking distance of the courthouse.

Progressivism enjoyed an Indian summer in the early 1920s. South Carolina modified by statute the common law concept of couverture, whereby a married woman could sue only through her husband. Heretofore, under this principle, when a man and woman married they became one person legally and the husband was that person. The husband was responsible for the wife's wrongdoings and she was bound to obey him at the peril of corporal punishment. Single women suffered no such legal subjugation.

At the annual meeting of the state bar in 1920, President Philip A. Willcox spoke against reform, especially against passage of the Eighteenth and Nineteenth amendments. "There are two instances—prohibition and women suffrage—which can be particularly referred to as examples of assault. They would not be successful but for the wave of hysteria, as a result of emotional excitement, consequent upon reaction from the world of conflict."

The Roaring Twenties were a wild cultural mélange of bathtub gin, jazz music, the Charleston dance, and F. Scott Fitzgerald's *The Great Gatsby*. The automobile be-

The United States' entry into World War I brought an enormous expansion to the Charleston Naval Yard. The naval base was an important part of the local economy until its closure during the Clinton administration.

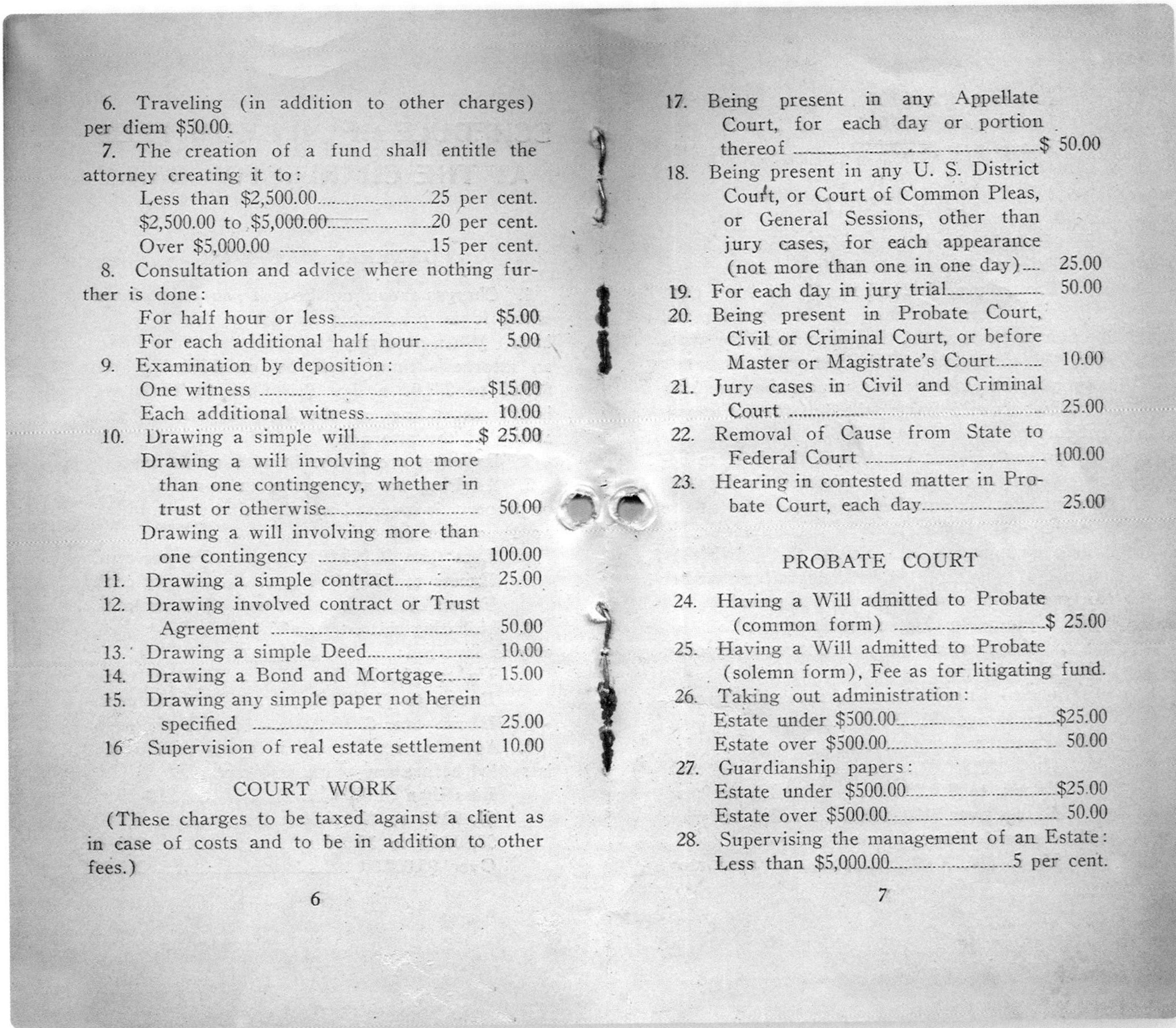

6. Traveling (in addition to other charges) per diem $50.00.

7. The creation of a fund shall entitle the attorney creating it to:

Less than $2,500.00....................25 per cent.
$2,500.00 to $5,000.00....................20 per cent.
Over $5,000.00....................15 per cent.

8. Consultation and advice where nothing further is done:

For half hour or less.................... $5.00
For each additional half hour.................... 5.00

9. Examination by deposition:

One witness....................$15.00
Each additional witness.................... 10.00

10. Drawing a simple will....................$ 25.00
Drawing a will involving not more than one contingency, whether in trust or otherwise.................... 50.00
Drawing a will involving more than one contingency.................... 100.00

11. Drawing a simple contract.................... 25.00

12. Drawing involved contract or Trust Agreement.................... 50.00

13. Drawing a simple Deed.................... 10.00

14. Drawing a Bond and Mortgage.................... 15.00

15. Drawing any simple paper not herein specified.................... 25.00

16 Supervision of real estate settlement 10.00

COURT WORK

(These charges to be taxed against a client as in case of costs and to be in addition to other fees.)

6

17. Being present in any Appellate Court, for each day or portion thereof....................$ 50.00

18. Being present in any U. S. District Court, or Court of Common Pleas, or General Sessions, other than jury cases, for each appearance (not more than one in one day).... 25.00

19. For each day in jury trial.................... 50.00

20. Being present in Probate Court, Civil or Criminal Court, or before Master or Magistrate's Court.................... 10.00

21. Jury cases in Civil and Criminal Court.................... 25.00

22. Removal of Cause from State to Federal Court.................... 100.00

23. Hearing in contested matter in Probate Court, each day.................... 25.00

PROBATE COURT

24. Having a Will admitted to Probate (common form)....................$ 25.00

25. Having a Will admitted to Probate (solemn form), Fee as for litigating fund.

26. Taking out administration:

Estate under $500.00....................$25.00
Estate over $500.00.................... 50.00

27. Guardianship papers:

Estate under $500.00....................$25.00
Estate over $500.00.................... 50.00

28. Supervising the management of an Estate:

Less than $5,000.00....................5 per cent.

7

came the technological icon of the twentieth century. It stimulated new cultural values and also new kinds of legal activity. However, in Charleston the stark reality of the era was economic distress. In the first six months of 1921, cotton prices in the state were around 40 cents a pound, but, by December, prices had collapsed to 13 and a half cents a pound. Hard times in the secular world and hard-shell Biblical notions of religion and morals largely kept the Roaring Twenties at bay in most of the state, with the exception of its chief port city.

As it had often been in the past, Charleston was a small oasis of libertinism. Lawyers and law enforcement officers paid little attention to federal prohibition laws. The state Supreme Court's decision in *State v. Schiadaressi, 100 S.C. 91 (1915)* recognized that the "people of Charleston are not law-abiding." With such attitudes on the bench,

These two pages are from the Schedule of Minimun Fees of Attorneys at Law in Charleston, S.C., *published in 1920. Attorneys were advised that "charges should not be made on a time basis when it is practicable to charge on a value basis."*

Charleston's defense attorneys could and did argue successfully that their clients' various misconducts complied with the customs of the community.

Charleston gained worldwide attention in the early 1920s with a dance craze. All-black stage revues became the rage in New York City's Broadway. "Shuffle Along" (1921), "Liza" (1922), and "Running Wild" (1923) paved the way for a new dance called the "Charleston." In 1921, the president of the state bar, William D. Melton of Columbia, worried about jazz dancing in his annual address.

"(U)unrest that seems to have possession of the people everywhere in society, was apparent at all levels....The stately Minuet and graceful waltz had to be supplemented by the Camel walk, the bunny-hug and the cheek dance."

The Charleston dance craze, named after the city in which it originated, swept the nation in the 1920s. The Charleston reigned supreme for ten years.

The Broadway revue *Liza* featured a dynamic chorus number titled "The Charleston Dancy." *The New York World* hailed it as the "fastest dancing show ever seen on Broadway." One critic reported that the agile black performers "dance with their hands, legs and bodies and no steps seem too difficult for them to do in unison."

The *Running Wild* review in 1923 was generally credited with creating the Charleston. *The Times* agreed that it excelled in "eccentric dancing ...some of the most exciting steps of the season (steps is not always the word, for knees were more often used than ankles)." For almost ten years, until replaced by the Black Bottom, the Charleston reigned supreme. In 1925, Boston's Pickwick Club collapsed under the vibrations created by the movements and 50 revelers perished. The dance gyrations became so frantic in England that some halls displayed signs stating "Please Charleston Quietly."

In 1922, the Charleston Bar had 77 members. The next year, the Nathans and Sinkler law firm was established and its members became leading attorneys in the twentieth century. For the first time in its history, the membership roll reached 100 lawyers in 1927.

Attorney Arthur G. Howe told a story of a quartet of Charleston lawyers known as "The Four Horsemen." They were Mayor Thomas P. Stoney, United States District Attorney J. D. Ernest Meyer, State Solicitor A. Russell McGowan, and City Attorney James Allan. Early one morning, Meyer knocked on the mayor's door and told His Honor that he (Meyer) was about to be indicted. Stoney said, "How can that be? You are the U.S. District Attorney, our friend, Russell McGowan is State Solicitor, and our cohort, James Allan, is City Attorney. There is no one else who could issue an indictment." Meyer confessed that a federal indictment was coming down upon him from Washington, D.C. for falsifying travel vouchers. Meyer's nephew, U.S. Senator and attorney Ernest "Fritz" Hollings, does not believe this story is true. "A deal was worked out with Washington for Meyer to leave the state and retire from the practice of law. Meyer relocated to the mountains of Tennessee where he opened a gambling casino. After the passage of a few years, Meyer came back to Charleston and resumed his law practice," said Howe.

In reaction to Charles Darwin's theory of human evolution, there was a crusade in the South to return to religious fundamentalism. In 1921, an anti-evolution clause was attached to a financial bill in the General Assembly. Another bill was introduced to withhold money from schools that taught "the cult known as Darwinism." Both of these failed to pass, but a similar one became law in Tennessee. On July 7, 1925, a Charleston newspaper headlined the "Battle of the Century." The article referred to a trial soon to begin in Dayton, Tennessee. The litigation grew from a coffee shop plot by two lawyers, a mining engineer, the county superintendent of education, and a pharmacist, who was head of the county Board of Education. A newspaper story reported that the American Civil Liberties Union (ACLU) would finance a court test of the Tennessee anti-evolution law. The coffee shop quintet surmised that such a trial would be good for local business and put their little town on the map. They persuaded John T. Scopes, a 24-year-old biology teacher, to confess to violating the law and to surrender to an arrest warrant. They sent a wire to the ACLU inviting the organization to come to town and defend him.

Reporters came from all over the world, even from Charleston. Charleston lawyers read the *News and Courier*

FIRST WOMAN ATTORNEY IN CHARLESTON

by Natalie Parker Bluestein

CHARLESTON'S FIRST WOMAN LAWYER WAS Hannah Rubinrott Axelman, the wife of the Rabbi at the orthodox synagogue in Charleston. She was considered an anomaly because of her profession and because she was a red-haired Yankee.

Born in New York in 1902, Hannah Rubinrott graduated from New York University Law School in 1923. After graduation, she clerked for an attorney, a step necessary to qualify for the New York bar exam. In 1926, she married Rabbi Benjamin C. Axelman, who had also attended law school. The Axelmans arrived in Charleston in 1926 when Rabbi Axelman accepted his position as Rabbi for the congregation at B'rith Shalom Beth Israel. Hannah immediately hung a sign outside of the house proclaiming, "Hannah R. Axelman, Attorney at Law."

Hannah Rubinrott Axelman, the wife of an orthodox Rabbi, became Charleston's first female attorney when she opened a law practice in 1926.

Local opinions varied on the Rabbi's wife having her own career. One congregant indignantly stated, "I could not believe the nerve of her, to be an attorney!" Hannah's son, Judge Joseph Axelman, who now resides in Virginia, remembers his mother receiving legal fees paid in vegetables. He also remembers that his mother was often appointed by Charleston mayors to serve on committees and panels as "the token woman."

In the 1930s, oratory was a required class at the High School of Charleston and Hannah tutored teenagers in public speaking in addition to her religious, civic, professional, and family responsibilities. Local attorney Jack Brickman recalled Mrs. Axelman asking him to be the try-out audience for her students. Other attorneys, including the late Charleston County Probate Judge Gus H. Pearlman, remembered as teenagers going to hear Mrs. Axelman argue in the Court of Common Pleas.

Hannah Axelman's personal behavior was subject to the strictures of the orthodox Jewish faith. Under the laws of orthodox Judaism, men are not allowed to touch a married woman and therefore, Mrs. Axelman did not shake hands with men. She also did not practice law on Saturday which was the Sabbath. Still, she persevered and garnered much respect from the legal community.

The Axelmans moved to Baltimore, Maryland, in 1943. Although the Maryland Supreme Court heard motions for admissions to the bar only on Saturdays, it made an exception for Hannah Axelman and her motion for admission was heard on Friday morning. Once admitted, Mrs. Axelman continued to practice law. She died in 1959, and her pioneering career is appreciated by every woman lawyer practicing in Charleston today. Her portrait now hangs in the library of the recently restored 1792 Charleston County courthouse.

headlines, "Who's Who in Monkeyville," "(Clarence) Darrow Objects to Daily Prayer," "Much Excitement," and "Darrow and (William Jennings) Bryan on Trial," and "Scopes Found Guilty." They then vicariously reargued the case in Broad Street coffee shops, in the lobby of the Timrod Hotel at the corner of Court House Square and Meeting Street, and at Tracy Becker's at 61 Broad Street.

On Big Thursday, October 24, 1929, the annual football game between the University of South Carolina and Clemson College was played at the State Fairground in Columbia. Nearly every Charleston lawyer was an alumnus of one of those institutions. Clemson was undefeated and Carolina had suffered only one loss. Each team was in contention for the Southern Conference championship. Fourteen thousand screaming spectators crowded into an old wooden stadium and excitement was so high that no one paid attention to the collapsing New York stock market. Clemson won the game, 21 to 14, but Big Thursday immediately became Black Thursday, setting off an economic crisis so serious that the state's financial structure collapsed. The agricultural depression that had gripped the South for a decade became part of a global economic

During the Depression, noted Charleston attorney Augustine T. Smythe instructed his stenographer not to use the office light "unless you are typing."

disaster that affected the state and nation on a scale that equaled the Civil War of the previous century.

The Great Depression of the 1930s impoverished white collar professionals and blue-collar wage-earners alike. The average annual income, if a family had one, was between 500 hundred and 1,000 dollars. The number of marriages dropped 40 percent from the previous decade. A significant factor in the nation's recovery and, incidentally, in the advancement of the legal profession was the election of Franklin D. Roosevelt as president of the United States on November 8, 1932. His numerous New Deal programs expanded the size and power of the federal government beyond all previous eras in United States history.

Anecdotes about the practice of law in Charleston during the Great Depression spotlight hard times. On Saturdays, most lawyers kept their office open all day and courthouses were open until one in the afternoon. No trial courts were in session from May to late September and Benjamin Alston Moore, a leading attorney, was heard to say that he feared his family would starve if he couldn't try a case in those summer months. As late as the 1950s, stories were told of depression-era lawyers stationing observers at the office of the recorder of deeds and mortgages during real estate closings. These folks kept an eye out for last-minute judgments and to see if sellers or mortgagors were trying to convey or mortgage properties twice in one day.

About the only bright spot for attorneys during this time was in foreclosure and bankruptcy actions, and there were many of them. In these proceedings, court costs and lawyer's fees were paid first if there was any money to be distributed. Most lawyers had a secretary to whom they could not pay a salary and who worked just to have something to do. To save on utility bills, attorneys cut off the office lights unless they were necessary. Augustine T. Smythe, Esquire, told his stenographer, "Daughter, don't turn on the office light unless you are typing."

During Roosevelt's first 100 days in office, the Federal Housing Act made federally insured loans available to home buyers. These insured loans multiplied the number of homeowners in Charleston County, putting bread and meat on the tables of real estate lawyers. The Farm Credit Act made loans available to farmers for seed money in exchange for using a mortgage on a piece of personal property, such as a tractor, as collateral.

By 1935, the New Deal included the Works Progress Administration Act and the Social Security Act, which provided retirement, unemployment, and welfare benefits for those unable to work. The practice of Social Security Administration law became a legal specialty, and continues to the present day.

When Roosevelt ran for reelection in 1936, South Carolina cast 98 percent of its votes for him, "Oh, Roosevelt's picture was everywhere, in every law office," said T. Allen Legare, who entered the bar in 1941. "It was right there where the clients could see it beside the Bible and the picture of Lincoln and his dictum, 'A lawyer's time and advice are his stock in trade.'"

On the state level, an important piece of New Deal legislation was the Workers' Compensation Act of 1935. This law provided a state forum to enforce the strict liability of employers, regardless of fault, to compensate employees for injuries arising from and in the course of employment. Legal practice in that area has led to a professional specialty, workers' compensation law.

During the 1930s, almost every South Carolina law office displayed, in addition to a portrait of President Roosevelt, this Abraham Lincoln portrait and quotation.

The emancipation of married women was enhanced in 1938, when the South Carolina Supreme Court was asked to abrogate the legal fiction of *couverture*, the oneness of husband and wife, in *Bryant v. Smith et ux, 187 SC 448, 198 SE 20 (1938)*. This challenge was based on a 1925 act giving married women higher liberties with a balance of responsibilities. At issue in *Bryant v. Smith et ux* was the common law issue of a husband's liability for the acts of his wife. Couverture was a vestige of seventeenth- and eighteenth-century British common law and a strange anachronism in modern law.

The repercussions of the Great Depression did not fully dissipate until World War II and the harsh economy certainly affected the expectations of all attorneys. Several of them had no noteworthy career until well after this decade and until after the war.

CHAPTER VII

WORLD WAR II AND ITS AFTERMATH

As President Franklin Roosevelt's New Deal gradually eased the United States out of the Great Depression, Nazi Germany actively prepared for war. In 1938 and 1939, the German Führer, Adolf Hitler, commenced aggression, seizing neighboring territory and extinguishing the governments of sovereign nations. By the end of 1940, he had drawn most of Europe into brutal military conflict. Japanese imperialism increased in the Far East as that nation invaded China and South Asia. The United States maintained a policy of quasi-neutrality toward the Axis nations of Germany, Italy, and Japan until December 7, 1941, when the Japanese bombed Pearl Harbor, Hawaii. Within a few days, the United States declared war on both Japan and the Axis nations of Europe.

By the start of hostilities, more than a year's anticipation of war had reduced the male population in American colleges and universities. Congress enacted the Selective Service System, recalled National Reserve officers, and activated the National Guard, moves that decimated male student bodies throughout the state. There were 95 law students at the University of South Carolina in 1941 but only 28 in 1944. In 1942, the Charleston Bar numbered 84 members, but two years later, only 61 remained. Senior members of local law firms exempt from service because of their age or health deferments served their firms' clients and held the legal business together during the war years.

The Selective Service System, enacted before the United States entered the war, created a tremendous labor shortage on the home front. The military draft forced many men to arrange or rearrange their personal legal affairs with little advance notice. To provide some measure of protection for them, the U.S. Congress passed an act protecting armed forces personnel from certain civil proceedings by giving them stays from court-ordered appearances. Specifically, the act included evictions, mortgages, leases, insurance payments, taxes, and domestic relations. Moreover, newly inducted personnel needed wills and powers of attorney. These young men created a great demand for legal counsel. Although James F. Byrnes, a United States senator from South Carolina, was nominated to the United States Supreme Court in

OPPOSITE PAGE: *Former U.S. senator and Supreme Court justice James F. Byrnes served as director of war mobilization and later as Secretary of State.* ABOVE: *World War II soldiers relax at an Army camp in Greenville, S.C. Congress passed an act protecting armed forces personnel from certain civil proceedings by giving them stays from court-ordered appearances.*

On March 16, 1943, Secretary of War Henry L. Stimson approved a legal assistance plan put forward by the Judge Advocate General (JAG) Department and the America Bar Association, thus instituting, for the first time in the history of the armed forces, a uniform, comprehensive system for making legal advice and assistance available to military personnel and their dependents. To the credit of the profession, members of the Charleston Bar served in this JAG Corps. At 3 a.m. on June 6, 1944, Charleston's radio station, WTMA, announced that the Allied Forces had invaded France. The bells of St. Michael's Episcopal Church pealed for the greatest amphibious landing in history.

The war so consumed the legal profession that, in 1945, the State Bar Association did not even hold its annual meeting. The imperatives of World War II had a distinct effect on the Charleston Bar. It was a time when a large transitory population, and therefore many attorneys, were temporary residents of the county.

Charleston's Navy Yard became the largest employer, public or private, this state had ever known. When Germany invaded Poland in 1939, the shipyard had 2,400 workers. In 1941, employment jumped to 9,000, and by the summer of 1943, 25,943 people were working three daily shifts at the yard. These workers needed housing and legal services in the North Area, the region surrounding the Navy Yard and Navy Base, a situation that gave rise to the county's first suburban law offices. In 1944, Edward B. Friday, a lanky, itinerant 64-year-old from Orangeburg, was the first lawyer to open an office there. Four nights a week he stayed in Cabin 11 at the Cottage Court and went back home on Friday nights. He rented office space on East Montague Street, in a building that became North Charleston's first city hall.

The North Area got its first permanent law firm in July 1948, when "Furman & Stevenson, Attorneys at Law"

January 1942 by President Roosevelt, the pressures of war were so great that, at the request of the president, he resigned the following year to become director of war mobilization. Byrnes had been born in Charleston but he had never practiced law there.

BROAD STREET BLUES OF 1946

THE FOLLOWING POEM WAS PRINTED IN THE Ashley Cooper column of the *News and Courier* in the 1950s and the columnist noted that the author is unknown.

As a lad I would dream of a legal career
Of logic profound, and an argument clear,
Of an office impressive, well filled with great books,
And a cute secretary, with brains and good looks.

So, I struggled and saved, and to law school I went,
And made acquaintance of Blackstone and Kent,
And passed my exams, and with nerves all a-tingle,
I rented an office and hung out a shingle.

At first I was filled with the ancient obsession,
That law was the highest and noblest profession,
But experience sad demonstrates that this science,
Is not worth a damn in the absence of clients.

I've trudged to Police Court and waited around,
In the hope that a client by chance might be found,
But Seideman had been there an hour already,
And so had Al Hamer and husky old Eddie.

Collections, I've tried, and subscribed to the listings,
In hopes that by strenuous turning and twisting
I'd handle some claims, maybe Macy or Grimbel,
But no, that's all sewed up by Seymour and Grimball.

My urge for insurance adjusting was fierce,
But here I found Bammy and Corbin and Pearce
And Baron and Coming and Nathan and Frank,
And my hopes to the bottom again promptly sank.

For damage suit practice my soul was on fire
Until I discovered that J.C. and Meyer
Had most of that nailed, and the real estate old cronies
Of Figg's or Cosgrove's or Crosland's or Stoney's.

In the old court of Sessions, I've sat by the week,
With never a customer surly or meek.
Each went, thief or killer or simple assaulter,
To Russell or Bussey or O.T. or Walter.

At corporate targets my shafts have I loosed,
Forgetting that all were the clients of Buist,
On remembering too late, with horrible shivers,
That this field was taken by Waring and Rivers.

Now wills and estates seemed a line very steady,
But I hadn't figured on Harry or Freddie
Or G.L.B. Rivers or tough Colonel Nat
Who had all the business pinned down to the mat.

I'd hope for a fee at the old R.M.C.,
But title examining wasn't for me.
For, try as I may, I just get in the way
Of Shimel and Bowman and Hartz and McCrae.

For torts and for contracts I've baited my hooks,
I've studied the Code and I've read all the books;
But though I have worked like all hell and damnation,
My labor to date is without compensation.

I've pined broken-hearted, for sight of a fee,
But nothing like that ever happens to me.
The brethren of Broad Street have all done me wrong,
From Arthur and Austin to Cosgrove and Long.

If a client is poor, he may knock at the door
Of Legge or McMillan or Heyward or Moore,
But if he is rich, the son of a bitch'll
Nine times out of ten go to Sinkler or Mitchell.

L'Envoi
Retainers aren't for fools like me,
And only Gaud can make a fee.

hung out their business sign. Two returning veterans, J. Heyward Furman, Jr. and Norman Stevenson, started their practice at 208 Cherry Street and much of their business came from the expanding local real estate market. Charleston's returning veteran lawyers included Morris Rosen, Charles Gibbs, Gedney M. Howe, Jr., Gus H. Pearlman, T. Allen Legare, Jr., J. C. Hare, Nathaniel Cabell, Clarence Singletary, Edward Buckley, and Joe Cabaniss.

Among the prominent Charleston attorneys returning as veterans from World War II were T. Allen Legare, Jr., (left) and Morris D. Rosen (right), seen here many years later at a McCants Firm St. Patrick's Day party. Between them is attorney Arthur G. Howe, who has served as both an Assistant United States Attorney and as a Circuit Solicitor.

The G.I. Bill of Rights, enacted in 1944, and victory in 1945, brought a wave of returning veterans to colleges and universities. By 1947, there were 328 students enrolled in the University of South Carolina Law School in a building adequate for only 75 people. The law faculty began offering three full semesters a year. Returning veterans brought with them motivation for change and high hopes to better themselves and their society. One returning Charleston veteran, John Wrighten, an African American, applied for admission to the University law school on June 30, 1946. His application was rejected, and the following year a legal action was filed on his behalf. The court ruled that if the state was going to offer a separate but equal legal education, it must provide a school for Wrighten. Judge J. Waties Waring presided over the case as he did over many other key South Carolina civil rights cases. Wrighten's case was not appealed to the United States Supreme Court. Instead, the state established a law school for African Americans at South Carolina State College in Orangeburg.

A memorable event for the legal profession occurred in 1947 when this state tried its last lynching case. Presiding Judge J. Robert Martin, Jr. always provided the bar with stories of his prickly personality. A *New Yorker* magazine story on the trial described Judge Martin as "...very local. He knows all about the rhetoric and opera. His speech arouses wonder as to how the best sort of stenographer, who takes down by sounds and not by sense, is not wholly baffled in the South, where 'You gentlemen must apportion your time' is converted into 'You g'men must appo'tion yo' taiaime', with magnificent vibrato on the diphthongs and strong melodic line to the whole. He is so good that though he is local, he expands the local meaning, and recalls that great Southerners are great men in the whole world. He has humor, but hates a clown." The *New Yorker* article concluded, "When the jury returned a verdict of 'not guilty' as to all defendants, Judge Martin stood, thought for a minute, turned and walked out of the courtroom. He did not thank the jury, as was his custom." "Judge Martin's curt finish to this trial was the talk of all Broad Street," recalled Morris Rosen.

A South Carolina anachronism was its distinction, in 1948, of being the only state that prohibited divorce. The major item on the November 1948 ballot was the presidential candidacy of J. Strom Thurmond of the Dixiecrat Party. A proposal to amend the 1895 constitution to permit divorce as a cause of action was also on the ballot. Not surprisingly, there was a heavy turnout and the amendment passed, bringing South Carolina into the twentieth century with 56,014 votes favoring divorce to 41,757 against. When the amendment was ratified by the General Assembly, divorce actions became such a large

OLIVER THORNWELL WALLACE

(1903-1979)

Oliver Thornwell "O.T." Wallace was a self-educated lawyer. His son, Robert Buford Wallace, is an attorney, a solicitor, and plantation owner. O.T.'s grandson, Robert Bruce Wallace, is an attorney and an alumni of the University of Virginia—a gentleman Cavalier. This succession is a good example of true American aspirations.

Wallace was born in 1903. His father died when O.T. was young and his mother bought a house on Francis Street, near Hampton Park. When O.T. was 12 years old, he quit school to help support the family but discovered that he had made a mistake because the public school system would not readmit him. A man in his church congregation recognized O.T.'s potential and paid the fees for him to enter a private school, Porter Military Academy. There he mastered Greek and Latin in the same semester. After graduation, the railroad that had employed his father offered him a job and by 1930 he was enrolled in LaSalle Correspondence Law School. He moved up to be assistant manager of a local insurance firm and then clerk in the law office of John Charles Long.

Political leaders of this era rode a democratic wave of "populism" and O.T.'s values were formed by it. Local kingpins had forceful personalities, oratorical talent, and the ability to make and hold friends. O.T. inspired the devotion of factory workers and domestic servants when he gave these voters recognition and equality.

Self-educated lawyer Oliver Thornwell "O.T." Wallace spent 35 years in public service, including nine years as a state senator.

O.T. helped the upcountry populist, Olin D. Johnston, when elected as governor in 1936, and for his aid, was appointed clerk of court of Charleston County. The appointment began a career of 35 years in public service, including nine years as a state senator. Wallace succeeded in removing the toll from the Cooper River bridge, convinced the state to build a hospital in Charleston for the Medical University, lifted the toll from the Folly beach highway, and secured many other benefits for Charleston County residents. He put so much enthusiasm into the senator's job that he had to keep his law office open all day on Saturdays to assist his clients. O.T. was at his best before a jury or on the senate floor, where he had a twinkle in his eye and talked with his hands. He could literally hop up and down in his intensity of purpose. One observer called him a "bull in a china shop."

He left the Senate to become Master-in-Equity for Charleston County. At that time there was no Family Court, and the Master heard, among other issues, domestic relations cases. On one occasion, he heard arguments by counsel in a custody case. The two attorneys pursued him to his Broad Street coffee shop, pressing for a decision, and he replied. "the custody of a three year old is not decided over a cup of coffee."

After his retirement, he had the pleasure of practicing law with his son, Robert, and in helping Robert try his first case.

part of the practice of law that a whole court system was created around it.

Before the end of the decade, the South Carolina General Assembly modernized requirements for admission to the bar. Each year, law students flocked to the legislature to persuade their House and Senate members to oppose the state bar's intention to declare null and void the "diploma privilege." This privilege allowed all graduates of the state's law school to be admitted to the bar without taking its examination. "The students had more influence than the Bar Association," said retired Chief Justice Bruce Littlejohn. "Finally some wise legislators came up with the idea that the bill should be enacted effective three years hence. This called off the lobbying, and the act passed requiring all applicants to stand the bar exam after December 13, 1950. It was the general belief among students then that the motive force behind the legislation was to undermine the education and admission to the bar of students from the black law school at Orangeburg.

George Lamb Buist was a fourth-generation member of one of Charleston's most distinguished legal families. He joined the firm of Buist and Buist in 1914. The firm became Buist, Buist, Smythe and Smythe in 1961.

Hugh Hefner, publisher of *Playboy* magazine, wrote in its twenty-fifth anniversary edition in 1975 that, "the early fifties was an era of conformity and repression—Eisenhower and Senator Joe McCarthy—the result of two decades of depression and war. But it was also a period of reawakening in America with reemphasis on the importance of the individual, on his rights and opportunities in a free society—a period of increasing affluence and leisure time." This decade of the 1950s began with the membership of the Charleston County Bar Association having increased to 96 members.

The State Bar Association had in the 1940s voted on three occasions to endorse a legislative bill to require all lawyers to be members of the bar association and to create a fully racially integrated bar, but the proposal never made headway in the General Assembly. The 1953 state bar meeting was a turning point. The association voted substantial changes in its constitution that raised the status of the state bar from purely a social fraternity to a professional organization. However, it was not until 1967 that the bar achieved racial integration.

Despite considerable resistance to change, modernization did occur in the 1950s. From 1895 to that time, all persons, including lawyers seeking admission to the bar, had to swear in their constitutional oath of office not to settle disputes by dueling. At James F. Byrnes's inauguration as governor in 1951, he took the customary antiquated oath not to settle disputes in that fashion. Because Byrnes had previously held such prestigious positions as justice of the U.S. Supreme Court and Secretary of State, many of his Washington colleagues attended the ceremony. Chief Justice Bruce Littlejohn wrote in his *Political Memories* that, "It is said that the dueling oath was removed from the Constitution upon the insistence of James F. Byrnes....The story goes that some of Byrnes's friends from Washington came to the inauguration and teased him about having to swear that he would not participate in a duel. He seemed embarrassed about it and, as a result, advocated and helped bring about the elimination of this provision of the Constitution." An amendment to remove the anti-dueling clause in the state oath from the constitution appeared on the November 1954 ballot. The electorate approved the amendment and the General Assembly ratified the change in February 1955. Section 26, Article III, of the constitution was amended to read: "The Oath of Office to be Taken...I do solemnly swear (or affirm) that I am duly qualified, according to the Constitution of the State, to exercise the duties of the office to which I have been elected or appointed, and that I will, to the best of my

JUDGE J. WATIES WARING

Charleston Bar member Judge Waties Waring played a major role in the 1954 precedent-shattering United States Supreme Court decision which held that racial segregation itself was unconstitutional. He acquired his legal education by reading law with John Pendleton Kennedy Bryan, a brilliant Broad Street trial lawyer. In 1914, Waring was appointed Assistant District Attorney, and later served as City Attorney for Mayor Burnet R. Maybank. It was with then Senator Maybank's recommendation that Waring was elevated to the federal bench in 1942.

Judge J. Waties Waring presided over many civil right cases, most importantly Briggs v. Elliott.

Three years later, Waring's private domestic life became the subject of public discourse. Waring had asked his wife of 30 years for a divorce. Because divorce was illegal in South Carolina at that time, she complied by going to Florida to obtain it, whereupon he quickly married a new wife. Charleston society closed its doors to the couple in support of his first wife. Some people came to believe that Waring's civil rights decisions were retribution for the actions of Charleston society, whereas others believed his progressive civil rights views were the natural evolution of his thinking.

In 1946, Waring ruled that African-American and white school teachers were entitled to equal pay and, in another case, he ordered the state to provide law school education for African Americans. In the early 1950s, a suit was filed in Waring's court seeking an end to school segregation in Clarendon County, and, in a pretrial hearing, he suggested to the plaintiff's attorney, Thurgood Marshall, that the complaint be rewritten to raise the basic issue that segregation itself was unconstitutional. Waring ruled for the plaintiff in *Briggs v. Elliott* and the defendant appealed to the United States Supreme Court. There it was combined with four other cases and became known as *Brown v. Board of Education,* the case that struck down racial segregation as public policy in America.

ability, discharge the duties thereof, and preserve, protect and defend the Constitution of this state and of the United States. So help me God."

Another event of much greater significance in 1954 was the United States Supreme Court's ruling in *Brown v. Board of Education* that the racial segregation doctrine of a "separate but equal" American public education was unconstitutional. This decision had a tumultuous, historic, and dramatic impact on public and private education nationwide and it set the stage for the destruction of all Jim Crow laws and customs. It is noteworthy that the ruling marked the beginning of the end for the law school for African Americans at South Carolina State College. Henceforth, the University of South Carolina was required to admit black applicants and the other school became redundant.

South Carolina's jury system also took a step toward the modern age. On September 9, 1957, the U.S. Congress passed Congressional Public Law 85-315, "To provide means of further securing and protecting the civil rights of persons within the jurisdiction of the United States." The law was popularly known as the Civil Rights Act of 1957. Section 152 amended Section 1861 of the previous code to govern "Qualifications of Federal jurors. Any citizen of the United States who has attained the age of twenty-one and who has resided for a period of one year within the judicial district is competent to serve as grand or petit jurors unless...he has been convicted of a crime punishable by imprisonment of more than one year...he is unable to read...he is incapable by reason of mental or physical infirmities to render efficient jury service."

Assistant U.S. Attorney Arthur G. Howe was prepared to present criminal indictments before Judge George Bell Timmerman when he received a copy of Public Law 85-315. Howe concluded that this legislation required that African Americans and women be included in the federal jury venire. He then presented an order to that effect to Judge Timmerman, who was holding court in Columbia. Howe recalled that Judge Timmerman signed the order reluctantly and then quashed all the indictments pending in his court.

South Carolina attorney Robert McCormick Figg, Jr., represented the Clarendon County school board in Briggs v. Elliott. *On appeal to the U.S. Supreme Court, the case became part of* Brown v. Board of Education.

At that time, the federal clerk of court was required to "canvas" the district for the names of prospective jurors. Clerk of Court Ernest F. Allen solicited prospective names from lawyers and preachers. Howe saw Allen specifically including the names of African Americans in the list for the petit and grand jury and told him "You can not intentionally include African Americans for jury duty just as you can not intentionally exclude them."

Elimination of the custom of "reading law" was another modernization. On June 18, 1957, Governor Byrnes signed legislation giving the Supreme Court authority to fix qualifications for admission to the bar. In November 1957, the court established the rule that no person should be admitted to the practice of law "who was not a graduate of the law school at the University of South Carolina, the law school of South Carolina State College, or a law school approved by the council of legal education of the American Bar Association." These rules provided a window of time to exempt those individuals already engaged in reading law. By 1958, membership in the Charleston Bar had jumped to 135 members, according to the City Directory for that year.

Medieval relics and vestiges of traditions from London's Inns of Court remained in local courts and in the legal profession during the 1950s. One Charleston legacy from London's criminal court of Old Bailey was the dock, a wooden enclosure about four or five feet square with the upper half of the box open. There, an alleged criminal would sit or stand during his arraignment while the charge was read to him and he was asked to plead "guilty" or "not guilty." South Carolina Circuit Rule 35 prescribed the use of the dock but the Supreme Court abolished the rule in January 1984. The Charleston County Courthouse dock was destroyed in 1989 when Hurricane Hugo collapsed the roof and ceiling upon it.

Another courtroom fixture eliminated by modernization of the courthouse was the brass spittoon. Spittoons were provided next to the tables of the attorneys for the plaintiff and defendant. Spittoons were also placed among the spectators. Lawyers did not smoke during a trial but they could chew tobacco and spit into the receptacle. As soon as the judge walked out of the courtroom, attorneys lit up their cigarettes and the brass cuspidors became ashtrays. If the judge wanted to smoke during a trial, he stood in the courtroom doorway and blew smoke into the hall.

The South Carolina Code Section 14-7-270 provided that a child under the age of ten or a totally blind person was qualified to draw the jury from among potential jurors' names placed in small capsules and deposited in a rotating drum. The courts generally used a blind man to draw the jury, but, from time to time, a child performed the duty. The clerk of court and attorneys had a callous habit of addressing the jury selector as "the blind man." The clerk would announce to the courtroom, "The blind man will now draw the jury."

When A. Arthur Rosenblum was a solicitor in Berkeley and Charleston counties in the early 1980s, he instructed the clerk to address the blind man by his name. The current custom is for the clerk to announce, "There being no objection, (that is, no objection to the absence of a child or blind person) the clerk will now draw the jury."

All court terms began with a prayer. Usually a local minister attended at the request of the presiding judge or clerk. Most of the time, those present in the courtroom rose and stood for the invocation, but sometimes the audience remained seated, bowed their heads, and closed their eyes. There were no kneelers. In 1982, prayer became a constitutional issue in federal courts. On appeal, the court ruled that the prayers had to cease, "because each minister composes his own prayer, its content is beyond control of the judge..."

Before chief administrative judges took control of the civil court docket, it was managed by the Charleston Bar Association. The week before a term of court began, the association met in the courtroom and either the president or the clerk read aloud the names of the pending cases and asked if they were ready for trial. It was not uncommon for the bar president to call upon the judge and report that all the scheduled cases had been settled or continued.

The court reporter's responsibility was to take down each word of a trial in shorthand on a standard five-inch-by-eight-inch shorthand notebook held together by a spiral binding at the top. Reporters generally read back portions of the record at the request of the judge or an attorney. On at least one occasion during a trial, the court reporter got up from his seat and stood in the doorway smoking a cigarette. A lawyer called the reporter's behavior to the judge's attention, whereupon the judge replied, "the

South Carolina law allowed either a child or a blind person to draw jurors' names. Here, 5-year-old Pamela Hughes draws names under the supervision of clerk Lloyd Fleming.

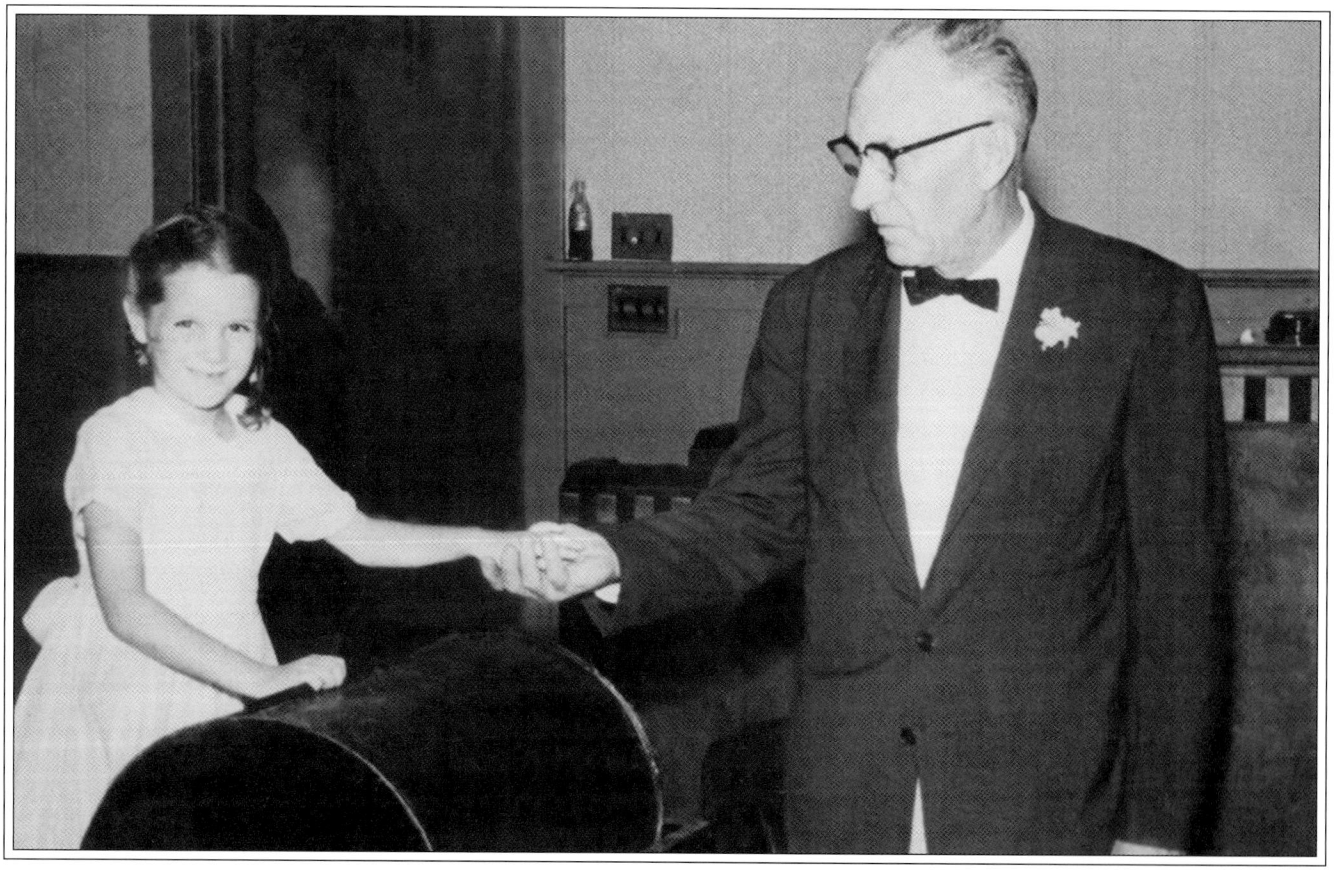

LOCAL MAGISTRATE MAKES *TIME* MAGAZINE

By St. Peter, and By St. Paul,
If this man is guilty, Let the bible fall.
—Judge Eugene Herron, Magistrate

On many occasions, North Area magistrate Eugene Herron, would administer substantive justice with the help of his old black bible. The judge's routine would be this: "How do you plead, guilty or not guilty?" "Not guilty." "Do you want to be tried by a jury or by the Bible?" "By the Bible." Judge Herron's bible was wrapped in rows and rows of strings lengthwise and across its width. He had a brass skeleton key which was about four inches long and the lock part was tied into the strings around the bible. To be "tried by the Bible," the accused and His honor would each hold the head of the brass key by their right index finger. The two fingers would touch through the ring. If either party moved their finger ever so slightly, the bible would drop, and the accused was presumed guilty.

A description of this form of justice was reported in a sidebar story of *Time* magazine in the 1950s. "Judge Herron got a lot of confessions with that strategy," recalls his former clerk, Margie Cannon.

Attorney Samuel H. Altman watched Judge Herron get a confession using his bible in this way. 'How do you plead, guilty or not guilty?" "Not guilty." "Come on over here and put your hand on the Bible. I'm going to ask you some questions. If your hand trembles, you are guilty. If your hand doesn't tremble, you are not guilty." The accused then changed his plea to guilty, and the judge said, "Five days or five dollars." Attorney Arthur Howe said, "If Gene Herron had been educated, he would have made a great jurist."

reporter is listening." It was a giant step forward when stenotype machines became available and were installed in local courtrooms.

Until sometime in the 1960s, the Charleston County Courthouse closed for the funeral of a lawyer as an officer of the court. The author remembers promising the Probate Court clerks that she would have her funeral on a Friday afternoon. This tradition eventually changed from the whole courthouse being closed to standing at ease during the funeral. In addition, two officers of the county bar association personally offered condolences to bereaved families.

Charleston County lawyers also practiced in the adjacent Berkeley County Courthouse, where this rural community modified courthouse customs to its small-town ways. The Berkeley County Courthouse at Moncks Corner had a tradition that the author believes was unique in this state. The practice began during the era of Jim Crow segregation of restaurants. Criminal court terms were held every spring and fall and enterprising local African Americans set up a portable eating establishment on the courthouse lawn. They cooked and served rice and fish sandwiches and sold milk, orange juice, and soft drinks from coolers. Several cooks began frying fish in the morning and cooking rice on a cast-iron wood-burning stove. The old stove had a chimney pipe but the aroma pervaded the courthouse. When Oxford-educated Judge James A. Spruill presided in Moncks Corner, he called Solicitor Arthur Howe into his chambers and asked, "What is that smell in the courtroom?"

Berkeley County clerks of court, "Buster" Williams and Calvin N. Clark, kept a tin tub of ice and free soft drinks in their office for the lawyers and the judge. Vending machines were of a future age. The jury room had such thin walls that the lawyers and the judge could listen to their deliberations. "Sometimes they would get into a right spirited discussion," said attorney Bill Shipley. The floor of the 1896 courtroom had been laid with green lumber, and as it dried out, gaps appeared in the floor. Folks in the courtroom watched through the cracks what went on in the sheriff's office below.

The fifties set the stage for the shift between World War II and the turbulent sixties, but still enjoyed some of the old-fashioned ways of the practice of law in a bygone era.

CHAPTER VIII

THE TURBULENT SIXTIES

THROUGHOUT THE 1960S, the nation experienced extensive cultural turmoil. The civil rights movement, the Vietnam War and the opposition to the war, the quest to discover the Age of Aquarius, growing sexual freedom, and the second wave of feminism were some of the social movements that made up that chaotic era. Despite these and other tumultuous societal changes and legal reforms, Charleston's legal community seemed unaffected by them until the end of the decade.

The bar examination of 1960 was the last opportunity South Carolinians had to enter the profession by "reading law" or studying under the tutelage of a bar member. In the 1950s, the General Assembly gave the Supreme Court authority to determine requirements for admission to the practice of law in the state. The court altered Supreme Court Rule 5 and henceforth restricted admission to applicants who had graduated from a law school approved by the American Bar Association.

The effects of *Brown v. Board of Education* extended to passage of the Civil Rights Act of 1964 and inevitably made themselves felt in South Carolina. Ernest F. "Fritz" Hollings, a Charleston lawyer and governor in 1963, admonished the General Assembly that its Jim Crow doctrine of "separate but equal" public education had run its course. "There were to be no more lawsuits, for the state has run out of appeal courts. The General Assembly must make clear South Carolina's choice, a government of law rather than a government of men." African-American students entered the University of South Carolina and its law school for the first time since Reconstruction. The "separate but equal" South Carolina State College law school closed in 1966.

Desegregation in education and public accommodations did not automatically desegregate the state's bar associations or court facilities. In 1968, the author watched as about 35 young African-American men and women marched through the Charleston County Courthouse. When they left the building, all of the "Colored" signs on bathroom doors and water fountains had disappeared. Bystanders made no protest, and the signs were never replaced.

Amid the civil rights struggle, the civil turbulence of the anti-Vietnam War protest, and social disorder, the Charleston and the State Bar associations slowly moved into the second half of the twentieth century. Every General Assembly from 1949 until 1966 had considered and then rejected legislation permitting women to serve on juries. Legislation to authorize a constitutional amendment was finally forced upon the state by a federal court decision in Alabama. Allegedly, the major objection to women jurors was the weak excuse that it was too expensive to provide sufficient numbers of acceptable jury restrooms, two for males and two for women, in each case one each for "Coloreds" and "Whites." No longer providing racially segregated restrooms had, in this rationale, lessened the expense of providing separate men's and women's facilities!

In 1965, C. Heyward Belser, Chairman of the House Judiciary Committee and Charleston lawyer Joseph H. McGee led another movement to grant women the basic right of serving on a jury. Before the 1966 session of the legislature could consider the matter, a federal district court in Montgomery, Alabama, ruled in the case of *White v. Crook* that Alabama's statutory exclusion of women from jury service was an unconstitutional violation of the equal protection clause of the Fourteenth Amendment. Belser and McGee had warned the legislature that there was a substantial likelihood that federal courts would reverse convictions of female criminals if appellants demonstrated that females were excluded from juries. The chairman of the Senate Judiciary Committee argued that he did not want women to serve on juries with illiterates. Therefore, a bill was passed that jurors must have at least a sixth-grade education. On November 8, 1966, South Carolina's

OPPOSITE PAGE: *Charleston lawyer and governor Ernest F. "Fritz" Hollings urged an end to the era of segregated education in South Carolina.* BELOW: *Charleston mostly escaped the turmoil of the Civil Rights era. One exception was the Charleston hospital workers' strike of 1969. Black hospital workers struck for the right to organize with help from Dr. Ralph Abernathy (front row, fourth from right) of the SCLC, and Walter Reuther (front row, fourth from left) of the UAW.*

voters endorsed a constitutional amendment and it was ratified on March 1, 1967.

The most important single decision affecting the power of the accused to understand and exercise his rights and to have protection from overbearing police investigation was rendered June 13, 1966, by the United States Supreme Court in the case of *Miranda v. Arizona, U.S. 384 426 (1966).* The Chief Municipal Judge for the towns of Mount Pleasant and Sullivan's Island, J. Lawrence Duffy, described the effects of *Miranda* and other civil protections:

> *Miranda was a Mexican-American boy accused of a crime. He was denied sleep by the police until he 'freely' confessed to the alleged crime. He didn't understand that he had rights. Once he was in custody and before he was questioned, he was entitled to know and understand his rights to be protected from overbearing police. The case of* Carol vs. Illinois *protects our vehicles from searches and seizures.* Mapp vs. Ohio *held that the police have to get a warrant to search and seize our vehicles and home. The mid-1960s was an enlightened period in this country when the United States Supreme Court gave us resounding decisions protecting individual rights. It was a fantastic period. That court is now (2006) gradually whittling those rights away.*

J. Lawrence Duffy served as the Chief Municipal Judge for Mount Pleasant and Sullivan's Island. As an attorney, he and deRosset Myers did the background legal work in the Ussury case, helping win what was at the time the largest judgement against one defendant in South Carolina history.

Another blemish upon South Carolina's legal practice, "trial by ambush," was eliminated in the late 1960s. Prior to 1968, court rules pertaining to discovery of the adversary's position were very limited. They permitted stunning an opposing attorney with surprise evidence and witnesses. After 1968, the state Supreme Court adopted federal rules of court procedure, including the taking of depositions. These reforms eliminated "ambushes" but have added greatly to the cost of preparing for trials. For example, in January 2001, a plaintiff in a medical malpractice action had to spend $120,000 in legal costs to prepare for his day in court. Charleston attorney William B. Regan has asserted that such high costs have contributed to the growth in the number of big law firms and the demise of "boutique" partnerships. Large law firms generally can look to their defense clients to advance funds to pay for discovery. When discovery rules were imposed, law firms started receiving quantities of paperwork that had to be read and understood. As part of court preparation, A. Arthur Rosenblum, a Charleston litigator, said that, "Discovery has more than quadrupled the work of legal preparation of a case for trial."

Early in the use of discovery, Sam Craven, a lawyer in solo practice, was served with ten interrogatory questions in a case he had against J. Rutledge Young of the large law firm Young, Clement, Rivers and Tisdale. Months went by and Craven did not answer the interrogatories. When their paths crossed, Rutledge asked him when the answers could be expected. Finally, Craven asked Rutledge if he had a book on interrogatories in his office that his secretary could copy. "Certainly, she can come by any time," said Rutledge. Craven's secretary, who was also his wife, spent three days copying from the book before the days of photocopiers. A week later, Craven served Rutledge with 100 interrogatories.

Increasing numbers of female attorneys started practicing law in many specialties—criminal defense, criminal prosecution, civil litigation, appellant causes, and tax

The name parners of the firm of Sinkler, Gibbs and Simmons, left to right, Charles Gibbs, Huger Sinkler, and Albert Simmons, photographed in the 1960s.

law, to name a few. A class action suit filed against the Fairfax County Bar Association and the Virginia State Bar alleged that their minimum fee schedule constituted price-fixing in violation of the Sherman Antitrust Act of 1890. The plaintiff sought injunctive relief and damages from the members. That suit, like the first shot at Fort Sumter, was heard around the world, at least around the insular world of the American legal profession.

The Charleston County Bar Association and other county bar associations had traditionally printed minimum fee schedules and updated them from time to time. Charleston lawyers had published the schedules since the 1790s, probably in imitation of a contemporaneous British practice. But the tradition collapsed as a result of the Virginia decision.

Irvin J. Slotchiver, a Charleston tax attorney, has preserved his copy of the Charleston Bar Association's last minimum fee schedule: "At a meeting of the Charleston County Bar Association held on July 2, 1970, it was resolved by the members present that the within Schedule of Minimum Fees be approved and adopted, effective August 3, 1970. Coming Ball Gibbs, Jr., Secretary."

Fees for 62 professional services were grouped under the following titles: Admiralty, collections, contracts, corporations, criminal law, depositions, domestic relations, estates, general matters, litigation, personal injury claims and actions, and real estate. Sample fees included:

- Trial of crime involving death penalty: Twelve (12) months earnings, but no less than $2,500.00
- Drawing simple will: $35
- Divorce or annulment, uncontested: $250
- Litigation of matters in which a fund or property is involved up to $5,000: 20%
- Personal injury actions, the plaintiff on contingency: 33%
- Drawing simple deed: $35
- Drawing a simple note and mortgage: $25.

To understand the real value of these fee rates, it is worth observing that in 1970, coffee was 69 cents per pound; five pounds of sugar cost 39 cents; 25 pounds of grits sold for $1.98; a Hoover vacuum cleaner was $159.95;

A virtual "Who's Who" of South Carolina politics posed for this photograph, probably at the Carolina Cup in Camden, S.C., in the 1960s. From left to right, James F. Byrnes, Strom Thurmond, Lieutenant Governor (and future governor) John West, and Edgar Brown. West noted on the back of the photo, "It is the first time Strom Thurmond and Edgar Brown had a picture together since Thurmond defeated Brown in the 1954 Senatorial election as a write-in candidate."

and Sears sold a seven-horsepower tractor for $388. Ten dollars in 1970 had the buying power of $49.20 in 2004.

When the Charleston Bar Association learned that this class action had been filed in Fairfax, Virginia, it hastily called a meeting early in 1972 to consider how to respond to a similar legal action. Harvard-educated attorney Robert Hollings raised the legal theory of "conscious parallelism." He explained that members who continued to use the fee schedule informally after it was abolished might be individually liable for violating the antitrust act. Gedney M. Howe, Jr. made a motion that the Charleston County Bar Association had never had a minimum fee schedule. Everyone knew the motion was bunkum, but it put a smile on members' faces. They unanimously passed Howe's motion and the meeting adjourned.

The United States Supreme Court took *certiorari* jurisdiction of the Virginia case and rendered a unanimous opinion against the bar in *Goldfarb et ux v. Virginia State Bar et al (1975)*. The issue before the court involved a prescribed minimum fee for examination of a real estate title.

The Supreme Court considered the argument that minimum fee schedules were exempt from the antitrust act because they involved a "learned profession." Heretofore, judges had recognized a limited exclusion of "learned professions" from the scope of the antitrust laws because the profession was not within the terms of "trade and commerce." Fairfax County also maintained that competition is inconsistent with the practice of a profession because "enhancing profit is not the goal of professional activities."

Chief Justice Warren Burger, writing the opinion of the court, said "The exchange of such service for money is 'commerce' in the most common use of the word. It is no disparagement of the practice of law as a profession to acknowledge that it has this business aspect." The court found the county bar's minimum fee schedule had created a pricing system, a classic example of price-fixing. It further held that neither the nature nor the public service aspect of the professional practice provided sanctuary. Anti-competitive conduct of the lawyers in the state and county bar was within the reach of the Sherman Act. The court concluded: "The interest of the states in regulating lawyers is especially great since lawyers are essential to the primary government function of administering justice, and have historically been 'officers of the court.'

The decision affected income from the practice of law. In the author's real estate law practice, she quickly learned that some lawyers had begun charging less for real estate work than the fees listed on the Charleston Bar schedule. Other lawyers had to cut their fees because clients were calling law offices shopping for lower fees.

In 1972, some Charleston lawyers won the biggest civil judgment ever assessed against one defendant in the state's judicial history. Sitting in the witness stand, Artie Curtis Ussery took off his dark glasses to show the jury his pupilless eye sockets. "I'm the only guy around with psychedelic eyes," he said. Ussery was a prisoner at the maximum security detention center of the South Carolina Department of Corrections. He had had a disagreement with one of the prison guards as to when he would be

Attorneys of the firm of Steinburg, Levkoff and Spitz, left to right, David T. Pearlman, Irving Steinburg, Hugo M. Spitz, Charles S. Goldberg, and Irving Levkoff, celebrate at a Christmas party in the 1970s.

allowed to do his job as keeper of the plants and flowers in the main yard. The dispute turned into a scuffle and another guard threatened Ussery with his tear gas billy club, an instrument that can be used either as a billy club or to discharge a tear gas canister. In the heat of the argument, the canister accidentally discharged and the flame burnt Ussery's eyes. He was awarded a jury verdict of $600,000 on March 2, 1972.

William McG. Morrison, Jr., Ussery's attorney, brought an action against the Federal Laboratories in Saltsburg, Pennsylvania. Lawyers J. Lawrence Duffy and deRosset Myers did all the background legal work. In court, Morrison established that the weapon had been poorly designed, that the company had not subjected it to definitive tests, and had refused to take action after five other people had been blinded by the malfunctioning canister. It would be another decade before a million-dollar verdict was rendered in Charleston County.

Between 1960 and 1974, the membership of the Charleston Bar jumped from about 150 lawyers to 200, according to the City Directory for 1974. During the last quarter of the twentieth century, the number of attorneys in Charleston County grew to more than 1,000. In addition to the boom in the number of attorneys, intrinsic changes in legal practice not only enhanced professionalism and diversified membership in the bar, but also maintained traditions of professional courtesy and civility.

GEDNEY M. HOWE, JR.

By Donald H. Howe

In this his beloved Charleston,
he was the preeminent trial lawyer
of the 20th century; yet his reach
was broader than the law

From a monument erected at the entrance of Charleston County Courthouse by friends of Gedney M. Howe, Jr.

I KNOW OF NO LAWYER WHO WAS HELD IN HIGHER esteem at the Bar and Bench than Gedney Howe. He was truly a lawyer's lawyer. He set an example in integrity and learning....Gedney Howe was a great architect of the law....He (as solicitor) considered himself as an officer of the court to insure that each person charged with an offense received justice with mercy," said Morris D. Rosen in his eulogy before the Charleston Coun-ty Bar Association on July 25, 2002. Howe was elected Solicitor for Berkeley and Charleston counties, succeeding Robert McCormick Figg in 1946, and served for ten years.

In a speech at a Trial Lawyers Association convention, Howe reminisced about the afternoon he assisted Figg in some Berkeley County criminal pleas when the presiding judge was giving every guilty plea a sentence of seven years. Figg and Howe talked privately to the judge about his rulings and the judge said, "Seven is my lucky number." The next day Figg and Howe brought the same defendants before the same judge, who was in a better humor than the day before. They represented each of those defendants to the court and the same judge gave them fair and measured sentences. Howe concluded his comments with, "All this is the kind of thing you can't tell at the Kiwanis Club or anything that occurs in court. So I know you all will keep it a secret. I've always found with two or three hundred lawyers you can depend on things to be kept quiet...I pass this along to you because in many ways the good old days were good old days and in many ways it was the human element that went in to make the court system what it was—it was personal, it was honest." When Gedney was scheduled to cross-examine or to talk to the jury, all the young lawyers would flock to the courtroom to hear him.

"Gedney had a very generous streak in him," said Coming B. Gibbs. "Gedney had an uncanny sense of when to throw money at a problem," said Marybelle H. Howe, his wife.

"David (Zidlick) said that many times, at Carolina, Big Gedney's check arrived at just the right moment," said Irene H. Zidlick, Howe's secretary.

Charleston judge Joseph S. Mendelsohn, rented his law office from Gedney and swears that every month Big Gedney referred enough fee-generating cases to Joe to cover his secretary's salary and his rent of 90 dollars a month, which included utilities. Gedney himself had a hard time sending bills.

William B. Regan claimed, "Gedney had a big law firm and it included Leonard

ABOVE: *A "lawyer's lawyer," Gedney M. Howe, Jr., was one of the most respected and influential attorneys of his generation.* OPPOSITE PAGE: *Following his death in 2002, Gedney Howe's friends erected this monument to him at the entrance to the Charleston County Courthouse.*

Long, Coming B. Gibbs, Jr., Arthur Rosenblum, Morris Rosen, Joe Mendelsohn, Charles M. Gibson, Barry Baker, and others. In reality, they were not a law firm. They were his acolytes, followers of Big Gedney, to whom he referred some fee-generating cases and some free cases." The author noticed that after Big Gedney's death, these acolytes had adopted many of his expressions and body and hand movements. Gedney would idle away some of his time by just standing on Broad Street, talking to any or all persons who walked by. In a sidewalk conversation, lawyer Larry Duffy explained that he had a complicated case. Gedney invited Duffy to bring over his complaint to see if he could help. Sure enough, Gedney helped Duffy redraft it and would not take a dime for his professional services. Stories like Duffy's are legend.

While Gedney never desired to hold public office after his decade as solicitor, he was active in every political campaign and always as a good Democrat. If candidates had Gedney's blessings, chances were good that they got elected. Outsiders labeled these lawyers—Gedney, Morris Rosen, Allen Legare, and O.T. Wallace—as the Broad Street Ring. On election nights, Gedney didn't go to the winner's party; he and Morris Rosen made house calls on the losers. Even in the days when Gedney was an undergraduate at the College of Charleston, he was the person the candidate went to for help.

All four of Big Gedney's children became attorneys. They called his household sermons "Howe's Little Home Lectures." "When asked if he talked about his court cases at home, his son, Donald Howe, answered, "Every single minute detail."

CHAPTER IX

THE BANNER YEARS THAT ENDED WITH A BANG

The most significant year in the history of the South Carolina Bar was not 1861 or 1895 but 1975, for it was in that year that the two formerly segregated bar associations merged and brought African Americans and women into full professional equality. Subsequent years were celebrated or mourned for many other reasons but equal justice within the bar was no longer an unrealized hope.

A committee cannot write a poem and a committee cannot manage a judicial system. Until 1975, the state court system had no administrative head and was, like many other South Carolina institutions, dominated by 170 members of the General Assembly. In 1959, the legislature gave the chief justice of the state supreme court full authority to operate the judicial system but did not provide any funds to carry out this mandate. The 1895 constitution had been amended many times but the judicial system was outdated and most lawyers agreed that the articles governing the judicial system badly needed amendment. Article V was simply inadequate to meet the needs of modern procedures. In 1966, Lieutenant Governor John C. West, a Camden and Hilton Head attorney and future governor, chaired a special committee of the General Assembly to make recommendations for needed amendments. He and two other lawyer-legislators began drafting an amendment to Article V.

The General Assembly voted to put the amendment to a vote by the electorate. A public forum called the Citizens Conference on Modernization of the Judicial System was held in Charleston. This conference reached a consensus that "the important feature of the unified court system is the ability of the chief justice, with the assistance of an administrator, to assign judges where they are needed, when they are needed." The conference received good publicity and there appeared to be a groundswell of interest in judicial reform. At the next election, the state's voters approved the amendment.

The amended Article V gave the General Assembly authority to elect nine new judges. One new judge was allotted to Charleston and bar member Klyde Robinson was elected on July 22, 1976. Judge Robinson was sworn in by Justice Julius B. Ness at a special meeting on August 6, 1976 at the courthouse followed by a social hour of the Charleston Bar held at the Hibernian Society. The revised article further mandated changes to create a "unified court system." Before 1976, there was little unifor-

The 1980s concluded with one of the most significant events in the history of the city and the state: Hurricane Hugo. It profoundly affected all aspects of life in Charleston, including the practice of law.

mity in record-keeping in different county courthouses and the constantly shifting caseloads in each local bar association were unsupervised. The Family Court structure was created in 1976. These courts were given exclusive jurisdiction over cases involving divorces, separate maintenance, support, alimony, adoptions, change of names, and criminal cases where juveniles were defendants. These cases were to be tried by a judge, not by juries. "The handling of domestic relations cases has become an important specialty," wrote former Chief Justice Littlejohn in *Littlejohn's Half Century at the Bench and Bar (1936-1986)*, published by the South Carolina Bar Foundation.

> *The establishment of these courts is one of the most significant changes brought about in my experience at the Bench and Bar. Without the family courts, circuit courts would be hopelessly inundated with litigation. Forty-six judges serve the Family Court; only thirty-one judges try both civil and criminal cases in the circuit courts.... In the early 1980s the Supreme Court adopted a Rule, already in effect in most other states, permitting a family court judge to divide marital property equitably. This is now an important part of the work of this court. The rule imposes upon the judge the authority to substitute for a jury and divide property accumulated during the time of marriage.... We have every reason to expect that the work of this court will increase.*

Prior to the creation of the Family Court, Charleston County had a Domestic Relations Court where Clarence Pearce was the first judge, followed by James Craven as chief judge and Robert R. Mallard as Associate Judge. The Family Court called for a complement of four judges: James Craven, Robert R. Mallard, Richard Fields, and Joseph Newell. The county government created a Charleston county court that could try cases which had a value up to 25,000 dollars. That court was superseded and Judge Theodore DuBose Stoney was its last justice.

Nineteen seventy-five was a banner year for the legal profession for another reason. Membership in the South Carolina Bar became mandatory for all attorneys practicing in the state. The South Carolina Bar Association began discussions in the 1960s to make membership compulsory. It was believed that the principal benefits of this action would be the improvement of professional standards of the association and the right to discipline members. Such a mandate would also be the beginning of a racially integrated bar. Legislation was enacted authorizing the Supreme Court to promulgate rules and regulations concerning mandatory membership by all attorneys. On December 14, 1967, the Supreme Court established the South Carolina State Bar, effective March 14, 1968. The South Carolina Bar Association continued in existence to organize attorneys' social activities. As it was a voluntary association, it could use funds in ways otherwise prohibited to the State Bar. For example, it could hire a lobbyist to manage the court reform legislation in the General Assembly. The association thus remained racially segregated.

Local attorneys in the Charleston County Bar Association were not governed by either of the state groups. In the 1950s, members of the local bar invited Richard Fields, an African-American attorney, to become a member. Fields recalled that in those years there were fewer than ten African-American attorneys in the whole state. The small group met on its own and sponsored its own continuing legal education programs. One of these meetings was at the Charleston County Public Library and was addressed by such luminaries as attorney Gedney M. Howe, Jr. and Judge Clarence E. Singletary.

Racial integration was unquestionable evidence of the acceptance of social change. At a 1973 business meeting of the State Bar, Charleston attorney and bar president, Henry B. Smythe, admitted that in 1968 he had thought separate bar associations were appropriate. Since then, he had come to believe that the two groups should merge, but another year and a half were required to accomplish the merger. The movement gained strength and at a joint meeting at Hilton Head on January 31, 1975, both bars approved the merger. The separate voluntary associations would be phased out and all their activities taken up by the South Carolina State Bar. The word "state" was dropped from the name and it became the South Carolina Bar. Since 1975, the South Carolina Bar operated with a minimum of control by the court and vital reforms were implemented through the efforts of the association. But it struggled to keep pace as court dockets, especially in the number of appeals to the Supreme Court, became clogged.

Recognizing the growing volume of appeals, the General Assembly created a Court of Appeals in 1979 and gave it constitutional status. This court had appellate jurisdiction but was not a court of last resort in cases which involved the death penalty, utility rates, significant constitutional questions, bond issues, and election contests. The court opened for business in the fall of 1983, with Alex M. Sanders, Jr., a future Charleston Bar member, as chief judge.

The Charleston County Bar took pride in having supplied presidents of the South Carolina Bar Association on several occasions during these eventful years. Charleston presidents were Morris D. Rosen (1979-1980),

TOP: *Judge Richard Fields was one of the first judges of the newly structured Family Court. In the 1950s, he had been invited to join the local bar.* ABOVE: *Charleston attorney and bar president Henry B. Smythe came to believe that the two bar associations should be merged.*

THE LAST CASE OF BREACH TO PROMISE TO MARRY

"The facts in this case weave a web of tangled love affairs," wrote Justice David W. Harwell in the case of Christine Bradley v. David Somers, 322 S.E. 2nd. 665 (1984).

ON HER APPOINTED wedding day, June 20, 1982, Christine Bradley, the expectant bride was wearing her new wedding dress and shoes and carrying her specially ordered silk bouquet. The guests had gathered in the church. The organ of the First Presbyterian Church at Hilton Head began to play and continued to play the same song over and over again. The time for the ceremony passed and the audience became uncomfortable. Finally, the pastor announced to the guests that the wedding would not take place.

Attorneys Ann M. Stirling (above) and Michael P. O'Connell represented Christine Bradley.

The pastor had called the bride and groom into his office to sign the marriage license where the groom announced that he could not go through with the marriage, and that "there is someone else." The groom's daughter was standing nearby dressed in sweatpants and a swimsuit. The groom testified that he had not told his daughter about the wedding and that, as a matter of fact, the daughter preferred his father's new girlfriend to Christine. The bride was humiliated, nauseated, and, shortly thereafter, suicidal.

Charleston Bar members Ann Stirling and Michael O'Connell represented the bride and Coming Ball Gibbs, of Gibbs and Holmes, represented the groom in the state's last "breach of promise to marry" lawsuit. The couple had met, begun to date, and have sexual intercourse while each was married to someone else. They agreed to divorce their spouses and marry each other. In preparation for the wedding, the bride and groom had ordered wedding bands from the Smithsonian Institution and arranged for the ceremony to take place in the First Presbyterian Church in Hilton Head. The parties also engaged an organist, caterer, photographer, florist, and baker. In preparation for the wedding, the bride had not only purchased her wedding gown and accessories and a nightgown, but also a Cross pen set for the groom bearing the engraving "David W. Somers, Jr., June 20, 1982." In addition to these expenses, the bride incurred $3,000 in psychiatric treatment after the abortive ceremony. The bride testified that, "to this day, she is not normal, has fits of raving, and has a severe distrust of men."

When this case was heard in the Court of Common Pleas, the jury gave the bride a judgment against the defendant for $60,000, an amount that included the damage the bride received in the break-up of her first marriage. After the groom abandoned the bride at the church, he made another offer to marry her and she refused.

In the appeal to the Supreme Court, the justices remanded the case for another trial solely on the issue of the cost of the damages the bride suffered because of the breach of promise to marry and directed the jury not to take into consideration the damage done to her first marriage as the bride was not entitled to be compensated for the injury done to that marriage. The court found that the groom's second proposal to marry did not mitigate the damages the bride suffered from the breach of the first promise. The case was eventually settled for less than the original verdict of $60,000.

The groom's attorney also asked the Supreme Court to abolish "breach of promise to marry" as a cause of action. The justices refused saying that other states had done so by statute not by court decision.

Thomas S. Tisdale (1981-1982), and Wade H. Logan III (1989-90). Attorney Gaines W. Smith was president of the Charleston Bar from 1975 to 1976 and remembered that the county had about 200 attorneys at that time. While Smith was president, the bar was called upon to entertain three members of the Supreme Court of Great Britain.

As best I can recall, the justices were in this country for a conference and these three made a visit to Charleston after their official conference. The local bar association had at least two dinner parties for them, one was held at the home of member Frank H. Bailey and one at the home of another attorney, Ben Scott Whaley.

In the last quarter of the twentieth century, there was a movement away from solo practices in small towns to the establishment of large firms in urban centers. Julius McKay of Columbia and Theodore Guerard of Charleston merged their firms. They then merged with a Greenville partnership and became Haynsworth, Perry, Bryant, Marion, McKay & Guerard. This firm had 35 partners, 27 associates, and four members of counsel, for a total of 66 lawyers with offices in Greenville, Columbia, and Charleston. Ness, Motley, Loadholt, Richardson and Poole, had offices in Charleston, Barnwell, and Providence, Rhode Island, with 29 partners, 12 associates, for a total staff of 41.

Thomas S. Tisdale was one of several members of the Charleston County Bar to serve as president of the South Carolina Bar Association. He served from 1981 to 1982.

In 1980 a new era began for many members of the bar. The United States Supreme Court decided a case that had arisen in the state of Arizona. Its opinion held that the First Amendment demanded that lawyers be permitted to advertise in the print media. The First Amendment reads:

Congress shall make no law respecting an establishment of a religion, or prohibiting the free exercise thereof; or abridging the freedom of speech, or of the press, or the right of the people peaceably to assemble, and to petition the government for a redress of grievances.

Chief Justice Bruce Littlejohn expressed his opinion on this subject.

Over the years, it had been considered unethical and improper for members of the Bar to advertise for business. It was against the code of professional conduct, and any lawyer who advertised in the conventional sense of the word might find himself appearing before the bar's grievance committee. It was considered unlawyer-like and certainly unprofessional.... While it is now legal to advertise, most of the older lawyers, and a good many of the younger lawyers too, refrain from it. I predict that as time passes there will be more and more advertising.... (W)ithout violating the Bar's code of ethics, (lawyers) have advertised and attempted to drum up business by such things as speech-making at civic cubs, joining a particular church, joining a civic club, visiting people in the hospital and attending funerals.

Five years later, the rules were amended to allow lawyers to advertise on television and radio. The rise of advertising created a need to recognize law practice specializations. Some appropriate authority would have the responsibility of examining an attorney and determining if he or she was truly qualified in a specific field. To permit an attorney to declare and advertise herself or himself as a specialist in one field or the other when he or she is not, cannot be permitted by the court. False advertising would not be tolerated by any court. Specialties were recognized by the South Carolina Supreme Court Rules in 1985. The first specialties were estate planning and probate law, taxation, and employment and labor law.

At that time, attorneys charged hourly rates for their professional services. A senior member of the bar, Charles S. Bernstein, observed:

The hourly fee is the worst thing that has happened to the law practice. It makes a lawyer cognizant of what they are earning, rather than the need to bring the law suit to a conclusion. Hourly rates came before advertising. Hourly rates have destroyed a cost-effective practice. Actually discovery is being used to intimidate

Two members of Buist Moore Smythe McGee have served as president of the Charleston Bar: Joseph H. McGee (1980-81, seated, left) and Benjamin A. Moore (1987-88, seated, right). Also pictured in this current photo of Buist Moore Smythe McGee are (standing, left to right) Susan M. Smythe, W. Foster Gaillard, Henry B. Smythe, Jr., and C. Allen Gibson, Jr.

and harass. The purpose was to avoid surprise, but it is being used as a weapon instead of a tool.

Joseph H. McGee was president of the Charleston County Bar Association from 1980 to 1981. He oversaw publication of a bar association directory and wrote in its foreword:

The Charleston County Bar Association has grown to nearly four hundred and fifty members, more than twice what it was twenty-five years ago. No longer is it possible for all Charleston lawyers to know one another. The suggestion that the Bar Association publish a membership directory with pictures was received by the Executive Committee approximately one year ago and it has taken since then to bring this idea to fruition.... We hope, however, that the membership...will find the directory a useful office resource and an aid to putting names and faces together.

A. Arthur Rosenblum succeeded McGee as president. He and his Executive Committee held the last annual meeting when the association was small enough to have a seated dinner and speaker. At that last dinner, Judge C. Weston Houck of Florence, recently sworn in as a United States District Court judge, was the main speaker. By 1983, the membership had jumped to about 700 lawyers and there was no place in Charleston County large enough to serve dinner to the full membership.

Attorney Joseph H. Cabaniss succeeded Rosenblum as president. His administration had to change the format of the annual meeting to a cocktail party with hors d'oeuvres instead of dinner. The meeting was held in a ballroom of the Charleston Omni Hotel and spouses were invited. There was no speaker. When asked if his administration would deal with the issue of building a new county courthouse or adding to the colonial courthouse, Cabaniss replied, "indeed I think the bar has been consumed with that topic for the past fifty years."

During the fiscal year of 1988 to 1989, Charles Goldberg served as president of the bar. He appointed Benjamin Goldberg to chair a committee to establish local continuing legal education courses. Prior to that year, lawyers had to travel to Columbia or watch closed circuit television to complete these required courses. He also had a committee examine the need for more space in the old courthouse.

Benjamin Goldberg succeeded Charles Goldberg (no relation) in 1989. Ben Gold-berg increased the number of local Continuing Legal Education (CLE) courses and continued to work on the issue of expanding the old courthouse. He also published a new Charleston County Bar Association pictorial membership directory. In his foreword President Goldberg wrote:

Benjamin Goldberg served as president of the Charleston County Bar Association from 1989 to 1990. During his term, he published a pictorial membership directory for the Bar Association.

> *On May 1, 1981, when the last directory was published, there were 450 members of the Charleston County Bar Association. Today, there are 694. As was said by President McGee in 1981, "No longer is it possible for all Charleston lawyers to know one another." This is certainly true today. This growth has had an adverse effect on the feeling of camaraderie for which the Charleston Bar has been known. The Bar Association is planning a series of projects and events in an effort to meliorate that condition.*

Hurricane Hugo, the biggest disaster to face the Charleston Bar in 150 years, blew into the city on the night of Thursday, September 21, 1989. Thursday morning's headlines in the *News and Courier* read, "Hugo Could Hit Tonight," "Schools Cancel Classes, Events," "Local Hospitals Preparing For the Worst," and "Gov. Campbell Declares State Emergency." All the plywood and batteries in Charleston were sold by noon.

On Thursday, September 21, Linda Lombard, local attorney and chairman of the County Council, was in trial in the Family Court with Judge Judy Bridges presiding. At every break in the case, Lombard received an update on the status of the hurricane. She approached the bench at noon and informed Judge Bridges that she needed to be at the emergency center on Leeds Avenue. Immediately, Judge Bridges responded, "go do your job" and continued the case.

Lombard checked in at the emergency center and went to the county jail, where Sheriff Al Cannon told her, "We know that the jail will flood and Lieber Correctional Institute has agreed to take our prisoners, but now, they are saying they can't do it because they are only allowed to take convicted criminals." After considerable negotiations between Lombard, Cannon, and the authorities at Lieber, the prison agreed to house Charleston County inmates during the storm.

Law offices began to close and all the courthouse employees were sent home. The courthouse was quiet except for the Court of Common Pleas. The presiding judge, a known workaholic, did not stop the trial of the case before him until six o'clock on Thursday evening.

Council chairman Lombard assumed responsibilities given to her by Governor Campbell's martial law decree. On the eleven o'clock television evening news on September 21, she made a climactic announcement urging everyone to evacuate the cities and county immediately. Also that day, Mayor Joseph P. Riley of Charleston declared that evacuation was required for city residents who lived in one-story homes. Attorney Lombard said that her hardest job was to decide when and under what weather conditions to command everyone to evacuate and stay away. Lombard sat out the hurricane in the Emergency Center on Leeds Avenue with television reporters from the national networks.

Some nonbelievers claimed, "hurricanes go to Myrtle Beach; they don't come to Charleston." Many residents, especially attorneys, questioned whether the old courthouse would survive one more hurricane. Others said, "let it be destroyed." By noon on the 21st, the city was quiet. The few residents who remained had put their cars in high-rise parking garages, renewed needed prescriptions,

Top and Above: *On the night of September 21, 1989, Hurricane Hugo struck Charleston with winds reaching 145 mph. Downtown Charleston suffered extensive damage, but the northern suburbs were even harder hit. Sullivan's Island and the Isle of Palms were disconnected from the mainland by the destruction of their bridges. The cost of the storm in the United States was estimated at $7 billion.*

bought supplies at the supermarket, cut down trees close to the houses, and sat down to wait out the hurricane.

Mayor Riley, also a member of the local bar, decided to sit out the storm in City Hall. With him that night were the city attorney, the Public Relations Officer, the Building Inspector, the Director of Administrative Services, two of the mayor's Executive Assistants, and representatives of the police and fire departments. Over in the Hollings Judicial Center, United States Federal District Judge Charles E. Simons, Jr. chose to spend the hurricane night in the new federal courthouse.

As expected, the rains began at sundown on September 21. The winds blew harder and harder and the rain grew very severe. By 7:30 p.m., the storm had damaged enough power lines for the whole area to lose electricity. The storm escalated to the degree that the wooden parts of the old courthouse began to give way. Gusts would actually push the courthouse a bit from east to west and then the building would ease back into its place. A young lawyer said that "the buildings and homes in Charleston were rocking and rolling."

At midnight, the winds and rain stopped. Hurricane Hugo's eye was passing over the city. Those who stayed had no room to doubt that they were directly in the hurricane's path. During the lull, Judge Simons took his flashlight and walked outside. All was quiet. Less than half an hour later, the hurricane's fury returned, bringing wind and rain at 145 miles per hour. It was morning before Lombard could observe the damage to the courthouse.

CHAPTER X

THE COURTHOUSE THE BAR BUILT

On the morning of September 22, 1989, the sun bathed the old courthouse and Broad Street in golden rays of sunshine. Charleston was exhausted and silent. Fallen trees, downed power and telephone lines, peeled-off roofs, and dead squirrels blocked the streets. Telephone, electricity, and water service had ceased to function. When Chairman Lombard and the county administrator entered the old courthouse, they could not go upstairs beyond the second floor because of the debris in the stairwells. The chairman was forced to condemn the building as unfit for human habitation, thereby canceling the civil trial docket in session and the term of the criminal court which was scheduled to begin on October 2.

Even before Hurricane Hugo, this old courthouse leaked badly. The Family Court in the newer O. T. Wallace Office Building next door had fared better in the storm, although 600 window panes were broken. Without electricity, the Family Court could not process and mail out child-support checks. The judges concluded that holding court would be difficult if not impossible without electricity. Mayor Riley declared a curfew from 7 p.m. to 7 a.m. for the indefinite future.

The county jail suffered no structural damage during Hugo but there had been a crisis when the jail's emergency power went out. More than 90 serious offenders had been loaded onto buses to be taken to other prisons. Sheriff Al Cannon said, "We had another thirty inmates in a hallway when the power went out, so we had to get them back in their cells in the dark and we had to help those buses pass through an electrically powered security gate. That left a little room at the jail for suspected looters and curfew violators as well as the usual criminals."

U.S. District Judge Sol Blatt, Jr. said that he barely heard Hugo's fury as he spent the night in the new Hollings federal courthouse. Leaks occurred where the $9 million courthouse was attached to the old post office, but the judge managed to catch some of the water in trash cans. The practice of law ceased temporarily and the court system came to a halt. Attorney Bart Daniel recalled that, "After Hugo blew through, I was assured that my family was safe, then I headed down town to check on some of the historic buildings. As I hiked over fallen trees and other debris in the street, I came upon other lawyers also headed for the Four Corners of Law to check on their beloved buildings. I teared up when I saw the county courthouse with its roof gone, bricks and wood scattered about, and gaping holes in the walls."

Bar President Ben Goldberg immediately began to investigate what the Bar Association could do for this helpless community. He contacted Bradish J. Waring, Charleston attorney for BellSouth and mortgagee of the Francis

Marion Hotel, and asked him to talk with his clients about setting up an emergency telephone bank in the hotel's ballroom. Goldberg lined up attorneys to man the telephones and give free legal advice. The telephone company took some of their linemen off other repair jobs to install 16 telephones in the ballroom and by Monday, September 25, this emergency Legal Assistance Center was up and running. News of the Center's activity was published in *The News and Courier* and *The Evening Post.* Volunteer attorneys answered callers' questions about how to apply for quick loans from the Federal Emergency Management Agency to repair their homes.

The Charleston Bar's heroic effort was recognized by a Certificate of Merit from the American Bar Association, commending the bar for "an outstanding partnership program which promotes greater understanding of the justice system and enhances the profession's service to both clients and their communities."

Another emergency was to find a place for the courts to meet. Lombard and the county administrator located an old navy facilities building on Melbourne Street in North Charleston, but it would take more than 90 days to prepare it for court use. The ersatz judges' benches were built of plywood and painted to make them look like mahogany. Circuit Judge Ralph King Anderson was Chief Administrative Judge of the Ninth Judicial Circuit, which includes Charleston and Berkeley counties. Three weeks after Hugo, he began to hear attorneys' motions at the Days Inn Motel at 155 Meeting Street. He then cleaned out a room on the fourth floor of the Wallace Building to hear nonjury matters. "Ben Goldberg and I went out to Melbourne Street, at least on three occasions, to review where the county was planning to provide courtrooms. We found that the construction team had built the witness chair fifty feet from the jury, " said Anderson. "In the

Severely damaged by Hurricane Hugo in 1989, the 1756 Charleston County Courthouse, one of the "Four Corners of Law," underwent a decade-long reconstruction and restoration with major support from the Charleston County Bar Association and its Friends of the Courthouse committee.

meantime, the docket of cases was getting further and further behind," Goldberg remarked. "The bar has got to get these courts up and running. Even before Hugo, the docket here was the second longest docket in the state." "It was a novel judicial situation and we had to come up with novel solutions. Ben Goldberg did a magnificent job working with the bar," said Anderson. One judge objected to not having a private bathroom at the Melbourne Street courthouse. The unhappy judge was spared hearing the county administrator's response. The judges had to use the public bathrooms.

John Bleecker, president of the Charleston Bar Association from 1994 to 1995, was one of the prime movers in the effort to restore the old county courthouse in the wake of Hurricane Hugo, and to establish a new judicial center in downtown Charleston.

A week after Hurricane Hugo, Governor Campbell and the state insurance commissioner discussed the possibility of economic panic if insurance companies collapsed under the weight of hurricane claims. "It really could have happened," the insurance commissioner said. "A domino-like collapse of insurers would have shaken the public's confidence in the whole industry during already traumatic times." Eventually, insurers paid out $3.2 billion in claims—$8 million a day—to South Carolina home and car owners, businesses, and shrimp boatmen. At one point, 5,600 adjustors blanketed the Hugo-affected areas. With few exceptions, insurers did not seek rate increases to cover hurricane losses. Hugo rewrote the book on hurricanes and it made insurers rethink their exposure in the hurricane belt.

A year later, a dozen insurance groups representing 42 companies said they would no longer write home or auto policies in South Carolina. Yet, South Carolina was fortunate that its policyholders did not have to pick up the full tab. The cost was spread out through industry reinsurance pools and company-wide disaster reserves which topped $13 billon. The main problems were disputes over tree removal and food spoilage and disputes over water- or wind-caused damage.

Working right along with Ben Goldberg was John M. Bleecker, Jr., the Bar Association's liaison officer to the courts. Bleecker remembered that, in August 1989, he and Ben Goldberg met the county administrator and the county's capital facilities manager, Carl Simmons. The purpose of the meeting was to emphasize to the county the pressing need for better judicial facilities. At that meeting, Simmons called the old 1756 courthouse "a grand old lady" and prophetically added that "she would never survive a 'Force Four' hurricane." Just a few weeks later, Hugo proved him right and destroyed this "grand old lady." After this meeting and before Hurricane Hugo, the county did enter into a contract to have the walls sealed to keep out moisture and mold. These contracts were made with the local firm of Liollio Associates, Inc. and with John Milner Associates of Pennsylvania, who had the reputation of working on European castles. After Hugo, these contracts had to be renegotiated.

The Charleston County Bar took up the cause of the courthouse repairs and new construction. It persisted for a decade to defeat interference and obstruction and the county's facilities are testimony to the bar's vision. A committee was formed and named Friends of the Courthouse. Its purpose was to raise money to purchase interior furnishings for the courthouse, items which the county was unable to provide. They began with a $125,000 matching grant from the Edward J. Nobles Foundation. A grandson of Nobles, the Beech Nut chewing gum king, was a neighbor of attorney Bradish Waring. The committee eventually raised over one million dollars in the ten-year period. The central committee of this group included Bradish J. Waring, Nancy Hawk, Jonathan H. Poston, Bart Daniel, Robert Rosen, Charlton DeSaussure, Jr., and William Cathcart, the only nonlawyer among the group.

Eventually, the Circuit Court became operational using the County Council chambers in the Wallace Building. The Probate Court was assigned a space which the county had used as a conference room. On one occasion, Ben Goldberg walked by this room and saw the judge sitting on a chair in the hall. He and Bleecker went to the county administrator and said, "The best probate judge in the state is having to sit in a chair in the hall, this is certainly not acceptable!" Some county employees had needed conference space and had temporarily moved His Honor out into the hallway.

Two generations of the Rosen family of attorneys are represented in this photograph, left to right, Richard Rosen, his father, Morris D. Rosen, and his brother, Robert Rosen. Robert Rosen was a leader of the Bar Association's effort to preserve and restore the historic Charleston County Courthouse.

Three months after Hugo, the bar began to try cases at Melbourne Street. The first jury trial was a Kiawah Island construction litigation involving seven lawyers. Bar members remembered this case because the trial lasted two weeks with the noise of hammering just outside the door. The foreman of the jury was a fellow attorney, Donald Williams of the McNair Law Firm. All seven opposing trial lawyers agreed that Williams would be a fair juror. The judge appointed Williams foreman of the jury and later said, "I could not have tried this case without the assistance of Williams."

Robert L. Clement, Jr. was elected president of the bar for the year after Hurricane Hugo, 1990 to 1991. He said, "The continuing problems which extended throughout the year as a consequence of Hurricane Hugo affected every aspect of the Association's year. Also a prodigious amount of work was done by the Law Library committee, chaired by John Linton, which concluded that the library would remain indefinitely in the temporary court on Melbourne Street in North Charleston. Maintenance and upkeep of the library was an ongoing challenge. Resident Circuit Judge William A. Howard generously agreed to have his law clerks contribute to this effort."

John Bleecker, who continued on the Executive Committee, reported that there was a glimmer of hope that some comprehensive Judicial Center would ultimately be built back at the Four Corners of Law. The County Council appointed a blue-ribbon committee to study possibilities for permanent court facilities. Seven of its 15 members were lawyers, including Clement and Bleecker. Clement helped draft the committee's report which urged development of a comprehensive plan for restoration or construction of the courthouse. The County Council was receiving nationwide responses to its request for advice about renovation of the historic courthouse at the corner of Broad and Meeting streets. "Due to Hugo, it was a year of mullet and hominy rather than one of wine and roses," concluded Clement.

During the year of 1990 to 1991, all the regular committees of the bar began to function again. Chair Elliott Halio drafted "Guidelines for Professional Cooperation," a project jointly sponsored with the Charleston Medical Society. Elliott Barrow and Capers Barr started to work on a code of professional courtesy which culminated in adoption of standards years later.

In the coming year, the words "judicial center" began to be used synonymously with the word "courthouse." Capers G. Barr, III, was elected president for the year 1991 to 1992. He and the bar recognized a continuing need to monitor the County Council's plans to restore the old courthouse and to build a new judicial center. The issue centered around where to build it. The bar was adamant in wanting it constructed in the historic district.

A decision was made to demolish the twentieth-century addition to the 1750s courthouse. After this was accomplished, archeologists dug trenches and pits to excavate items of historical interest, which included shards of ceramics, a variety of ink, wine, medicine, South Carolina Dispensary bottles, and tobacco artifacts. A privy on the northwest corner of the property had been used since 1893 and was filled with some wine glass shards and numerous wine or spirit bottles.

"We were upward of 1,000 members and approaching 1,200," said Elliott Halio, president for the year 1992 to 1993. The main issue I had to deal with was building the Judicial Center. I did go to a couple of council meetings and listened to what they had to say. Our presence was necessary to indicate to them how much we were interested in the building. Otherwise, there were just routine matters that came before the executive committee."

"We met with County Council on more than one occasion, and the entire bar was behind that project," said Coming B. Gibbs, president for the year 1993 to 1994. Robert Rosen took the lead on the preservation and restoration of the historic courthouse while John Bleecker led the bar's efforts to keep the courthouse complex downtown and to create the present judicial center. John worked closely with the architects and they were very helpful. Additionally, attorneys William M. Youngblood and Charlton DeSaussure, Jr., experts in municipal finance, lent their help concerning certain tactical issues. Their friendship with or influence with certain members of County Council was helpful."

John Bleecker, president of the bar in the year 1994 to 1995, recalled, "During that year, the Charleston County Bar was very involved with the plans for the judicial center as well as the old courthouse. The Executive Committee of the bar also faced the high cost of maintaining the law library. Almost half of the revenue from dues was used for it. In this year, efforts were started for another photo directory, but it wasn't printed until a couple of years later. The Bar did commission an oil portrait of Gus Pearlman, judge of the probate court."

"A highlight of my year as Bar president," said Bleecker, "was the honor of turning the gavel over to Lee Robinson, the first woman to serve as president of the Charleston County Bar Association." "As president, I never felt any objection to my being a woman president of the bar," said Robinson. "The membership had grown so much at that time, that the executive committee organized a program to match a young attorney with an older attorney as a mentor, someone to whom an inexperienced lawyer could go with questions."

THE RULES OF EVIDENCE

What you want to say most
is inadmissible.
Say it anyway.
Say it again.
What they tell you is irrelevant
can't be denied and will
eventually be heard.
Every question
is a leading question.
Ask it anyway, then expect
what you don't get.
There is no such thing
as the original
so you'll have to make do
with a reasonable facsimile.
The history of the world
is hearsay. Hear it.
The whole truth
Is unspeakable
and nothing but the truth
is a lie.
I swear this.
My oath is a kiss.
I swear
by everything
incredible.

By Lee Robinson, Poet
President, Charleston Bar, 1995-1996

SISTERS IN LAW

Women Lawyers of the Charleston Bar

A HIGHLIGHT OF THE TWENTIeth century was the recognition that women could pursue any vocation they chose. The first wave of feminism occurred about the time of World War I when most women were united under one umbrella, the fight for the right to vote. Out of that movement came a drive to admit women to the practice of law. On Valentine's Day 1918, South Carolina changed its admission policy to the bar to include women.

The first woman to practice law in Charleston was Hannah Axelman, who was admitted to the bar on December 18, 1931. In that same decade, two others stepped up to the bar: Mary Stewart Allan and Mary Polhemus. The South Carolina Supreme Court emancipated married women in 1938. Next, Ruth Williams opened a practice in 1954.

The second wave of feminism occurred in the 1960s and early 1970s. With it came the right of women to sit on juries—and a kindergarten miss could draw the jury. For the first time, female litigators tried cases in the courtrooms and women attorneys moved into every legal specialty of law. More women became local attorneys: Helen Ehrhardt Clawson; Ann Elizabeth Fleischli; Margaret Elizabeth Brown; Patricia O'Dell Brehmer; Ann Mary Stirling; Constance Beth Ackerman; and Suzanne Pendarvis Ravenel.

Since the second wave of feminism, the Charleston County Bar Association has elected women to be president. Carol B. Ervin was president in 2003 and Cheryl D. Shoun is currently president-elect. Women lawyers have served and are serving as judges in every courtroom from positions as magistrates to justices of the South Carolina Supreme Court.

There are currently over 500 women in Charleston County practicing law, including Chief Justice Jean Hoefer Toal. Every door is open and there is no longer a glass ceiling for women attorneys in Charleston County.

ABOVE LEFT: *Ruth Williams opened her law practice in 1954.* LEFT: *Attorney Helen Ehrhardt Clawson.*

Robinson had been a member of the bar for 20 years. She recalled that some senior members were especially helpful when she was new to the practice of law. "Arthur Howe, 'Big' Gedney Howe, and Coming Ball Gibbs were especially supportive. Once, right in the middle of trial, an ethical issue presented itself. When the case recessed, I called Arthur Howe to discuss the problem. He told me to 'come on over and we'd settle it,' and he helped me to solve my question. In 1996, Robinson won a national award from the American Bar Association for the best essay on a subject of the legal profession. The title of her essay was *Looking at the Case from the Child's Point of View.*

"The two most important issues that were resolved during my tenure as president and the next few years thereafter were the selection of the location of the Charleston County Judicial Center and its funding," said E. Bart Daniel, president of the bar from 1996 to 1997. "Both issues had remained unresolved since 1989. Both proved to be contentious, time-consuming, and drawn out. As a result, I was asked to continue to chair the Judicial Center and Historic Courthouse Committee for the County Bar." "Unbeknown to the legal community, the Council had preliminarily decided to move the Judicial Center to an area outside of the Charleston business and legal district, namely to either county-owned property on Morrison Drive or the vacant Charlestowne Square Mall in North Charleston. Through the efforts of many in the legal community and Mayor Joe Riley, those wanting to keep the judicial center in the legal, business, and historic district persevered. After that final vote, we turned our attention to funding this enormous county project which would cost substantially more once the decision was made to build it in the heart of the historic district," said Daniel.

The Charleston County Bar Association's Judicial Center and Historic Courthouse Committee worked hard to ensure that the new Charleston County Judicial Center would be located downtown, near the Four Corners of Law. The effort succeeded, and the $46,000,000 center opened on August 30, 2002.

"When I was selected by the presidential search committee to serve as its president, I was told that my selection was because I was a Republican. At that time, the Charleston County Council consisted of nine Republicans and no Democrats. Ultimately, the County Council, which had no lawyers on it, was convinced to spend $46,000,000 for construction of the Charleston County judicial center," concluded Daniel.

"The overarching issues for the bar that year were the final decision regarding the establishment of a judicial center, either downtown or elsewhere in the county, and the decision regarding renovation of the historic courthouse. The old courthouse had been in disrepair since Hugo, therefore another issue was the difficulty in creating a judicial center at the Four Corners of Law. Ultimately, the plans for the judicial center were reduced in height by a floor and its mass was reduced as well. A series of public presentations were made to educate all interested parties about the benefits of maintaining the judicial complex downtown," said John P. Linton, president of the local bar from 1997 to 1998. "My recollection is that the bar membership was approaching, if not exceeding, 1,000, that year I was president," said Linton.

Andy Savage, a well respected attorney and former Charleston County Council member, led presentations of the final proposal of the Judicial Center. He was chairman of an Ad Hoc Committee to woo all public officials and citizens to the project. The biggest event of the campaign was held at the Charleston Visitor Center, and was attended by virtually all of the public figures involved and a great majority of the bar. Following this occasion, the Judicial Center received final funding and approval by the County Council.

Linton added that, "the decision to move forward with the judicial center also brought in focus the need to reevaluate the longstanding commitment to the Charleston Bar Law Library. The advances in electronic technology for legal research convinced the bar that housing a huge book library was no longer feasible," said Linton. "Moreover, the space requirements for such a library would not be available in a new courthouse. The decision to discontinue the law library permitted the bar to increase continuing legal education courses, have financial support for more pro bono projects and various civic undertakings."

"One of the challenges during that year was to have a number of social gatherings for the purpose of maintaining as much collegiality as could be achieved with a growing bar. These were typically held after a legal educational seminar," concluded Linton.

Frances Cantwell, president from 1998 to 1999, said that in her term as president the decision had been made to build the judicial center downtown between Broad, Meeting, Queen, and King streets. It was to be built in the middle of that block so that its modern façade could not be seen in the historic district. The judicial center would also be adjacent to the old courthouse. The next hurdle was to get the approval of the City of Charleston's Board of Architectural Review. The board altered the plans and required it to have a door on the King Street side. The county was on a financial shoestring and would not finance the costs of providing security personnel and machinery for a King Street door. Skilled in mediation, Cantwell and other experienced lawyers solved the problem. The King Street door was built but does not open.

South Carolina Supreme Court Chief Justice Jean Toal, seen here making an address to the Charleston School of Law, is the first, and thus far the only, woman to have served on the South Carolina Supreme Court. Reelected in 2004, her term as Chief Justice will expire in 2014.

"Finally there was a groundbreaking ceremony for the new courthouse, and I attended as president of the Bar. It was on July 30, 1999," said M. Dawes Cooke, Jr., who was president was from 1999 to 2000. "That year, we also published a new Bar Legal Directory, which I noticed came one hundred years after the popular picture that many people have in their law offices entitled, 'Bench and Bar of Charleston, South Carolina, 1899,' comprising the photographs of 82 members of the Bar from that year," said Cooke. "It was a direct ancestor to this new directory," Cook wrote in the forward of the new directory. "Most of the surnames in the 1899 directory are familiar to us today. Fully a quarter or more of them appear in our directory, including Barnwell, Buist, DeSaussure, Hagood, Hastie, Hollings, Legare, Logan, Rivers, Simons, Sinkler, Smythe, Walker, and Young." The new directory contained over 1,000 names. "The only controversy that I recall was that at our annual meeting of the Bar we passed a resolution favoring removal of the Confederate flag from the roof of the State House. I received complaints about that from two members of the Bar Association," said Cooke.

Chief Justice of the South Carolina Supreme Court Jean Toal swore in Michael A. Molony as president of the Charleston County Bar for the year 2000 to 2001. In that year, the bar still had to work closely with the County Council to ensure that the judicial system would remain near the Four Corners of Law. The president and executive committee worked closely with the Friends of the Courthouse in raising money for the furnishings. During that year, the bar held a reception for the newly elected Circuit Judge, Deadra Jefferson, and the bar sponsored its first South Carolina Circuit Judges reception.

The many activities of the bar for that year included the establishment of a website and a membership list which included members' e-mail addresses. Continuing Legal Education courses, offered by the county bar, were arranged in conjunction with other activities, such as Riverdogs baseball games or oyster roasts. At the end of Molony's year in office, the county bar held its annual meeting in the South Carolina Aquarium.

Precedent was broken when J. Brady Hair was elected president of the bar for the year 2001 to 2002. For the first time in the history of this bar, an attorney was elected president of the bar who did not have a home or office in downtown Charleston. The association at that time had between 1,200 and 1,300 members. Hair, a man who had the ability to make complicated issues comprehensible, was born, raised, and practiced law in North Charleston. That city had begun life as an industrial suburb to Charleston and was home to the Charleston Navy Base and Navy Shipyard. Hair's respect at the bar polished the image of that hard-working municipality. He conducted the annual meeting in North Charleston at its celebrated convention center and was proud to give the recognition to his hometown. By the twenty-first century, many members of the local legal profession had opened law offices in the Charleston suburbs where their clients lived and worked. Law offices had very few walk-in clients. They arrived in automobiles and expected to have a parking space.

J. Brady Hair, elected in 2001, was the first president of the Bar Association not to have a home or office in downtown Charleston. A native of North Charleston, he also has his law practice there.

At the dawn of the twenty-first century, the old courthouse looked better than it ever had in its 247 years. The Friends of the Courthouse had furnished it with framed portraits of early members of the bar, the judiciary important to the history of the Charleston County Bar from the eighteenth, nineteenth, and twentieth centuries, a few distinguished citizens, and some prints relating to the history of the Charleston County legal profession. The Friends raised funds to purchase window trimmings, rugs, and furniture befitting a courtroom of 1790s vintage but still useable today. Attorney Bart Daniel greeted visitors at the open house for the restored old courthouse. "When that big door would open, each time you'd hear people gasp and catch their breath because it's truly that beautiful," he said.

All the members of the Charleston Bar have stories to tell about the positive impact of the judicial center on the administration of justice, verdicts, and respect for the law. Milton Stratos observed that the décor and aura of the courtrooms are such that he and clients see this as a "real court, not a temporary hangout." Larry Duffy reported that when he and his clients enter the judicial center, they always know they are in an important place.

To honor the restoration of the old courthouse to its 1790s grandeur, the South Carolina Supreme Court held a session of court in it on March 19, 2002. All five justices assembled in the James Louis Petigru Law Library and ceremonially entered the historic second floor courtroom. That courtroom overlooks the famous corner of Meeting and Broad streets.

Judicial arguments were presented first by the attorney for the appellant. The respondent then had an equal amount of time to answer, and both sides had five minutes rebuttal. Each case took about 40 minutes to present. All of the cases docketed for that day were represented by members of the Charleston Bar. The first case was presented by attorneys Carl H. Jacobson and Trenholm Walker. It was a workers' compensation matter. The second case involved a procedural issue and was argued by Justin Lucey and Henry Grimball. The third and final case was a City of Charleston annexation issue argued by Gregg E. Myers with Frances Cantwell and William B. Regan representing the city. Regan felt that the experiences of arguing a case in that courtroom was "awesome."

When the newly restored Charleston County Courthouse opened on March 19, 2002, the South Carolina Supreme Court held a session in the historic second floor courtroom (above). William B. Regan, who argued a case that day, described it as "a highlight of my career."

He was aware of the history that had preceded his presence there. "It was a highlight of my career."

Watching this courtroom drama, the author stood just inside the court door and imagined that the room was haunted by the lawyers of previous generations. The windows would have been open so that the rooms were filled with the smell of the meat market across the street and the sound of conversations and of horses along Meeting and Broad streets. She could see young John Rutledge standing before the judicial bench taking his oath to become a member of the Charleston Bar. Rutledge appeared wearing the regalia of a proper English barrister which he had had tailor-made for himself on Regent Street in London. He was wearing a new horsehair wig, deeply powdered in dead white. The white ruching around the neck and delicate cuffs of French lace adorned his brocaded silk black gown. She thought about August 5, 1776, when the members of the privy council and lower house marched out of this courtroom to stand before the local militia on Broad Street where the Declaration of Independence was read aloud for the first time and changed its legal status from a colony to a state. After the court adjourned, Henry Grimball's daughter, Emily, asked the chief justice to sign a note to excuse her from school that day.

For several decades, the bar had relied on nonprofit organizations to help it meet its obligations to provide indigent individuals fair access to the judicial system. The Neighborhood Legal Assistance System had been founded here in 1967, but, with the loss of federal funds in 2001, it was forced to close. After it ceased to operate, Neighborhood Legal Assistance sold its King Street real estate for over one million dollars and the net proceeds of the sale were $915,000. The federal agency claimed its funds had purchased the property and therefore it had a resulting right to the funds. Charleston attorneys Frank McCann, Gerry Kaynard, and George Kefalos brokered a compromise with the federal government. Under the settlement agreement, the bar agreed to establish a nonprofit corporation to administer free legal services in the Charleston area to clients meeting Neighborhood Legal Assistance Program guidelines.

Mark Tanenbaum was president of the Charleston Bar for the year 2002 to 2003. The bar then had a membership of 1,353, 62 of whom were new applicants admitted at the 2003 annual meeting in February. Moving into the twenty-first century, Tanenbaum had the bar's web page updated and the new "courtrooms are interactive, that is they are equipped with metal detectors and are lap-top compatible with drop-down screens for Power Point presentations. Plus, in this year, the Bar had great continuing legal education courses." All the chief justices of the state's court of appeals met in Charleston and the bar entertained them with a reception at 51 Meeting Street, the 1808 historic Russell House and gardens," said Tanenbaum. Justice Kaye G. Hearn, Chief Justice of the South Carolina Court of Appeals in South Carolina, was the hostess.

In April 2003, a group of lawyers announced the opening of a for-profit law school in Charleston. Spokesman for the group was Judge Alex Sanders, Charleston attorney, former chief judge of the South Carolina Court of Appeals, and president emeritus of the College of Charleston. "South Carolina has the lowest number of lawyers per 100,000 population than any other southern state," Sanders said. "It has 185 lawyers per hundred thousand."

Other members of the Charleston Bar are also founders of the school: U.S. magistrate Robert Carr; U.S. District

ABOVE: *Gerry Kaynard was one of three attorneys who forged a compromise with the Federal government concerning the Neighborhood Legal Assistance Program.* BELOW: *First-year students pose in front of the new Charleston School of Law.* OPPOSITE PAGE ABOVE: *Judge Alex Sanders has served as spokesman for the founders of the Charleston School of Law.*

Judge Patrick Michael Duffy; Gedney Howe, III; Richard Fields, retired state judge; magistrate George Kosko; U.S. District Judge David Norton; attorney and Mayor Joseph P. Riley; Edward Westbrook; and Deadra Jefferson, state circuit court judge. The founders took an assignment of an 1825 charter to The Forensic Club, a society of Charleston lawyers established to hire a local lecturer in law. The assignment of this charter was signed by Thomas G. Buist, Esquire, a descendent of an original founder of The Forensic Club. This club was the first law school in the South and predated Harvard Law School which was founded in 1817 but did not matriculate students until 1829.

The Charleston School of Law will assist the local bar. Richard Gershon, dean of the new school, stated that, "the library of the law school will be available to the local bar for doing research. The school will be housed at its building at 81 Mary Street. In addition, the students will be involved with pro bono programs and internships with local lawyers and judges. The Charleston Bar will be invited to attend special lectures on aspects of the law." For the year 2003 to 2004, Carol B. Ervin was elected president of the bar with a mission to lead it further into the twenty-first century.

Attorney Lloyd "Student" Willcox, the first member of the bar to reach 100 years of age, said, "There is no finer company than the company of other lawyers." Any member of the Charleston Bar would echo that sentiment. *The Journal*, a magazine of the American Bar Association, highlighted this collegiality in its September 2001 issue. Lawyer Ted Hostetter says that he had been a member of the Richland Bar before relocating to Charleston where he immediately felt the comity of the local bar. The cover of the magazine featured the article with these headlines, "Southern Collegiality, Lawyers still practice with old-fashioned civility in Charleston, S.C."

"Here, your word is your bond," Eduardo Curry stated in a quote featured on the magazine cover. The author of the article wrote, "The practice of law in this city still embraces traditions and the values of civility and collegiality that in some places have become relics of the past." It identified Broad Street as "lawyer's row." Brady Hair, who was president of the bar at the time, is quoted as saying, "While many lawyers are housed all over downtown and the suburbs, Broad Street remains a central gathering place for the area's attorneys."

On weekday mornings, lawyers cluster around a large rectangular table at Brent's on Broad Street for camara-

Breakfast at Brent's on Broad Street is a Charleston legal tradition. In the front row, left to right, Richard Hanckel, III, Larry Sexton, and Ruth Cupp; in the back row, left to right, Judge Joseph Mendelsohn, Steve Steinert, Robert A. Bernstein, Donald M. Williams, and G. Sims McDowell, III.

HENRY WILLIAM DESAUSSURE

A friend of George Washington in one generation and mentor to John C. Calhoun in the next, Henry William DeSaussure lived in two critical eras of the state and nation. Born on August 16, 1763, at Pocotaligo in Beaufort County, he served his country as a soldier and civil servant and his state as a legislator and judge. He also served his city of Charleston as a soldier and as intendant (mayor) in the 1790s.

At the age of 17, he was captured when Charleston fell to the British in May 1780. Exiled to Philadelphia in 1781, he took the advice of his merchant father, Daniel DeSaussure, and studied law with Jared Ingersoll. He was admitted to the bar of Philadelphia in 1784 and became a member of the South Carolina Bar when he returned to Charleston in 1785.

Henry DeSaussure married Elizabeth Ford of Morristown, New Jersey, whose parents were acquainted with George Washington. Through this family connection, this former prisoner of war had the honor of meeting his commanding officer. The men became friends and political allies. President Washington appointed Henry W. DeSaussure director of the United States Mint in 1795. Later that year, he returned to his beloved South Carolina where he continued his public service and his private law practice. As intendant of Charleston in the 1790s, he presided over the city during a time of economic hardships and bitter political strife between Federalists and Republicans.

According to *Generations of Lawyers, A History of the South Carolina Bar*, "Henry W. DeSaussure and his brother-in-law Timothy Ford were reputed to be the best teachers for those aspiring to be admitted to the bar...." Presumably for this reason, John C. Calhoun entered the partnership of DeSaussure and Ford as a student for 100 guineas on December 24, 1804.

In addition to service in the General Assembly, DeSaussure was a founding chancellor of South Carolina College (1801). His colleagues in the General Assembly elected him a judge of the Court of Equity in 1808 and he held that office for almost three decades. Named President of the Court of Appeals in 1817, Henry W. DeSaussure left a prolific legacy on the Equity Court. From 1809 to 1829, nearly half of the 2,000 decrees and opinions handed down by the court were delivered by Judge DeSaussure. His four-volume *Reports of the Court of Chancery and Court of Equity in South Carolina*...(1817-19) codified the state's equity law.

Among his other public service, DeSaussure was a trustee of the College of Charleston and South Carolina College and Commissioner of the Charleston Orphan House. He was a member of the Society of the Cincinnati and a Unionist during the nullification crisis. He died on March 26, 1839.

derie, a mug of coffee, and sometimes breakfast. Names like Howe, Mendelsohn, Goldberg, Rosenblum, Altman, Bernstein, Cupp, Krell, Steinert, Maybank, Williams, Berlinsky, and others are regulars. For fresh air in the group, some nonlawyer members are Hanckel, Campbell, Ratner, Lybrand, Sexton, and Bailey.

Brady Hair also said, "The majority of the lawyers here would rather help someone along than compete for clients, believing such good works will come back to them in the form of future referrals from that colleague. Longtime members of the bar work hard to show newcomers the way things are done by lawyers in Charleston."

There are concerns that things may be changing. Sol Blatt, Jr. who has been a U.S. District Court Judge in Charleston for over 30 years, stated, "lawyers appearing before me sometimes are more contentious and less polite in court than they were when I became a federal judge in 1971. Nevertheless, things haven't gotten anywhere near as bad as I hear from other judges in other places. The lawyers who appear before me are as collegial as they can be. I don't ever call a lawyer down in front of his client unless I have to, and it's very rare."

The *Journal* noted, "That spirit of inclusion of new lawyers is a pivotal and important memory for many lawyers who practice here." A visiting businessman noticed a unique practice at the Charleston Bar, that of referring fee-generating cases. The man was familiar with many bar associations throughout the South, but attorneys re-

William Henry DeSaussure served as Commissioner of the Charleston Orphan House. Established in 1790, it was the oldest municipal orphanage in the United States.

The DeSaussure family's legal tradition continued as Henry Alexander DeSaussure (1788-1865) followed his father in the practice of law. He died in Columbia at the age of 75. In the next generation, his son, Wilmot Gibbes DeSaussure, graduated from South Carolina College in 1840 and read law in his father's office. Admitted to the South Carolina Bar in 1843, he practiced as a partner in the firm, DeSaussure and Son.

The life and practice of Wilmot DeSaussure was changed by the Civil War. In 1861, after Colonel Robert Anderson evacuated Fort Moultrie, General DeSaussure of the South Carolina Forces was placed in charge of the abandoned fort. At the bombardment of Fort Sumter on April 12, 1861, he commanded the artillery at Cummings' Point. He later led reserve troops in the defense of Charleston and was also State Adjutant General.

Succeeding generations of DeSaussures branched out into other endeavors, notably military service and the medical profession. In the War of 1812, the Civil War, both World Wars, Korea, and Vietnam, they served the state and the nation in emulation of Henry William DeSaussure's service in the Revolutionary War.

In the first half of the twentieth century, Henry William DeSaussure practiced medicine in Charleston, contributing much time and personal resources to the Charleston Orphanage House and the Florence Crittendon Home for Unwed Mothers. During the second half of the twentieth century, Charlton DeSaussure, followed his cousin not only in the practice of medicine, but also in public service as President of the Medical Society of South Carolina and Professor of Medicine at the Medical University of South Carolina.

In the present generation, Charlton DeSaussure, Jr. returned the family name to the practice of law. Admitted to the bar in 1978, he combines public service with the private practice of law through his work with The Gibbes Museum of Art, the Community Foundation serving South Carolina, and the Friends of the Charleston County Historic Courthouse, and as past president of the South Carolina Historical Society. In 2003, DeSaussure was appointed Corporation Counsel to the City of Charleston by Mayor Joseph P. Riley, Jr. He now serves the Mayor, City Council, and the citizens of Charleston in City Hall where six generations and more than two centuries ago his grandfather had been intendant.

ferring fee-generating cases to other members of the bar was a courtesy he had never witnessed at another bar.

In 1974, Ann Stirling was the first female litigator at the Charleston Bar. Still, she was made to feel welcome. A leader of the bar, "Big" Gedney Howe, introduced her as "his lawyer." His son, another Gedney Howe, claimed, "Relationships trump technicalities in Charleston. I get a lot of calls from younger lawyers asking how much a particular case is worth or seeking assurance that a settlement offer is fair. One thing Charleston lawyers go to great lengths to avoid is filing default motions against other attorneys. You just don't put someone in default. Somebody calls you and says, 'I missed this filing date. Will you support my motion for an extension?' and you say, yes, because you know it's bound to happen to you sometime." Coming Ball Gibbs underscored this thought. "That sort of honor system has worked in Charleston for a long time. Even today with the influx of 'out-of-towners,' they understand the importance of relationships over legal maneuvering. Judges encourage this sense of compromise and fair play."

Current President Francis X. McCann and President-Elect Cheryl D. Shoun will take the bar forward from this history and when the next generations enter the judicial center that this bar built, they can think about the lawyers who loved their profession and who have preserved, since the 1760s, William Pitt's words in marble, "Where law ends, tyranny begins."

ATTORNEYS

From Charles Town to Charleston

LAW FIRM HISTORIES

This historic account of Charleston's legal profession would not be complete without including descriptive profiles about the men and women who make up this notable profession. Working within a firm or as a solo practitioner, attorneys stretching from West of the Ashley to East of the Cooper have influenced the growth and development of not only the legal profession, but also the Lowcountry as a whole. Although the following profiles describe the areas in which these firms and lawyers practice, the histories are not intended to be representative of quality of service.

Though the niches they carve for themselves may be varied, the attorneys all bring to their profession a time-honored duty in representing their clients. This sense of integrity often extends to other parts of their lives and the people, organizations, businesses, and communities to which they contribute are stronger for the association. The Charleston Bar Association is comprised of lawyers who continue to leave positive imprints in the historic Lowcountry landscape. Men and women of shining character, these counselors are active public servants contributing to the common good of the generations who will follow them.

Almost destroyed by Hurricane Hugo in 1989, the historic Charleston County Courthouse still stands beautifully restored as one of the Four Corners of Law, thanks in large part to the efforts of the members and firms of the Charleston County Bar Association.

CHARLESTON COUNTY BAR ASSOCIATION

FROM 35 MEMBERS TO MORE THAN 1700, FROM AN AMIABLE fraternity to a professional organization upholding the counselor creed of integrity, the Charleston County Bar Association embodies the growth and prestige of its namesake city. However, more than a mirror of its historical environment, the Charleston County Bar Association has throughout its history been a catalyst, a driving force in the development of the city.

The modern Charleston County Bar Association dates back to January 10, 1924, when 35 members of the County Bar assembled at the courthouse to discuss a proposal for the establishment of a County Court. At that meeting, a motion was unanimously adopted that "a Charleston County Bar Association be established forthwith." The first annual meeting of the Association was held at Fort Sumter Hotel on June 28, 1924. The noble purposes set forth for this new organization have been its guiding principles for nearly a century, steering the Charleston County Bar Association into the new millennium.

At the helm is Charleston County Bar Association president, Francis McCann. Priorities on his agenda include a plan to help fathers incarcerated for falling behind on child support get back to work, a plan to limit attorney advertising, and a film project with the local college.

This composite portrait of Charleston lawyers at the end of the nineteenth century is titled "Bench and Bar of Charleston, South Carolina, 1899."

A 1977 graduate of the University of South Carolina School of Law, McCann is the former assistant solicitor in Richland and Charleston counties. Today, he specializes in personal injury and criminal law. McCann also has experience organizing activist efforts, including active roles in the Lowcountry AIDS Legal Clinic, the Fee Dispute Committee, the Charleston Zoning Commission, and the Planning Commission for the City of Charleston.

Francis X. McCann is currently the president of the Charleston County Bar Association.

"I serve as Planning Chairman for the City of Charleston, where people appear before me and our commission. If I can keep my own involvement in the public sector and encourage other lawyers to bring their expertise to the government or community board rooms on a volunteer basis, that is what matters most," he said. "That is part of what we were trained to do and it is very rewarding."

One of the first items on the agenda is looking at ways to reduce long-term confinement of that small percentage of non-paying fathers who will never be able to make restitution. The Association feels that the Charleston jails are much too crowded already and that there is no chance of fathers making money to help their children while incarcerated. If the Association succeeds in its agreement to fund programs that may help the community to realize a solution, it would be the first in the state.

Second on the agenda is "helping to curtail the latest crop of advertisements by lawyers," which is considered to be the biggest challenge facing the profession today. In conjunction with the College of Charleston's Theatre Department, McCann is planning to launch a media project to chronicle some of Charleston's more senior lawyers, illustrating what it was like to practice law in South Carolina in the 1950s and 1960s.

"We have a duty to reclaim and protect the image that was given to us by the Charleston lawyers that came before us. They didn't see our profession as a business and we shouldn't either," McCann said. "We have 1700 people in this community who work really hard to protect the law and give people access to the law that may not have access."

The general sentiment among the members of the Association is that lawyer advertising has brought great disrepute to the profession and that it is imperative that information not be overshadowed by salesmanship.

"It has wiped out years of good will that our predecessors in the Bar have fostered before our time in the profession. We have to police ourselves," he said. "If we don't, we will suffer the deserved reputation that the TV lawyers project as a universal stigma."

As the Charleston County Bar Association, now second largest in the state of South Carolina, moves through 2005, McCann envisions lawyers around the community getting more involved in helping those with limited access to legal advice.

"The social side of the bar is important, but I think we need to move a little more into the activist side," he said. "We have been given the privilege of being members of the Association that gives us access to the law in a unique way."

McCann also places significant emphasis on "getting back to basics." The Charleston County Bar Association is growing by leaps and bounds. Each year, more than 100 new attorneys join and with the opening of the Charleston School of Law, South Carolina's newest law school, the numbers are likely to grow even more in the years to come. Part of the Bar Association's duty is merely to get the attorneys together.

As a means to help ensure this cohesiveness, all future federal court filings will be online. Also, there are plans to further utilize and enhance the Charleston County Bar Association's website by creating a viable medium of communication among members, as well as courts.

"With the growth, we have become fragmented—not knowing all the members and not seeing each other in person unless we are at the courthouse," McCann said. "Times have definitely changed. I just hope that we slow down and cultivate relationships the old-fashioned way."

The Charleston County Bar Association's rich history of professionalism, civic awareness, and tireless contribution to the quality of life in Charleston have earned it a deserved place at any table where important decisions about the city's future are discussed. The Association will respond to the challenges of the new millennium with the same spirit of innovation, cooperation, determination, and professional excellence that have brought it to its current position of respect within the community.

ANASTOPOULO & CLORE, LLC

SINCE ITS INCEPTION IN 1987, THE ANASTOPOULO Law Firm has been providing legal services to plaintiffs in all areas of personal injury law, including product liability, medical malpractice, auto accidents, slips and falls, and pharmaceuticals litigation.

Senior partner Akim Anastopoulo started the practice as a sole practitioner after working in the Charleston County Solicitor's Office. Soon after, his wife, attorney Constance Anastopoulo, joined him in practice. Today, the Anastopoulo Law Firm has a total of nine attorneys and is continuing to expand.

Mr. Anastopoulo ensures that the firm's focus is on providing individual attention and personalized service to all clients. Clients can expect to be treated like family members, he says. This type of service reflects one of Mr. Anastopoulo's original goals: to create an environment where "people could know that they could go to attorneys for help without being fearful."

The Anastopoulo Law Firm has been recognized for this personalized service in a variety of ways; but, as Mr. Anastopoulo explains, there has been one particularly meaningful form of recognition: "We've received honors, but probably the biggest thing that I take pride in is that I've had numerous clients name their children after me.... I think I regard that as the highest honor I could get."

A father of two daughters, Rossi and Hali, Mr. Anastopoulo was born and raised in Charleston with siblings Arthur, Angelo, and Patti. In keeping with a family tradition of success in tennis, all of the Anastopoulo children played tennis at the collegiate level and Mr. Anastopoulo was state champion. Today, he is grateful to be able to live and practice law in his hometown. "I enjoy practicing in Charleston," he says, "because of the relationships we have with other attorneys. A lot of the attorneys I grew up with in the city, playing tennis with them, and it's nice to have a working relationship with people that you trust and that you look up to."

Mr. Anastopoulo, who is a graduate of the University of Louisville and the University of South Carolina School of Law, plans to continue to develop these working relationships through the Anastopoulo Law Firm. The firm will continue to grow to meet the needs of its clients and to, as Mr. Anastopoulo says, "help as many people as possible." Mr. Anastopoulo recently added a law partner, Mark Clore, from Houston, Texas. The firm is now known as Anastopoulo & Clore, LLC. Mr. Anastopoulo is a member of the South Carolina Trial Lawyers Association and the American Trial Lawyers Association.

Akim Anastopoulo founded the Anastopoulo Law Firm in 1987. With the addition of law partner Mark Clore, the firm became Anastopoulo and Clore, LLC.

MELISSA F. BROWN, LLC

Melissa Brown opened her own practice in 1999. A frequent lecturer and author on family law, she represents clients in complex family court cases involving divorce, custody, child support, and paternity issues.

NATIVE CHARLESTONIAN Melissa Brown draws from her professional, educational, and personal background in representing clients in complex family court cases involving divorce, custody, child support, and paternity issues. She is a graduate of Ashley Hall School, the University of Virginia, and the University of South Carolina School of Law.

She gained valuable work experience as a law clerk for the Honorable William L. Howard; Lee M. Robinson, PA; Nexsen, Pruet, Jacobs and Pollard; and Andrews & Shull, PA. In 1999, she opened her own practice, Melissa F. Brown, LLC.

Mrs. Brown has served as the Chair of the Family Law Section of the South Carolina Bar Association and as Vice-Chair of the Law Practice Management Committee of the Family Section of the American Bar Association. She is a member of the South Carolina Women Lawyers Association and has served as Treasurer of the Charleston County Bar Association's Family Court Section. In law school, she was a member of the Order of Barristers, the National Moot Court Team, and the Moot Court Bar, and she also participated in the National Moot Court Competition.

Mrs. Brown frequently lectures about family court matters for the South Carolina Bar Association and the American Bar Association. She has published articles in the *American Journal of Family Law*, the *South Carolina Law Review*, the *South Carolina Lawyer*, the *South Carolina Trial Lawyer's magazine*, *The Law Journal*, *An Executive's Guide to the Law*, and the *Family Law Review*, a publication of the Family Law Section of the State Bar of Georgia. While Chair of the South Carolina Family Law Council, the Council published the first edition of *The South Carolina Family Lawyers' Trial Tool Kit*. She has also published many articles in continuing legal education manuals produced by the South Carolina Bar Association and the National Business Institute.

While Mrs. Brown handles many divorce and custody cases, she strongly supports marriage and tries to encourage her clients to reconcile where possible. She is married to Todd Brown, and they have two children, Ellen Hudson and Fleetwood.

ASBILL & BECK

When Mary Ann Asbill and Daniel A. Beck opened Asbill & Beck law firm in downtown Charleston 17 years ago, it wasn't long before the husband-and-wife team was earning recognition and awards for its pro bono work. Today, the still-small firm packs a powerful punch in its work to protect and help the small guy. "We're all about the underdog," says associate lawyer Etta K. Simons Collins, a 1997 graduate of the University of South Carolina (USC) School of Law, who joined Asbill & Beck eight years ago.

ASBILL & BECK

Lawyers Helping Injured People

Specializing in personal injury and workers' compensation cases, Asbill & Beck prides itself on its dedication to everyday people. "We look out for the working man," explains Beck, a 1977 graduate of the USC School of Law and former deputy public defender for both Charleston and Lexington counties. "We don't represent insurance companies, just working folks. They need good lawyers too." Beck decided to become a lawyer after seeing "To Kill a Mockingbird" as a teenager. He says Asbill, a 1984 graduate of the USC School of Law, provides uncannily accurate instincts that result in winning cases. Once one of the state's leading court-appointed guardian ad litems (GAL) for children, Asbill was pivotal in a case that led to the state Supreme Court recognizing the doctrine of immunity for GALs. "She's a great law partner," notes Beck. "Her instincts about people are better than anybody I ever met. She adds the human insight; I'm the tactician who does the strategy; and Etta's our book lawyer—she's the legal eagle," laughs Beck. "I couldn't do it without them."

THE BLEECKER LAW FIRM, LLC

Anne Frances Bleecker has always had a great love for the law profession and her hometown of Charleston, South Carolina. She incorporates her passions by managing her law firm in downtown Charleston and serving on the Charleston City Council.

Ms. Bleecker holds a B.A. degree from Smith College and a master's degree in Public Administration from the LBJ School of Public Affairs at the University of Texas at Austin. She received her law degree from the University of South Carolina Law School in 1991. After practicing with Nelson, Mullins, Riley & Scarborough in their Columbia and Charleston offices, Ms. Bleecker co-founded a small firm in 1995. In May 1998, she opened her own practice, exclusively in the Family Court. Her accomplishments include receiving the Compleat Lawyer Award from the University of South Carolina Law School in February 2000 in recognition of her civic and professional achievements.

As a member of Charleston's City Council, Ms. Bleecker represents West Ashley, Johns Island, and James Island residents. She is Chairperson of the Human Resources Committee and has created the Mayor's Office on Aging to focus on issues that affect older Charlestonians. Her love for her community has been evident in her active participation with such organizations as the Steering Committee for the International Museum of African-American History, The Citadel Business School Advisory Board, the Ashley Hall Alumnae Board, the Trident Urban League, and the Cathedral of St. John the Baptist. Without question, she is most proud of her children, Anne Brooks (14) and Joseph (9).

EDWARD M. BROWN & ASSOCIATES

THE YOUNGEST OF TEN CHILDREN, Edward Brown was born and raised on Wadmalaw Island, South Carolina. He attended Bishop College in Dallas, Texas and was awarded the Crown-Zellerbach fellowship, which allowed him to attend the University of California at Berkeley. Mr. Brown graduated from the University of California at Berkeley in 1971, and returned to Texas to attend the Thurgood Marshall School of Law at Texas Southern University where he was a Ford Foundation Fellow. After graduation, Mr. Brown settled in the Boston area but returned to Charleston in 1978. He has been practicing law in Charleston ever since.

In 1982, Mr. Brown started his own general practice. Today, as founder of Edward M. Brown & Associates, Mr. Brown maintains an active trial practice in the areas of family law, civil rights law, employment law, medical malpractice, constitutional law, and contract law, among other areas. He also handles estate administration, tort, military courts martial, product liability, personal injury, Merit System Protection Board, Federal Sector EEOC, and workers' compensation cases.

Mr. Brown is supported by his office manager and assistant of 20 years, Deborah Robinson. "She's very devoted, very loyal, and extremely good," says Mr. Brown.

Outside the practice of law, Mr. Brown enjoys spending time with his family and playing golf. He is a Civil War and World War II buff and a member of 100 Black Men of Charleston, Inc., an organization devoted to the enhancement of economic and educational opportunities for African Americans with a focus on assisting African-American youth.

BUIST, BYARS, PEARCE & TAYLOR, LLC

Tom Buist, Custus Byars, Dixon Pearce, and Gray Taylor.

BUIST, BYARS, PEARCE & TAYLOR, LLC is a Charleston, South Carolina-based law firm that focuses on real estate, representing clients in the purchase, sale, use, and development of residential and commercial properties, including real estate-related litigation. Additional practice areas include trust and estate planning. Firm attorneys have a depth of experience and guide customers through the entire real estate and estate planning process with ease.

The firm preserves the values of founder Thomas G. Buist, who for more than 45 years has provided legal services to the Charleston community. Though rooted in tradition, attorneys also employ state-of-the-art systems and technology to offer clients the best service at competitive rates. The firm holds an AV rating from the esteemed legal organization Martindale-Hubbell. An AV rating is the highest ranking, which reflects the professional accomplishments and integrity of the attorneys.

The attorneys at Buist, Byars, Pearce & Taylor assist clients with a number of real estate issues, including land acquisition and development, residential and commercial closings, master planned communities, foreclosure and condemnations, tax-free exchanges, and other types of real estate finance. Attorneys also represent homeowners' associations and provide counsel on the formation of corporations, partnerships, and limited liability companies, and handle litigation related to property matters.

The firm's trust and estate attorneys also handle estate planning, tax and probate matters for individuals and fiduciaries, and advise clients in the areas of estate tax, disability, and retirement planning.

Four office locations serve Mt. Pleasant, West Ashley, the resort islands of Kiawah and Seabrook and the Hilton Head/Bluffton area, and offer convenience and access for clients across the Lowcountry.

BUIST ▪ MOORE ▪ SMYTHE ▪ McGEE ▪ P.A.

BUIST MOORE SMYTHE MCGEE IS one of the oldest and largest general practice law firms in Charleston, South Carolina and one of the oldest in the country. The firm was established in November 1970, with the merger of two of Charleston's oldest law firms—Buist, Buist, Smythe & Smythe and Moore, Mouzon & McGee.

Buist Moore Smythe McGee began its partnership on Exchange Street, in a handsome old building on the east side of the Charleston peninsula, overlooking Charleston harbor. As the firm has expanded, so have its offices. A three-story office building adjacent to and connected to the old building was completed in mid-September 1989. The firm is currently in the planning stages for further expansion at this location.

Buist Moore Smythe McGee primarily handles civil law matters. Though its roots are in Charleston, the firm's attorneys have the experience to effectively manage any legal matter in any practice area for clients throughout the state, the region, and beyond. Business and commercial litigation represent practice areas in which the firm's lawyers forcefully demonstrate this wide-ranging experience. The firm serves a client base diverse in size, industry, and geography, with a broad mix ranging from Fortune 500 companies, to medium and large-sized enterprises, to individuals. Its attorneys handle a broad range of civil law matters including: admiralty and aviation, alternative dispute resolution, bankruptcy and creditors' rights, business and banking, civil litigation, construction, employment, environmental, health law, insurance, media law, product liability, real estate, taxation, and trusts and estates.

Along with the attorneys of Buist Moore Smythe McGee, the firm functions with a very well-organized and trained staff of more than 50 persons. They include the firm's administrator, legal assistants, secretaries, a librarian, client services director, and other support staff. "We have an outstanding group of lawyers who are very well-educated, industrious, committed, and totally and completely ethical,"

Buist Moore Smythe McGee, first row, left to right, Joseph H. McGee, B. Alston Moore, Jr., Susan M. Smythe, Gordon D. Schreck; second row, left to right, C. Allen Gibson, Cynthia Spieth Morton, J. H. Hines, Henry E. Grimball, Henry B. Smythe, Jr.; third row, left to right, Shawn M. Flanagan, Marshall J. Allen, David S. Cox, Charles J. Baker; fourth row, left to right, James D. Myrick, Morris A. Ellison, W. Foster Gaillard, William C. Cleveland, III, Kenneth F. Smith.

notes Ben Moore, one of Buist Moore Smythe McGee's founding principals. "We have a wonderful stable of clients, both corporate and individual, and in addition to representing the interests of our clients, we also take a very active part in the community."

The attorneys of Buist Moore Smythe McGee are involved with historic preservation and conservation, and with local schools, churches, civic organizations, and community activities throughout the Lowcountry. The firm is particularly proud of the fact that seven of its attorneys are listed in *The Best Lawyers in America.*

DAVIDSON BENNETT & WIGGER

The law firm of Davidson Bennett & Wigger was started in 1988 by Eric Davidson and L. Russell Bennett in James Island, South Carolina. At present, Davidson Bennett & Wigger has four partners and five associates. The other partners are Jarrel L. Wigger, Mark W. Weeks, and Rob Donaldson. Mr. Bennett retired in December 1998.

The firm practices in two primary areas, real estate and personal injury law, but also does employment law, wills and trusts, small business representation, and workers' compensation law.

With more real estate closings than any other firm in South Carolina, the attorneys of Davidson Bennett & Wigger have a very service-oriented practice and also perform many 1031 Tax Exchange transactions.

With a staff of 45, the firm has expanded its practice over the past 15 years with two additional locations. The firm's primary location is now in North Charleston and the James Island and Mt. Pleasant offices provide representation throughout the tri-county area for real estate, and statewide for personal injury matters.

Founded in 1988, the law firm of Davidson Bennett and Wiggins now has three offices. Pictured left to right are Mark Weeks, partner, Eric Davidson, partner, Jarrel Wigger, managing partner.

JOSEPH P. CERATO, P.A.

AT THE AGE OF 23, JOSEPH P. CERATO realized that he could be an effective and successful trial attorney. Unable to afford college, he opted instead to enlist in the United States Navy, where he was a Yeoman for seven years. During this time he served as staff for two admirals and received the Navy Achievement Medal in 1981. He was also able to attend college at the College of Charleston and, in 1986, he received his bachelor's degree from The George Washington University. In 1986, he was awarded the Marian Gressett Scholarship from the University of South Carolina School of Law which enabled him to pursue his law degree at the University of South Carolina School of Law, where he graduated in 1988.

After graduation, Mr. Cerato worked as an associate for Andrew J. Savage, III until starting his own practice in 1990. Since that time, he has worked extensively in the areas of family and criminal law. Most of his time is devoted to various aspects of family law, including child support and custody, prenuptial agreements, adoption, divorce, and other domestic disputes.

In the area of criminal law, Mr. Cerato has successfully defended numerous clients charged with a variety of crimes, from minor traffic violations to felonies, and also handles probation and parole violations. Whether in Family Court or General Sessions Court, he commits to handling each case "competently, zealously, and professionally" and, as a sole practitioner, is able to guarantee that he will personally handle all cases from beginning to end. Of his experience, Mr. Cerato says, "I believe that my working class background, good common sense, and aggressive nature provide me with the tools necessary to be a successful trial attorney."

CLEKIS & HRICIK, LLC

CLEKIS LAW FIRM, PA WAS ESTABlished in 1988 with a handful of clients. Over the years, the firm has represented thousands of clients. It is located in the Franke Building, a beautiful brick and wood beam building located in the historic Market District of downtown Charleston.

Founding partner, Nicholas J. Clekis received his B.S. degree from the College of Charleston in 1982 and his J.D. degree from the University of South Carolina School of Law in 1985. After working with such firms as Morris, Duffy & Boone and Grimball & Cabaniss, LLC, Mr. Clekis set out on his own, concentrating on personal injury, criminal, and family law.

Today, Mr. Clekis, as president and senior partner of the Clekis Law Firm, PA, has joined forces with Richard A. Hricik and the firm is now known as Clekis & Hricik, LLC. Also working with Clekis & Hricik is Cezar E. McKnight and Brian C. Johnson, Attorneys at Law. Jodi Underwood, Netha Kreamer, Amy Semken, and Cynthia Smith are the supporting staff for Clekis & Hricik. Clekis & Hricik works to provide quality legal service in the areas of general civil and criminal law, including auto accidents, workers' compensation claims, medical malpractice, product liability, and most other types of personal injury cases.

Mr. Clekis takes pride in representing clients pursuant to the contingency fee system which enables individuals otherwise unable to afford quality representation to hire private counsel for a percentage of the recovery. It also allows Clekis & Hricik to represent individuals of modest means against large corporations, insurance companies, and wealthy defendants. As Mr. Clekis sees it, providing quality representation to people who cannot afford a private lawyer is what makes plaintiff practice so rewarding.

LAW FIRM OF J. JOSEPH CONDON, JR.

JOE CONDON ALWAYS WANTED to go to law school. As a young graduate of the University of Notre Dame in 1973, he enrolled and started classes at the University of South Carolina's School of Law. But when family obligations called him back to his hometown of Charleston, he left law school to help his father in the local family retail business, Condon's Department Stores.

Twelve years later, he returned to the University of South Carolina Law School and graduated in 1988. He worked with Grimball & Cabaniss before starting his own general practice in 1993. "Working at my family's stores taught me a lot about dealing with the public," explains Condon. "It can be difficult, but it's also rewarding. What I learned from those years has really helped with my law career, because I realized that the average person is the backbone of America." His work focuses on personal injury, workers' compensation, and criminal and domestic law. "I think people are basically honest, and I like helping them," says Condon. "They get in jams or unfortunate situations in which they use poor judgment and it's my job to help them get back on the right course."

Mr. Condon is a member of the Charleston Bar and the South Carolina Bar. He is active in his church and has two children and one granddaughter.

DALLIS LAW FIRM, P.A.

DALLIS LAW FIRM, P.A., OFFERS A SIMPLE approach to the practice of law in an effort to provide its clients with high quality, yet cost-effective legal services to assist individuals and businesses in real estate matters of all sorts.

The firm originally began in 1986 at 124 Meeting Street under the name of Dallis & Dreyfoos as a partnership between W. Alex Dallis, Jr. and William Dreyfoos. The office was moved to 23 Broad Street in 1988 and to its current location in West Ashley in 1997.

As the son of an attorney and grandson of a civil engineer, W. Alex Dallis, Jr., was educated in both fields, but ultimately decided to pursue law as a career. He graduated from Princeton University in 1978 with a civil engineering degree and received his J.D. degree from the University of South Carolina in 1981. Mr. Dallis worked as an associate in a local Charleston law firm for several years before opening his own firm in 1986. In 1992, Dallis Law Firm, P.A., opened an office in Columbia and in 2003, an office in Summerville as well.

The firm concentrates on transactional versus trial practice, working primarily with real estate transactions, small business formations, and simple wills. In addition to Mr. Dallis, who works primarily in the firm's West Ashley office, the firm employees an associate in both the Columbia and Summerville offices. Mr. Dallis credits a knowledgeable and available staff as the means to maintaining the firm's reputation of providing quality, affordable services to its clients. "We've pulled together a good team of folks to provide clients with quality service at an affordable price, and I think people recognize that," he notes. "All our employees understand how important it is to be well-versed in the issues our clients face and they know that I will drop everything to ensure that they receive whatever guidance they need to successfully conclude our clients' transactions."

E. BART DANIEL

E. Bart Daniel, Attorney At Law in private practice, is active in white collar, health care, securities, environmental, and business litigation. He has successfully defended numerous white collar prosecutions including health care fraud, environmental crimes, and customs and securities violations. Bart recently obtained a Not Guilty verdict in a federal antitrust case alleging widespread price fixing and restraint of trade in the textile industry.

A Charleston native, Bart received his B.S. Degree in Business Administration from The Citadel in 1977 and his J.D. degree from the University of South Carolina Law School in 1980.

Following graduation, he served two years as Assistant State Attorney General assigned to the White Collar Crime Unit and later four years as Assistant United States Attorney prosecuting fraud, income tax, customs, and drug violations.

In 1985, Daniel entered private practice where he concentrated on white collar criminal defense and selected civil litigation. He accepted President George Bush's appointment as United States Attorney for the District of South Carolina and was confirmed in 1989. While in public office, he was universally admired for doubling the number of Federal Grand Juries by initiating Grand Juries in Charleston and Greenville.

Lauded for his outstanding achievements as a federal prosecutor, Bart was presented the highest award given to any United States Attorney: the United States Attorney's Flag Award. He returned to private practice in 1992 and was appointed President of the Charleston County Bar Association in 1994.

Daniel is well respected on both a state and national level for his public and private sector work in the area of white collar crime. He is a published author of numerous books on federal and state investigations and prosecutions. He is active in community not-for-profit organizations and his alma mater, The Citadel. Daniel has been married for 26 years and is the father of four children.

G. WELLS DICKSON, JR.

South Carolina native Wells Dickson has been a sole practitioner in Charleston since 1993, but his law career spans 30 years and covers much of his home state. He has full-time offices in Charleston in association with Lofton & Lofton, P.C. and in Kingstree with LeGrand Carraway, where he frequently serves as a Special Referee.

Mr. Dickson graduated from the University of South Carolina School of Law in 1974, after practicing as a Certified Public Accountant in Georgia and South Carolina. He served as a prosecutor for the U.S. Attorney's office, chief criminal prosecutor for the Attorney General's office, judge for the town of Kingstree, and was a partner with the Columbia firm of Collins & Lacey. Mr. Dickson is former chairman of the Lexington-Richland Counties Mental Health Association and former chairman of Community Care, an outreach organization in Columbia comprised of church volunteers.

He began his legal career as a general practitioner but now focuses on federal and state trials and appeals, criminal defense, personal injury, and civil litigation. Says Mr. Dickson, "My work at the U.S. Attorney's office concentrated on white collar crimes, tax violations, bank robberies, and drug prosecutions. At the Attorney General's office, I prosecuted public figures, murder, and drug cases. My expertise evolved from these experiences. I now spend a great deal of time litigating civil matters and became a certified circuit court Arbitrator and Mediator in 2004."

J. MATTHEW DILLON

Matt Dillon opened his practice in 1999 after having worked at two of Charleston's oldest law firms, Young, Clement, Rivers & Tisdale and Barnwell, Whaley, Patterson & Helms. Mr. Dillon moved to Charleston in 1991 from his hometown of Winston-Salem, North Carolina—where he began practicing in 1988—to join his wife Alison as she began her residency in Obstetrics at the Medical University of South Carolina. The Dillons fell in love with the area and today it is as much their hometown as it truly is for their two children, Matthew and Caroline.

Mr. Dillon received his B.S. degree from Guilford College in 1984 and graduated from the Campbell University School of Law in 1988. He went to work in one of Winston-Salem's busiest trial practices and within months of passing the bar found himself in the courtroom trying civil, domestic, and criminal cases.

The move to Charleston resulted in an instant immersion in complex civil litigation and experience with some of the city's best litigators. Mr. Dillon's involvement in cases ranging from crane accidents to the defense of medical malpractice to claims over the construction of nuclear steam generators gave him a unique degree of experience and a comfort level with serious and complex cases and with leading lawyers from around the country.

Drawing on this background, Mr. Dillon opened his own practice to provide personalized service to clients with contract, business, and fraud cases as well as serious injury and construction cases. Through his practice, Mr. Dillon has developed a reputation for his ability to successfully litigate consumer, bad faith, and insurance disputes in addition to other contract-related claims. Mr. Dillon is involved with the bar, the community, and his number one responsibility, his children.

SUSAN K. DUNN

Charleston attorney Susan K. Dunn is a sole practitioner emphasizing arbitration and mediation. She has practiced in Charleston since 1977. A graduate of the University of North Carolina School of Law and Duke University, Dunn chose her profession to "help those mired in disputes and to keep checks on those in power."

Ms. Dunn's career began at the Charleston firm of Shimel, Ackerman, Theos and Spar where she practiced predominantly domestic and real estate law. She spent a few years in a partnership with Lee M. Robinson and has been a sole practitioner ever since.

Ferguson et al v. the City of Charleston et al represents a landmark case for both Ms. Dunn's career and constitutional law. Over the past ten years, Ms. Dunn has represented ten women in a federal case that challenges the constitutionality of drug tests performed on pregnant and postpartum women at a public hospital. The U.S. Supreme Court and the 4th Circuit Court of Appeals have issued rulings that are favorable to the plaintiffs. "I knew taking this case was a professional gamble, but it was consistent with the reasons I became a lawyer," says Ms. Dunn.

Ms. Dunn's commitment to her profession has garnered her some of its top awards, including the 1998 Bissell Award from the South Carolina Women Lawyers Association.

Ms. Dunn serves as a part-time minister for the Circular Congregational Church. She is developing a program to cross-train ministers, therapists, and attorneys to understand how their respective professional cultures impact the effectiveness of the assistance they provide.

FINKEL & ALTMAN, LLC

FINKEL & ALTMAN, LLC IS A FULL SERVICE LAW FIRM THAT handles all types of litigation in state and federal court, residential and commercial real estate, corporate, finance, bankruptcy, foreclosure, and taxation matters. Gerald Finkel founded the firm in Columbia in 1970 and opened the Charleston office ten years later.

The attorneys of Finkel & Altman, LLC have made a conscious commitment to provide sophisticated legal services and to develop practice areas in the corporate and commercial litigation fields. Over the years, our lawyers have accepted a number of major cases of novel impression and have developed a reputation for handling complex cases such as antitrust cases, federal injunctive relief actions, unfair trade practice claims, corporate, business, and commercial litigation, foreclosure, bankruptcy, commercial and residential real estate, and banking-related matters.

The firm currently employs approximately 23 attorneys, 10 in the Charleston office and 13 in the Columbia office. Ralph C. McCullough, II, professor emeritus at the University of South Carolina School of Law and Provost of the Charleston School of Law, is of counsel to the firm. Elizabeth McCullough also serves as of counsel to the firm.

Finkel & Altman, LLC possesses a unique combination of experienced lawyers with backgrounds in various legal fields. Our junior lawyers are trained to use the latest discovery and trial techniques. All of our firm's members are dedicated to the practice and advancement of law in South Carolina. In fact, several of our attorneys teach at the University of South Carolina School of Law. In addition, our lawyers are active in continuing legal education and participate in the committees of the American Law Institute, the American Judicature Society, the American Bar Association, the American Bankruptcy Institute, the South Carolina Trial Lawyers Association, the South Carolina Bar Association, the Richland County Bar Association, and the Bankruptcy Section of the Richland County Bar Association. By remaining active in teaching and participating in the development of the legal profession, our firm remains on the cutting edge of legal thought and emerging trends in the law to best serve our clients' interests.

Finkel & Altman LLC began as a litigation firm, and litigation continues to be the firm's largest practice area. Many of the firm's members began their careers handling personal injury cases. The firm now engages in a wide variety of complex litigation. Jerry Finkel is a former president of the South Carolina Trial Lawyers Association. Ralph McCullough is one of the authors of the *Civil Trial Manual*, a standard reference work for trial lawyers. Ralph McCullough and Jerry Finkel co-authored the *South Carolina Law of Torts*, another reference work which is now in its fourth edition, and both have taught trial advocacy at the University of South Carolina School of Law. The firm's litigation practice ranges from personal injury and product liability cases, to antitrust cases (the firm's predecessor brought the first successful antitrust case in South Carolina), to appeals and constitutional issues (the firm represented David Lucas in *Lucas v. South Carolina Coastal Council*, a landmark Supreme Court decision on takings jurisprudence), and to franchise and commercial litigation.

Gerald Finkel is the founding member and the managing member of Finkel & Altman, LLC.

A 1970 graduate of the University of South Carolina School of Law, Mr. Finkel is a past president of the South Carolina Trial Lawyers Association and was a member of the House of Delegates of the South Carolina Bar, also serving on the Bar's board of governors. He has served as chairman of the Insurance, Negligence and Workers' Compensation Section of the South Carolina Bar. He has been a Special Judge for the Richland County Family Court and the Court of General Sessions for the Fifth Judicial Circuit. In 1981, he served on the Governor's Sentencing Guidelines Commission and the South Carolina Appellate Defense Commission. Mr. Finkel is an Adjunct Professor at the University of South Carolina School of Law where he teaches trial advocacy and insurance law, and a Visiting Professor at the Charleston School of Law. He has published extensively in the areas of business law, insurance law, and torts. He is a member of the American Law Institute where he has served on the Consultative Committees for the Restatement of Unfair Trade Practices and the Restatement of Torts 3rd. He is included in all published editions of *The Best Lawyers in America.*

Charleston native Charles S. Altman graduated from the University of South Carolina School of Law in 1969 and worked primarily as a sole practitioner until joining the firm 15 years ago. He was admitted to the South Carolina Bar, the United States District Court, the District of South Carolina in 1969, the United States Court of Appeals for the Fourth Circuit in 1974, and the United States Supreme Court in 1995. Mr. Altman graduated from the University of South Carolina with a B.S. degree in Accounting in 1966 and received his J. D. degree in 1969 from the University of South Carolina School of Law. While in law school, he was active in Phi Alpha Delta. Mr. Altman is currently a member of the Charleston County Bar Association and concentrates primarily in the areas of general business law, corporate law, commercial and residential real estate, creditor and debtor rights, bankruptcy, and complex litigation.

The South Carolina Bar Association named Finkel & Altman, LLC Pro Bono Law Firm of the Year in 1999. Because we have offices in Columbia, Charleston, and Georgetown, South Carolina, we can effectively serve our clients throughout the state.

GIBSON LAW FIRM, LLC

Don Gibson was born in 1943 in Union County, South Carolina and grew up just outside Lockhart, South Carolina. Following his graduation from Lockhart High School, Don attended Clemson University where he graduated with a B.A. in Mathematics in 1966. While subsequently serving as an officer with the United States Air Force, he attended graduate school at The George Washington University where he was awarded an M.S. in Administration in 1973. He was then accepted at the University of South Carolina School of Law where he obtained his J.D. degree in 1975. He was admitted to the South Carolina Bar in 1976 and opened his office as a sole practitioner in Charleston, South Carolina.

He is married to Mary Lois Pope of Norfolk, Virginia and they reside in Mount Pleasant. They have four children and two grandchildren.

The law firm has continued to grow and evolve, but remains fundamentally anchored to helping working folks. The South Carolina native says growing up in a small mill village in a working class family has always tilted his practice in the direction of providing assistance to average working citizens in their struggle to defend and assert their rights with insurance companies, corporations, and government. As a result, he states, "I am used to swimming upstream in waters where the advertising cliché 'one call, that's all!' used by some lawyers to promote their business, does not apply. I have never faced anything but hard work and struggle to protect my clients' rights." A plaintiff's attorney at heart, Gibson's present practice areas includes workers' compensation, personal injury, real estate, and business law with a smattering of criminal defense.

At age 59, Don was awarded his LL.M. degree in International Taxation from the Regent University School of Law. The firm has a bilingual staff and has developed a large Spanish clientele in an effort to prepare the practice for the population changes in society. Consistent with his philosophy of helping working folks, Gibson would like to expand his practice to include immigration law so that he can provide a more comprehensive service to his international clients. Having practiced in North Charleston for 29 years, he is more enthusiastic than ever about the practice of law in the new global world. "It is such a blessing to be able to work in the greatest legal system in the history of mankind"

Two milestone experiences have provided him with invaluable insights. One was a disappointing outcome on a civil case, a large case involving the death of a mother with two surviving children, where the client refused to accept a significant settlement offer. Though the jury returned a verdict in favor of his client, the amount was disappointing. "In my drawer, I keep a photo of those two children who were depending on me for a good verdict for their future. It serves as a constant reminder that I should have encouraged the client to accept the offer and it is never far from my reasoning in my advice to all clients. I also had the privilege of serving twice as a juror and that has done more for my judgment and legal practice than any other thing," says Gibson.

THE LAW OFFICES OF J. BRADY HAIR

THE LAW OFFICES OF J. BRADY HAIR IS A TRIAL AND appellate firm, comprised of attorneys Brady Hair and Derk Van Raalte. The firm focuses on federal white-collar criminal defense, state criminal defense, complex civil litigation, and state and local government regulatory matters.

A hybrid of public representation and private representation, the firm handles private civil and criminal cases and serves as legal counsel to the City of North Charleston, the third largest city in South Carolina. "Representing the city has been a lifelong love for me—part of it is that I have had a lifetime of governmental service that I enjoy," says Hair.

Brady Hair, a former Assistant United States Attorney, focuses his practice on federal and state criminal litigation, governmental law, and complex civil litigation. He currently serves as Corporate General Counsel for the City of North Charleston and has done so since 1995. Prior to beginning his private practice, Mr. Hair served for four and one half years as a federal prosecutor in the United States Attorney's Office. While there, he predominantly prosecuted bank fraud and other white-collar criminal cases.

"In 1995 I began my journey as counsel for the City of North Charleston, a position I hold today. In that role I act as the gatekeeper. I have been balancing a dual role in private practice and public service for a decade," says Hair.

Derk Van Raalte shares Mr. Hair's dual role in the public and private sectors of law. Prior to joining the private practice in 2002, Mr. Van Raalte served in the United States Attorney's Office (criminal division) and in various municipal government positions. He handles matters in State and Federal Courts, with a focus on appeals, state and federal criminal defense, and complex civil litigation.

The firm's expertise in criminal defense is well earned. Prior to entering private practice, both attorneys gained trial and appellate experience as federal and local government prosecutors. The firm's white-collar representations have included matters such as false claims act cases, health care cases, environmental cases, and various business crimes. The firm also defends more traditional state court crimes.

Mr. Hair and Mr. Van Raalte also accept complex and document-intensive civil matters. These have included cases ranging from class actions, employment cases, constitutional rights cases, professional negligence cases, fraud cases, and selected personal injury cases.

Mr. Hair holds the Martindale-Hubbell rating of AV. He received his B.A. degree from Francis Marion College in 1982 and his J.D. degree from the University of South Carolina Law School in 1986. He is a past president of the Charleston County Bar Association, and a member of a number of legal professional organizations. Mr. Van Raalte received his Bachelor of Science (Finance) degree from Clemson University cum laude in 1992, and his J.D. degree from Case Western Reserve University School of Law, cum laude, in 1995.

Mr. Hair and Mr. Van Raalte are published authors of white collar crime books and frequent national and state keynote speakers.

MARGARET D. FABRI

Margaret Fabri decided to enter law school at the age of 37 because she believed she could "make a difference in the world with a law degree." She attended Northern Illinois University College of Law and then the University of South Carolina School of Law, graduating cum laude in 1985.

Ms. Fabri began her law practice in January 1986. Emphasizing family law and plaintiff's employment law, Ms. Fabri considers her private practice to be an asset. "As a sole practitioner, I have had the luxury of taking on cases which I might not have been able to undertake in a law firm environment," she says.

She has had success at the Fourth Circuit including *Dennis v. Columbia Colleton Medical Center*, a sex discrimination case, and made state case law in *Moore v. Moore*, a 1990 custody case. "I am passionate about the cases I take on, and I never give up," Ms. Fabri says.

Ms. Fabri is also committed to public service. She ran for a seat on Charleston City Council in 1997, narrowly losing in a runoff. She is active in conservation groups, including the South Carolina Coastal Conservation League: "I realize what a precious resource we have here on the coast and I am determined to protect it." Ms. Fabri believes she is "very fortunate" to practice in Charleston, South Carolina. "As a solo practitioner in a small state, I have been able to pursue the rights of my clients at every level of our court system, both state and federal. "I believe I have made a difference."

HARRELL LAW FIRM, PA

Founded in 2001 by John D. Harrell, the Harrell Law Firm was established in an effort to return to the ideals of the traditional law firm with an emphasis on highly personalized client service. The attorneys that comprise Harrell Law Firm have made a commitment to maintain a firm that is small enough to develop personal relationships with its clients, yet comprehensive enough to handle complex litigation matters.

A Charleston native and Porter Gaud School graduate, Harrell founded and managed a large statewide government contracting firm upon graduation from the University of South Carolina with a Bachelor of Arts degree in English. Several years later, he completed his J.D. degree at Georgetown University Law Center. While in Washington, D.C., he became involved with an indigent public advocacy litigation clinic, which provided legal services to the underprivileged. Since returning to the Lowcountry, Harrell has been able to help many businesses and individual clients by guiding them through and serving as an advocate in bureaucratic and legislative forums. Before founding the Harrell Law Firm, he was an associate at one of the oldest firms serving the Charleston metropolitan area.

The Harrell Law Firm provides a broad spectrum of legal services that includes general civil litigation, personal injury, insurance defense, construction law, general business law, and commercial and residential real estate. Harrell's business background has influenced his mission at the firm, which is to provide personalized services and individual attention, even to the corporate client.

LAW OFFICE OF WARING S. HOWE, JR.

OVER 50 YEARS AFTER HIS FATHER established a private law practice in Charleston, South Carolina, Waring S. Howe, Jr. continues the tradition of representing everyday working people. From the same office his father opened in 1949 overlooking Broad Street, Mr. Howe practices three types of law: personal injury, workers' compensation, and some criminal defense.

A native of Charleston, Mr. Howe graduated from Clemson University in 1978. He received a B.A. degree in Political Science while also accepting awards for Outstanding Debater and the Trustees' Award Medal in 1978. He attended law school at the University of South Carolina, graduating with a J.D. degree in 1982. After spending two years in Germany, Mr. Howe moved back to Charleston in 1984 and began practicing with his father.

Well known for his involvement in politics, Mr. Howe serves on the Democratic National Committee and was a delegate to the Democratic National Convention in 1992, 1996, and 2000 and went as a "superdelegate" in 2004. He was also a regular panelist on Channel 5's popular television show, *Carolina Gang*, for two years (1999-2001).

Along with his political involvement, Mr. Howe has been active in other areas. He is currently chairman of the South Carolina Commission on Consumer Affairs. He served on the Board of Governors of the South Carolina Trial Lawyers Association for seven years (1992-99), and was a member of the Charleston County Aviation Authority for twelve years (1989-2001), for four of which he was chairman.

Defining his success, Mr. Howe says, "I've lived my life guided by the principle that the little people need a strong voice to assist them. I analogize my work this way: All of my clients oppose corporate interests. Corporate interests equate to Goliath, my clients are David and I am the slingshot."

MATTHEW R. HUBBELL

MATTHEW R. HUBBELL IS A SOLE PRACtitioner specializing in federal and state white-collar criminal cases. He works extensively on environmental crime, health care fraud, tax, antitrust, and customs cases in addition to general criminal defense and select personal injury cases.

Mr. Hubbell's background is well suited to his current practice. He was an assistant United States attorney in the District of South Carolina for almost ten years. During this time he gained significant experience in the areas of international securities fraud, computer crimes, wire and mail fraud, public corruption, environmental crime, health care fraud, immigration, tax, and money laundering. His prosecution of environmental crimes resulted in one of the first jail sentences ever in the District of South Carolina for an environmental crime. In 1996, he successfully prosecuted the District's very first health care fraud case. He also created the U.S. Attorney's Internet Child Exploitation ("ICE") Task Force, a task force designed to address the growing number of child predators utilizing the Internet as a vehicle for crime.

A 1988 graduate of The Citadel, Mr. Hubbell has served as an adjunct professor at The Citadel and frequently participates in The Citadel's mock trial and moot court programs. He is a frequent lecturer on criminal law issues and a member of the Executive Board of the Charleston County Bar. He is also coauthor of *Computer and Intellectual Property Crimes*, a book published by the South Carolina Bar in 2003. He and his wife, Susannah, and son, Matthew, are active members of Saint Michael's Episcopal Church.

HOOD LAW FIRM, LLC

The Hood Law Firm, left to right, founder Robert H. Hood, Sr., partner Molly Hood Craig, and partner Robert H. Hood, Jr.

THE HOOD LAW FIRM, LLC WAS FOUNDED BY ROBERT H. Hood, a graduate of the University of the South (B.A., 1966) and the University of South Carolina School of Law (J.D., 1969). Mr. Hood has been widely recognized for his achievements in civil trial advocacy. In 1983, he was featured in the first edition of *The Best Lawyers in America* in the categories of commercial litigation, personal injury, plaintiff and defense, and business litigation. Since that time he has been selected as a best lawyer in every edition of *The Best Lawyers in America*, including its current edition. Hood Law is listed in the *Bar Register of Preeminent Lawyers* as well as *Best's Guide to AAA Insurance Firms*. The Hood Law Firm is rated AV by Martindale-Hubbell, its highest rating.

Mr. Hood specializes in commercial litigation, insurance coverage issues, construction, medical and legal malpractice, personal injury, product liability, toxic torts, and general civil litigation. He was president of the South Carolina Defense Trial Attorneys Association from 1980 to 1981, chairman of the South Carolina Bar Ethics Advisory Committee from 1983 to 1990, and president of the Association of Defense Trial Attorneys from 1985 to 1986. He has also served on the Board of Directors (1987-1990) for the Defense Research Institute and served as president of the Charleston chapter of the American Board of Trial Advocates in 1997.

Mr. Hood is a member of the Charleston County and American Bar Associations, the South Carolina Bar, the South Carolina Defense Trial Attorneys Association, the Association of Defense Trial Attorneys, the Federation of Insurance and Corporate Counsel, and the International Association of Defense Counsel. He is also a Diplomate in the American Board of Trial Advocates, a member of the Defense Research Institute, and the Fourth Circuit Judicial Conference.

Presently, the Hood firm has 22 lawyers, including partners Molly Hood Craig and Robert H. Hood, Jr. The firm also has numerous paralegals and a committed support staff, including registered nurses. The firm plans to continue to grow in response to the needs of its clients.

Molly Hood Craig is on the executive committee of the South Carolina Defense Trial Attorneys Association, the Federation of Defense & Corporate Counsel, the Defense Research Institute Association, a member of the International Association of Defense Counsel, and the Association of Defense Trial Attorneys. She specializes in medical malpractice, employment law, nursing home litigation, and general negligence. Bobby Hood, Jr. is a member of the American Bar Association and South Carolina Defense Trial Attorneys Association. He specializes in product liability, construction, professional negligence including medical and legal malpractice, and general tort cases.

The firm is located in a historical building in downtown Charleston, South Carolina, three blocks from the state and federal courthouses.

LAW OFFICE OF GEDNEY M. HOWE, III, P.A.

THE HOWE LAW FIRM WAS established in 1937 by Gedney M. Howe, Jr. A native of Charleston, Mr. Howe was admitted to the South Carolina Bar in 1937 after receiving his J.D. degree from the University of South Carolina School of Law. He practiced law in Charleston until his death in 1981, except for four years' service in the U.S. Navy during World War II. He was known and respected among South Carolina Bar members as a "lawyer's lawyer" and a scholar. He was elected Circuit Solicitor of the Ninth Judicial Circuit in 1946 and served without opposition until his resignation in 1956.

Mr. Howe was recognized among circuit judges as the best solicitor in South Carolina and, although he never sought public office again, he remained very active in statewide politics. He was a great trial lawyer. The Charleston Bar would always crowd into the courtroom to hear him cross-examine a witness or make a jury speech. Jurors loved him, and he always obtained great results. No other lawyer was held in higher esteem at the bar and bench than Gedney M. Howe, Jr.

Gedney M. Howe, III began practice with his father, Gedney M. Howe, Jr., in 1973, after graduating from the University of South Carolina School of Law. His firm specializes in criminal and civil trial work in all state and federal courts.

Gedney M. Howe, III began practice with his father in 1973, after graduating from the University of South Carolina and the University of South Carolina School of Law. He has received Martindale-Hubbell's highest rating and is listed in the publication, *The Best Lawyers in America.* He is a member of the International Society of Barristers, the National Association of Criminal Defense Lawyers, and the National College of Criminal Defense Attorneys, and has lectured to the South and North Carolina, Georgia, Washington State, and Florida bars on the subject of trial practice. He represented the South Carolina State Senate in reapportionment litigation and has participated in numerous civil and criminal trials, with particular em-phasis in the areas of personal injury and product liability. He is a member of the Charleston County Bar Association, the South Carolina Bar Association, and the South Carolina Trial Lawyers Association.

Alvin Hammer, a partner with Mr. Howe, III, joined the firm in 1984. A graduate of the University of North Carolina and the University of South Carolina School of Law, and a native of Columbia, South Carolina, he began practice in 1973. He is a member of the Charleston Bar Association, the South Carolina Bar Association, and has received Martindale-Hubbell's highest rating. He has extensive experience in civil and criminal state and federal appellate work. He has been a member of the bar of the U.S. Court of Appeals for the Fourth Circuit since 1974, and a member of the U.S. Supreme Court Bar since 1980.

Caroline West graduated from the College of Charleston in 1993 with a bachelor's degrees in Economics and Political Science. She received her law degree from Cumberland School of Law at Samford University in 1996. She is a member of the Charleston County Bar, the South Carolina Bar, the South Carolina Women Lawyers Association, the South Carolina Trial Lawyers Association, and the Association of Trial Lawyers of America. She has been a member of the bar of the U.S. Court of Appeals for the Fourth Circuit since 1998.

The firm specializes in criminal and civil trial work in all state and federal courts with emphasis on wrongful death cases, vehicular accidents, drunk driving victims, product and premises liability, recreational accidents, airplane and train crash injuries, other accident injuries, business, probate, and estate litigation, and criminal defense.

R. WALTER HUNDLEY

R. Walter Hundley, a Charleston area attorney, has an extensive background in workers' compensation law in South Carolina. After handling the defense of workers' compensation claims at the firm of Young, Clement, Rivers & Tisdale, Mr. Hundley was appointed to serve as chairman of the Governor's Advisory Committee for Improvement of Workers' Compensation Laws from 1986 to 1989.

R. Walter Hundley served as chairman and commissioner of the South Carolina Workers' Compensation Commission before opening his own practice devoted to workers' compensation matters.

In 1989, Mr. Hundley was appointed chairman and commissioner of the South Carolina Workers' Compensation Commission, positions which he held until 1994. During his tenure on the Commission, he reviewed and substantially revised the Commission's regulations. These updated regulations were signed into law by Governor Carroll Campbell on September 2, 1990.

Mr. Hundley also served as president of the Southern Association of Workers' Compensation Administrators (SAWCA) from 1993 to 1994. While president, he and Burnet R. Maybank, III coauthored *Law of Workers' Compensation in South Carolina*, which was published by the South Carolina Bar. This book was the first of its kind in that it consolidated, organized, and detailed a wealth of information about workers' compensation law in South Carolina. Also during his term as SAWCA president, Mr. Hundley succeeded in instituting significant policy changes, such as modifications to assigned risk pool policy.

In 1995, Mr. Hundley opened his own practice, which is devoted solely to workers' compensation matters. His office is currently located in West Ashley. Although Mr. Hundley has had significant experience in the insurance industry and as a defense attorney, he has chosen to devote all of his time to representing injured workers. "One of the reasons I became a plaintiff's attorney," he says, "was because I felt like I just needed to represent people." Mr. Hundley underscores his desire to use his skills and experience to help those whose lives have been affected by a work-related injury by making a commitment to each and every client. As such, he has focused on providing individual attention to the clients he currently has rather than on marketing to get more clients. Mr. Hundley believes the growth his practice *has* seen is primarily the result of taking care of his existing clients. "I added more people [in my office] not to get more clients, but to take better care of my clients." According to Mr. Hundley, a satisfied client is the goal of his office: "I measure our success by how many satisfied clients we can have at the end of the day."

As a result of these efforts and the kind referrals of many area attorneys, the practice has continued to grow, leading Mr. Hundley to hire attorney E. Courtney Gruber in 2000. Mr. Hundley is assisted by Paralegal Wendy Garrison O'Connor and Office Manager Tabitha K. Weathers. Ms. Gruber is assisted by Legal Assistant Jennifer C. Savage. Mr. Hundley states that each and every one of his staff brings invaluable support and expertise to the practice.

JOYE LAW FIRM

THE JOYE LAW FIRM IS A CHARLESTON-BASED INJURY LAW firm that specializes in representing persons injured in accidents or by product defects. We have successfully advocated for clients throughout the state, including Columbia, Georgetown, Goose Creek, Hilton Head, Sumter, Moncks Corner, Myrtle Beach, Summerville, and Walterboro.

For over 30 years, the Joye Law Firm has been dedicated to defending our civil justice system against those who seek to destroy it. The depth of experience of the firm's ten attorneys—Reese I. Joye, Mark C. Joye, Ken W. Harrell, Angus M. Lawton, Christopher J. McCool, C. Andrew Carroll, Matthew W. Jackson, Tina A. Walker, Brian G. Burke, and Amy B. Rothschild—is complemented by an expert support staff of more than 20 paralegals and other staff members. The firm has received the highest rating available—the Martindale-Hubbell AV rating—as well as being one of the few law firms in the country that is a member of the Leaders' Forum of the Association of Trial Lawyers of America.

The attorneys of Joye Law Firm are known for being tough, aggressive, and thorough, and they strive to move cases toward speedy resolution, whether through trial, settlement, or alternative dispute resolution. With combined litigation experience of over 100 years, they possess the institutional knowledge and in-the-trenches legal abilities to ensure that their clients get a fair recovery when they have suffered injuries The focus of their work is on personal injury and product liability, specifically cases involving automobile accidents, defective products, work injuries, premises liability accidents, tractor-trailer collisions, and medical malpractice. Their tough-minded advocacy on behalf of the firm's clients enables them to reach a timely and successful resolution through negotiation and settlement. However, they do not hesitate to proceed to trial when it is in the best interest of their clients.

Reese Joye, a native of Bennettsville, South Carolina, founded the firm in North Charleston in 1970, after obtaining a B.S. degree in Mechanical Engineering from the University of South Carolina in Columbia in 1961 and graduating from the University of South Carolina School of Law in 1965. Joye worked as an in-house attorney for the Boeing Company in Seattle before returning to South Carolina in 1970 to begin his own law practice.

He is well known as a tenacious litigator who focuses on protecting the rights of individuals. He has tried hundreds of cases before juries during his 30-plus-year career and practices in the areas of wrongful death, personal injury, dram shop law, aviation, alcohol-related cases, and general criminal defense trial work. He is perhaps best known for his work on DUI cases and has taught attorneys from every state in the U.S. techniques and strategies to use in the defense of DUI cases. He has been a frequent lecturer at state bar association, trial lawyer association, and criminal defense association seminars on DUI defense. He, along with the late, great DUI defense attorney, Richard E. Erwin; professor, attorney and author Lawrence Taylor; attorney, lecturer, and author Donald H. Nichols; and engineer Dr. James Feldman organized and participated in a nationwide seminar tour featuring the best known attorneys in the defense of DUI cases entitled "Winning Strategies in DUI Defenses."

Joye is the author of several legal books that are known and studied by lawyers nationwide and is the founding president of the South Carolina Association of Criminal Defense Lawyers. He is a member of the South Carolina Bar and has been admitted to practice before the U.S. Federal Courts and the U.S. Supreme Court. He is a member of the American Board of Trial Advocates and the South Carolina Trial Lawyers Association. He was chair of the Aviation Section of the Association of Trial Lawyers of America from 1984 to 1985, and chair of the Criminal Law Section from 1989 to 1990.

He and his wife, Jackie, are long-time residents of Mount Pleasant, where they are active in community activities. They have three children, including firm partner Mark Joye, and five grandchildren.

Reese's son Mark Joye is also an attorney with the firm. He graduated from the University of North Carolina in Chapel Hill in 1985 and obtained his J.D. degree from the University of South Carolina School of Law in 1989. He is one of the preeminent trial lawyers in the state of South Carolina and nationwide and is a seasoned litigator who has represented plaintiffs injured from defective products, car crashes, tractor-trailer collisions, and falls. In 1997, Mark represented the parents of a young boy who was killed when ejected from the rear of a Chrysler minivan. The case, *Jiminez v. Chrysler*, resulted in a jury verdict of $262.5 million dollars, then the largest verdict ever returned against an automobile manufacturer. It remains the largest personal injury jury verdict ever in South Carolina history. The case also brought national attention to the firm and renewed pressure against Chrysler Corporation to fix the unsafe rear door latches on its minivans. Mark practices in the areas of product liability, wrongful death, and personal injury. He is a board-certified civil trial advocate by the National Board of Trial Advocacy.

He is a member of the South Carolina Bar and of the Executive Committee of the Charleston County Bar Association. Mark has been admitted to practice before the U.S. District Court and the 4th Circuit of the U.S. Court of Appeals. He is also a member of the Board of Governors and of the Executive Committee of the South Carolina Trial Lawyers Association. He is listed in *Who's Who in American Law* and has received an AV rating from Martindale-Hubbell.

Ken Harrell, a native of Waverly, Virginia, joined the law firm as its third equity partner in 1994. Ken is a graduate of James Madison University and the William & Mary School of Law. Prior to joining the law firm, he worked as a corporate defense lawyer for six years before deciding he was best-suited to represent individuals. Ken is the head of the firm's workers' compensation, Social Security disability, and mass torts practices, and he is a frequent lecturer at legal seminars.

Angus Lawton became the firm's fourth equity partner in 2005. Angus grew up in Allendale, South Carolina before obtaining degrees from Duke University and the University of South Carolina School of Law. After operating his own law firm for several years, he joined the Joye Law Firm, where he is the head of the firm's pre-litigation department.

Joye Law Firm is committed to providing its clients with the best representation possible. Joye attorneys are building on a solid foundation of excellence and determination built over 30 years. "We believe in treating our clients as individuals with unique needs and personally giving them the time and respect they deserve," says Mark Joye. His professional motto, which stems from his days as an Eagle Scout, has been disseminated to all his colleagues, "Be Prepared." Although the firm focuses on individual litigation, it is always prepared to take on big corporations that hurt people, and win.

"At the end of every day, we know we have helped persons who would be powerless to fight moneyed interests without quality legal representation," says firm attorney Reese Joye. "Certainly, as with every profession, there are bad apples that fit the stereotype of the 'greedy and dishonest' lawyer which multi-national corporations and the insurance conglomerates would have you believe that all of us are. In the end, I know that most trial lawyers are good people who truly enjoy working to promote the greater good that comes from holding careless manufacturers, corporate scam artists, and insurance conglomerates responsible."

The attorneys of Joye Law Firm are known for being tough, aggressive, and thorough. Pictured are (standing, left to right): Angus M. Lawton, Ken W. Harrell, and Mark C. Joye, and (seated): senior partner Reese I. Joye

KAHN LAW FIRM

The father and son team of Ellis I. Kahn and Justin S. Kahn established Kahn Law Firm on January 1, 1995 on Meeting Street in historic downtown Charleston.

Originally from Charleston, South Carolina, Ellis Kahn received his undergraduate degree from The Citadel in 1958 and a J.D. degree from the University of South Carolina Law School in 1961. He attended the graduate division of Southern Methodist University School of Law from 1962 to 1963. After school, Mr. Kahn joined the United States Air Force as a judge advocate. In 1964, he worked as a law clerk for U.S. District Judge Robert W. Hemphill and, in 1966, he began private law practice in Charleston.

Justin Kahn graduated in 1988 from Tulane University, New Orleans, Louisiana, with degrees in both psychology and communication. He received his J.D. degree from the University of South Carolina School of Law in 1992. Mr. Kahn began practice in Charleston as an associate with Solomon, Kahn, Budman and Stricker and is now a partner with Kahn Law Firm. The author of numerous publications, Mr. Kahn also presents lectures on the topic of law.

The Kahn law firm practices complex litigation, medical malpractice, product liability, and catastrophic injuries and is currently located in West Ashley.

GEORGE J. KEFALOS, P.A.

George Kefalos is a sole practitioner who for almost 30 years has emphasized plaintiff's personal injury, insurance, bad faith, and business fraud matters. He earned his bachelor's and law degrees at the University of Pittsburgh. He moved to Charleston after law school graduation in 1975, arriving by Greyhound bus with a bundle of resumes. It's a decision he calls "the luckiest move I ever made."

Mr. Kefalos began his career as a young associate with a local firm before going on to establish his Charleston-based practice, which has thrived ever since. "Although I am not from Charleston, I have spent the past two decades developing productive and effective relationships within Charleston's law community," says Mr. Kefalos. "In fact, most of my clients are referred to me by other attorneys. These relationships have been critical to my continued success." His skill in trial law recently earned Mr. Kefalos the distinction of being named a Fellow of the College of Trial Lawyers of America. "Trial law is like theater and literature," says Mr. Kefalos. "A trial is like a play. Every detail must be scripted and planned, from what you to say to how you act. If you don't prepare, you won't win."

Mr. Kefalos employs two full-time paralegals, which enables him to serve clients while maintaining his independent practice. He speaks regularly to the local and state bar associations about trial tactics and insurance law. He is named in the most recent addition of *The Best Lawyers in America.*

KERNODLE, TAYLOR & ROOT

SINCE ITS INCEPTION IN APRIL 1999, Kernodle, Taylor & Root has experienced rapid growth as a result of its commitment to client service. The firm, which now comprises seven attorneys, concentrates its practice in government law, employment law, construction defect claims, pest control operator defense, and motor vehicle product liability and warranty law.

Kernodle, Taylor & Root succeeded in winning the first nationally published decision in which the protection provided by *7 U.S.C. § 1926(b)* was applied to a fire protection district. Kernodle, Taylor & Root has also had the privilege of representing many governmental entities as general counsel and litigation counsel. The firm represents several well-known public officials in their individual capacities as well.

In addition to this extensive government law experience, the firm represents such national clients as Ford Motor Company, Lowe's, and Builder's First Choice, a national construction materials company, among many others. This national client base—a cornerstone of the firm—coupled with extensive local clients and contacts, makes the firm local in flavor but national in quality. Founding partner Trent Kernodle says, "Our goal is to grow and build an institution, providing efficient legal services characterized by proficiency and integrity."

Founding partner Trent Kernodle, of Kernodle, Taylor & Root, specializes in product liability, construction law, and government law. Kernodle, Taylor & Root has experienced rapid growth as a result of its commitment to client service.

Mr. Kernodle started the practice after working as a clerk for a Jackson, Tennessee federal court judge and as a partner with the former Charleston law firm Holmes & Thompson, L.L.P. A native of Milan, Tennessee, Mr. Kernodle attended the University of Tennessee (where he obtained B.A. and M.B.A. degrees) and Memphis State University School of Law (now the University of Memphis School of Law), where he was the recipient of the Law Alumni Scholarship, the Donnelly J. Hill Scholarship, and a full scholarship to the International Court of Justice. He also served as the associate editor of the *Memphis State University Law Review.*

Today, as founding partner at Kernodle, Taylor & Root, Mr. Kernodle specializes in product liability, construction law, and government law. He is a member of the South Carolina Bar House of Delegates, the Tennessee Bar Association, and the Charleston County Bar Association Executive Committee. Outside the professional arena, Mr. Kernodle enjoys automobile restoration and spending time at his farm in Cross, South Carolina. His pride is his family, which includes his wife, Kay, and four children: Alicia (also a South Carolina attorney), Bay, Sam, and Parker.

LAWRENCE KOBROVSKY

AFTER GRADUATING FROM HAVERFORD College (B.A., 1976) and the Benjamin N. Cardozo School of Law at Yeshiva University (J.D., 1980), Lawrence (Larry) C. Kobrovsky began practicing law in Charleston with Jimmy Stuckey as Stuckey & Kobrovsky in May 1980. In 1995, Mr. Kobrovsky started his own general practice law firm. His focus is on individual attention and Mr. Kobrovsky takes great pride in his client loyalty and satisfaction. Over time, the practice has represented several generations of the same families.

Mr. Kobrovsky served on the Charleston County School Board from 1993 to 1998, serving as Vice Chairman from 1996 to 1998 and as chairman of the Academic Policy Committee. During his time on the school board, Mr. Kobrovsky initiated and organized the annual Veterans Day and Memorial Day programs for Charleston County schoolchildren on the Yorktown at Patriot's Point as well as the 50th Anniversary of WWII Victory Parade. Mr. Kobrovsky's efforts in public education were recognized by Governor Mark Sanford, who appointed Mr. Kobrovsky to his statewide Education Task Force and as South Carolina's representative on the Education Commission of the States.

Mr. Kobrovsky is especially proud that as a result of his work to end the use of ethnic and racial quotas in the admission process of Charleston County magnet schools in *Deogburn et al. v. Charleston County School Board, Case #2:02-3680-08*, and *Cash et al. v. Charleston County School Board, Case #:2:02-4243-08*, neither race nor ethnic background can any longer play any role in the admission of students to any public school in Charleston County. Mr. Kobrovsky donated a portion of his attorney fees from those cases to an annual essay contest for students on the significance of the Fourteenth Amendment—Equal Protection Clause—of the United States Constitution.

Mr. Kobrovsky is a member of Synagogue Emanu-El and the Sons of the American Legion. Mr. Kobrovsky has also served on the Board of Directors of the Charleston Jewish Federation and the Addlestone Hebrew Academy. He and his wife, Susan, are the proud parents of daughters Valarie and Abby.

Mr. Harold M. Richman has been Mr. Kobrovsky's investigator for 20 years. Mr. Richman is a former Marine and D-Day Veteran. He was President Harry S. Truman's orderly at the Potsdam Conference. Mr. Richman is also the recipient of the South Carolina "Palmetto Award" from Governor Hodges.

Catherine D. Critser has served as a legal assistant to Mr. Kobrovsky for the past two years. She currently holds the position of president for the "Blue Star Mothers of the Tri County" as well as president for the "Summerville-Oakbrook Rotary."

KRAWCHECK & DAVIDSON, L.L.C.

THE LAW FIRM OF KRAWCHECK & DAVIDSON, L.L.C. is noted for its expertise in condominium and planning development law. Partners Leonard (Lenny) Krawcheck, Lydia Davidson, and Kenneth Krawcheck pack a lot of experience and influence into their small firm, consolidating their strengths to offer their clients close personal attention and high quality legal work. The firm's practice centers on real estate, community association law, construction, probate, and estate planning and litigation.

"For many years, we represented the developer of Seabrook Island—we were the original lawyers for the private island resort," explains Lenny Krawcheck. That successful venture sealed the firm's reputation and future in resort real estate. Krawcheck & Davidson has received the highest rating from Martindale-Hubbell, the national organization which assesses and rates attorneys.

A 1965 graduate of Tulane University's School of Law, Lenny Krawcheck headed his own practice before joining forces with Lydia Davidson in 1986, in the same office they occupy today on State Street, just steps away from Broad Street. "Lenny had practiced for 25 years, and was known as an excellent real estate attorney in the community,: says Davidson. The two realized they had similar legal interests and similar clients after Davidson rented office space from Krawcheck. "We recognized that joining together would more efficiently and successfully deliver services to our clients," explains Davidson, a 1981 graduate of the University of South Carolina's (USC) School of Law. Leonard's son Kenneth joined the firm in 1991 after serving as a law clerk for U.S. District Judge Sol Blatt, Jr. A 1988 graduate of USC's School of Law, he became a partner in 1997.

All three partners have held important positions in public service. "We try to give back, to make a contribution to the community, which has been very good to us," notes Krawcheck. Lenny Krawcheck served in the South Carolina House of Representatives for two terms, has been Chairman of the City of Charleston Zoning Board of Appeals since 1979, and chairman of the real estate section of the Charleston County Bar since 1992. He is a member of the Porter Gaud School Board of Trustees. Davidson served as Assistant Charleston County Attorney for 14 years, and on the Board of Directors of the local chapters of the American Heart Association and Junior Achievement. She is a member of the Mason Preparatory School Board. Kenneth Krawcheck was Chairman of the Board of Commissioners for the City of Charleston Housing Authority for three years, and presently serves as a member of the South Carolina Ethics Commission.

The law firm of Krawcheck & Davidson, clockwise from top left: Leonard Krawcheck, Lydia Davidson, Lydia Cowan, and Kenneth Krawcheck. The firm is noted for its expertise in condominium and planning development law.

The practice is complemented by a support staff of nine, many of whom have been with the firm for over ten years. "They're experts at what they do," says Lenny Krawcheck. He is married and three of his four children are attorneys. Davidson, who is also married, has one child who is a law student. Kenneth Krawcheck is married with one child.

LADDAGA-GARRETT, P.A.

The Laddaga-Garrett firm specializes in health law and ERISA litigation and primarily represents hospitals, physicians, rehabilitation facilities, and other healthcare providers.

The firm was founded in 1983 by Lawrence A. Laddaga, a graduate of the University of South Carolina (USC) (B.A., cum laude, Phi Beta Kappa, 1978) and the USC School of Law (J.D., 1981). Mr. Laddaga has been, and continues to be, an active member of the Healthcare Financial Managers Association (HFMA). He currently serves on the National Principles and Practices Board and was president of the South Carolina Chapter of HFMA from 1997 to 1998. He has been recognized by HFMA on numerous occasions for his professional accomplishments. In 1998, he received the H. Ray Everett Award for the most outstanding member and, in 1997, he won the Helen Yerger award for the best feature article published in the HFMA Journal in 1996.

Mr. Laddaga is joined at Laddaga-Garrett by native Charlestonian Linda C. Garrett. Ms. Garrett received her B.A. degree, summa cum laude, Phi Kappa Phi, from the College of Charleston in 1991 and her J.D. degree from USC School of Law in 1995. She served as an instructor in the Paralegal Certificate Program at USC Department of Education from 1994 to 1998. Ms. Garrett specializes in the counsel of health care providers regarding compliance in such matters as fraud and abuse, Stark II, Anti-Kickback, EMTALA, and HIPAA.

Mr. Laddaga notes that "a lot of firms that do health law tend to concentrate on medical malpractice or governance issues," but "because we started out doing work for hospital business offices, we are very well grounded in the business aspects of health care." Of this experience, Mr. Laddaga says, "when it comes to the financial aspects of how health care is paid for, there is no one else out there that knows more than we do."

LIZZI LAW FIRM, PC

After a 12-year stint in the navy, Christopher D. Lizzi decided to change direction and pursue a career in the field of law. Graduating from Charleston Southern University in 1987, he then moved to Columbia, South Carolina to attend law school at the University of South Carolina, graduating with a J.D. degree in 1991.

Stationed in Charleston while in the navy, Mr. Lizzi elected to come back to the Lowcountry to practice law. He began his career in the 9th Circuit Solicitors Office in Moncks Corner for two years. In 1993, Mr. Lizzi opened his own practice, Lizzi Law Firm, in North Charleston. Today, the firm still sits in the heart of North Charleston, two doors down from its original location, with a staff of two paralegals and a receptionist.

A native of Pittsburgh, Pennsylvania, Mr. Lizzi chose Charleston for his practice because he feels that a lot of things are evolving in South Carolina in terms of its legal system. Mr. Lizzi knows what it takes to be successful in his career and to continue to bring in clients on a large list of referrals. "I am as straightforward as it comes," he says. "I'll leave your money in your pocket if I don't think you should be doing something."

Lizzi Law firm is a trial practice, focusing on criminal law, family law, personal injury, and general litigation.

LOFTON & LOFTON, P.C.

Lionel Lofton graduated from Campbell University in Buies Creek, North Carolina in 1967. Following graduation, he taught school at Gaffney High School in Gaffney, South Carolina for one year prior to attending law school. Mr. Lofton received his J.D. degree from the University of South Carolina Law School in 1971 and was admitted to the South Carolina Bar that same year.

Mr. Lofton worked as the head of the criminal division for the United States Attorney's office in Charleston straight out of law school. He was an assistant United States Attorney until February 1983. During his tenure with the United States Attorney's office, Mr. Lofton took a six-month leave in 1975 to serve as legal advisor to Governor James B. Edwards.

In 1983, after 12 years as a federal prosecutor, Mr. Lofton decided to open a private practice, the Law Offices of Lionel S. Lofton. His experience and tenure in the United States Attorney's office facilitated the development of not only a statewide, but also a national, practice.

Frances Cain-Lofton, a graduate of the College of Charleston and the University of South Carolina Law School, worked as an assistant solicitor in Charleston County from 1983 to 1984 before joining the Law Offices of Lionel S. Lofton in 1984.

The two were married in 1990 and formed Lofton and Lofton, P.C. in the mid-1990s. Mr. Lofton practices federal and state criminal defense and personal injury law. Mrs. Cain-Lofton practices family law and personal injury law and also serves as a Charleston County Summary Court judge in their hometown, McClellanville, South Carolina. In 2004, Mr. Lofton's daughter, V. Lynn Lofton, joined the firm. Today, the firm sits in its original location downtown in Charleston, South Carolina.

LAW OFFICE OF ARTHUR C. McFARLAND

Judge Arthur C. McFarland, a Charleston native, has been practicing law for almost 32 years. As managing attorney with the firm, Mr. McFarland focuses his general practice on seven key disciplines of law: probate, real estate, family, personal injury, employment, civil rights, and commercial. He has been a Charleston municipal court judge for 29 years and the chief judge since 1978.

Judge McFarland graduated from Notre Dame University in 1970 and received his J.D. degree from the University of Virginia Law School three years later. He began his career with a fellowship at the NAACP Legal Defense Fund. His role as a prominent, local African American provides him a cultural familiarity that he uses to serve his clients and the community.

Judge McFarland emphasizes his commitment to community as much as his dedication to the law, striving to "assist as many people as possible" by mentoring young African-American lawyers and delivering free lectures about legal and community issues to schools, churches, prisons, and civic organizations. He has served on numerous local and national community boards and commissions. His South Carolina Bar services include the Judicial Qualifications Committee and lecturer for the Bridge the Gap Program. He is a member of the Medical University of South Carolina Health Sciences Foundation Board of Directors, the 100 Black Men of Charleston, Inc., and National President and CEO of the Knights of Peter Claver, Inc., the oldest African-American Catholic lay organization in the U.S.

Judge McFarland previously served as president of the Charleston Business and Professional Association, the Charleston Country Human Services Commission, and the Robert Shaw Boys and Girls Club. He has received dozens of awards and honors for his community service. He has appeared in numerous publications, on SCETV, ABC's *Nightline*, and radio talk shows. He is married to Elise Davis-McFarland, Ph.D. and they have two children.

MARTIN & MARTIN

THE FATHER AND SON TEAM OF Martin & Martin began more than 50 years ago with the dream of a young man from Bluffton, South Carolina. The son of John Henry Martin, a merchant marine and Rena Alethia Martin, a domestic worker, Daniel E. Martin, Sr. attended Penn High School on St. Helena Island, South Carolina. While there, he was inspired by his older brother Jacob's attempt to attend the then-segregated University of South Carolina School of Law. Jacob was initially accepted until it was discovered that he was an African American. He was ultimately denied admission.

Daniel decided to pursue his brother's dream. He obtained a B.S. degree from Allen University and began law school at Howard University before being called into military service. Undeterred, he ultimately returned to law school at South Carolina State College where he was one of the last students to graduate before the school was closed in 1966 in the name of integration.

Attorney Martin began his legal career in Charleston in 1966 and became director of the Neighborhood Legal Assistance Program, Inc. from 1967 to 1972. He served as Assistant Solicitor for the Ninth Judicial Circuit from 1974 to 1984 and was elected to the South Carolina General Assembly as a Representative for District 111 in 1984, serving until 1992 when he was elected circuit court judge for the Ninth Judicial Circuit. He served until his retirement in 2001.

Judge Martin represented the First Congressional District on the State Committee for Judicial Reform in 1976. He was a founder and for four years Director of the Neighborhood Legal Assistance Program, Inc. from 1967 to 1972. He was a founder and former member of the Board of Directors of the Public Defender Corporation of Charleston County.

Judge Martin is a member of the American Bar, the South Carolina Bar, Charleston County Bar, the U.S. Tax Court, the U.S. Court of Claims, the U.S. Court of Customs and Patent Appeals, the Federal District Court for the District of South Carolina, the Fourth Circuit Court of Appeals, and the U.S. Supreme Court.

Daniel E. Martin, Jr. decided to pursue a career in law early in life, graduating from Bishop England High School in 1980 and receiving his B.S. degree in Political Science from Howard University in 1985. He attended the University of South Carolina School of Law and earned his J.D. degree in 1988. He entered the practice of law with his father the same year and was appointed as a Charleston County Magistrate in 1989, resigning in 1993 to practice law full time. He served on the executive committee of the Charleston County Bar and as a member of the House of Delegates for the State Bar. He is the former treasurer of the South Carolina Black Lawyers Association and currently serves as a member of the Ninth Judicial Circuit Resolution of the Fee Disputes Board and as attorney for the town of Lincolnville, South Carolina. He is married to Reba Hough Martin of Hartsville, South Carolina and is the parent of Daniel, III and Zelena.

The legal team of Martin and Martin is engaged in the general practice of law with concentrations in real estate, personal injury, and domestic law.

GREGG MEYERS

AFTER GRADUATING FROM HAMLINE University School of Law, Gregg Meyers worked across the country for the Civil Rights Division of the Department of Justice. In 1987, he came to Charleston, where he practiced in the Charleston office of a Columbia law firm and later at Wise & Cole, now Pratt-Thomas, Epting & Walker, PA.

Since 1998, Mr. Meyers has been a sole practitioner specializing in sexual abuse cases, cases involving the federal False Claims Act, business and commercial litigation, and construction litigation. He has handled a number of appeals in state and federal appellate courts, particularly appeals designed to change sexual abuse law. He presently holds the largest jury verdicts ever awarded in both Charleston and Berkeley counties.

Mr. Meyers is happy to work as a sole practitioner because, he says, "I have the great luxury of taking cases I feel strongly about." These include the sexual abuse cases that now make up a large part of his practice. Of these he says, "I feel like at the end of the day I've done something positive."

Mr. Meyers is assisted in his practice by long-time assistant Jackie Lunsford, whom he describes as wonderful to work with, extremely reliable, and a real benefit to his practice.

Outside the law profession, Mr. Meyers has served on the Charleston County School Board since 1996 and served as its chairman from 2002 to 2003. He also has a busy family life with five children and his wife, Susan.

REGAN AND CANTWELL, LLC

REGAN AND CANTWELL, LLC BEGAN practice in 1990 as a partnership between William B. Regan and Frances I. Cantwell. The firm concentrates in zoning, land use, and governmental law issues.

Bill Regan is a 1963 graduate of the College of Charleston and a 1966 graduate of the University of South Carolina School of Law, where he was a member of the law review, a member of the national moot court team, and a member of the Wig and Robe National Honor Society. In his senior year, his fellow students concluded that he should receive the Claude N. Sapp Award for the best combination of scholarship, leadership, and industry in his class. He is a former president of the Charleston Lawyers Club, and from 1975 until 2002 he served as Corporation Counsel for the City of Charleston. In 2002, the South Carolina Law School Alumni Association named him as one of three recipients of the Platinum Compleat Lawyers Award. In 2004, members of the Charleston County Bar Association endowed the William Bennett Regan Award for Outstanding Leadership and Commitment to Public Service at the Charleston School of Law, which will be given each year to a graduating senior selected by the faculty.

Frances Cantwell is a 1976 graduate of Marquette University, where she was a member of the Phi Beta Kappa Honorary Scholastic Fraternity and a 1979 graduate of the University of South Carolina Law Center. She was a member of the Wig and Robe National Honor Society and represented the school in the national finals of the trial moot court competition. She served as an Assistant Corporation Counsel for the City of Charleston for 20 years, and is a past president of the Charleston County Bar Association and the South Carolina Municipal Attorneys Association. She currently serves on the South Carolina Supreme Court Ad Hoc Rules Committee.

MOTLEY RICE LLC

LOCATED ON THE SHORES OF THE COOPER RIVER, MOTLEY Rice's headquarters stand as a symbol of strength in the Charleston Harbor. The building's nautical design and close proximity to the water blend naturally into the Charleston seascape. From the building, one may observe an impressive view of Charleston and its many historic sites, including Fort Sumter and the U.S.S. *Yorktown*. The firm's other offices located in Barnwell, South Carolina, Hartford, Connecticut, and Providence, Rhode Island are also located in historic and beautiful areas. While the foundations of these buildings are strong, the ideas, convictions, and talents of the people inside the buildings stand as the true bedrock of Motley Rice LLC.

THE FOUNDATION

Founded on April 28, 2003, Motley Rice LLC is one of the nation's largest all plaintiffs' litigation firms. The attorneys, assisted by over 350 support personnel, are proven leaders in litigation, demonstrating extensive courtroom experience and an in-depth understanding of the law. Affiliated law firms rely on Motley Rice as a resource powerhouse and courtroom necessity. Clients express gratitude for our accessibility, responsiveness, and dependability.

The roots of Motley Rice LLC are deep, complex, and near-legendary. Founding members Ronald L. Motley and Joseph F. Rice have worked together for over 20 years, fearlessly investing long and hard hours in the construction and operation of a uniquely successful law practice.

Nearly 60 years ago in Barnwell, South Carolina, the law firm Blatt & Fales was established. As the law developed in the areas of product liability and tort, the firm expanded to meet the growing need. Ron Motley joined the Blatt & Fales team in 1977, which solidified the practice's specialty in product liability.

In the 1970s, when asbestos litigation was in its infancy, Motley began representing workers injured by the asbestos industry. In the late 1970s, his firm acquired the infamous Sumner Simpson papers, internal company documents dating back to the late 1920s that demonstrated manufacturer knowledge of the hazards of asbestos. Undaunted by the power

and strength of corporate opposition, Motley and a strong team of associates began a tenacious discovery effort against asbestos defendants. Eventually, Motley's work garnered widespread national recognition. He became known as "the man who forced the asbestos industry into bankruptcy."

In 1979, Motley recruited attorney Joe Rice to the firm. The partnership proved to be a perfect match. Many of their colleagues from throughout the legal community have an interesting way of describing the "marriage" between Motley and Rice. "Motley is born to try cases, Rice to negotiate the settlements. Ron tries the case and Joe cuts the deal," says lawyer Richard Scruggs.

The extensively researched medical information distinguishing tobacco and asbestos-related causes of lung cancer, along with a personal desire for moral, ethical, and social reform from tobacco producers in the United States created a bridge to a new litigation focus in the 1990s. Their exhaustive and inventive approach resulted in the discovery of highly incriminating evidence against the tobacco industry. With this knowledge, Motley led state litigation efforts against the tobacco industry. With a strong team working in the courtroom, Rice was well-positioned to lead negotiations. The result was the Master Settlement Agreement, a $246 billion accord with the four largest tobacco producers in the United States. This record-breaking settlement provided reimbursement to the states for publicly funded health care costs and imposed advertising and sponsorship restrictions. Today, the agreement continues to be the largest financial resolution of civil litigation in the history of United States jurisprudence.

When asked about how his interest in the tobacco settlements began, Rice said, "I was scared. Ron didn't care about the economics like I did...he was looking at this from a pure excitement, personal drive point of view." However, the duo decided it was worth the risk and continued onward.

Motley Rice attorneys have received awards and accolades for their efforts in tobacco-related litigation. More importantly, the outcome of the tobacco litigation has been viewed as one of the greatest accomplishments in public health during the 20th century.

In 1998, Motley was named Harry M. Philo Trial Lawyer of the Year by the 50,000-member Association of Trial Lawyers of America. The Campaign for Tobacco-Free Kids named him their Youth Advocate of the Year in 1999. Both Motley and Rice are past recipients of the President's Award of the National Association of Attorneys General. In 1999 and 2000, Rice served on the faculty at Duke University School of Law as a Senior Lecturing Fellow. In 2004, Corporate Legal Times named Joe Rice "one of the five most respected (and feared) plaintiffs' attorneys."

THE FUTURE

Today, Motley Rice attorneys and staff continue to seek justice in the areas of: catastrophic injury; complex case resolution; consumer and commercial fraud; environmental hazards and contamination; medical negligence and defects; occupational disease and toxic torts; and transportation defects and disasters. The Motley Rice LLC attorney group (with 15 members, also referred to as partners, and 45 associates at print time) is comprised of varied backgrounds, experiences, and personalities. Several were groomed by Ron and Joe, others were partners in their own firms before joining Motley Rice, and many were co-counsel who decided to become team players in a different environment. Regardless of their backgrounds, this team works together to build a strong culture for all of its employees, co-counsel, clients, and communities.

The firm and its attorneys and staff have committed time and resources to charitable organizations in the communities in which they have offices. The firm supports many national foundations, charities, and public interest and health organizations. Motley Rice takes pride in the fact that their attorneys and staff give back to the community by serving on committees, boards, and advisory groups or through volunteerism and other activities with not-for-profit organizations. Motley Rice employees have an enduring commitment to making a difference.

It is not a secret that Motley Rice is a young firm, with only three members over 50 years old. "To the lawyers of Motley Rice, it's about more than just the payoffs and rewards," said member Jack McConnell. "It's about making a difference in the legal world, one case at a time."

By continuing to take challenging cases that others fear, by giving back to their profession, their people, and their communities and by believing optimistically that just one person can bring about change, they believe that they will persevere for those who seek justice.

PRATT-THOMAS, EPTING & WALKER, P.A.

PRATT-THOMAS, EPTING & WALKER, P.A., based in Charleston, South Carolina, is a skilled litigation and business law firm whose attorneys strive for innovative solutions to complex legal issues on behalf of their clients.

The firm was founded in 1975. In 1996 it moved to its current location in an historic Greek Revival style-mansion in downtown Charleston, built circa 1835 by Robert Martin. The firm made extensive renovations to the property, preserving the original vision of the building and grounds while adapting its use to create a unique setting for the practice of law.

The attorneys of Pratt-Thomas, Epting & Walker offer clients years of experience and are highly skilled in their respective areas of practice. As a result, the firm has earned an AV rating, the highest possible designation from Martindale-Hubbell, an esteemed legal organization that facilitates a peer review process for rating lawyers and firms on legal ability and general ethical standards.

The firm emphasizes a client-centered, personal approach to cases, and its attorneys are known for being highly professional and approachable, yet assertive and thorough, determined to reach a favorable resolution of the legal matters facing their clients.

Pratt-Thomas, Epting & Walker occupies this 1835 mansion.

Attorneys are supported by an experienced staff and state-of-the-art technology, ensuring high-caliber representation, top-quality client service and advocacy, and fair billing. Instead of using extensive teams of paralegals, young attorneys, and support staff to manage projects, these tenured attorneys work directly with clients, getting to the heart of the matter and ensuring their needs are met in as efficient a manner as possible. As a result, the attorneys enjoy loyal and long-term relationships with their client base.

The firm handles cases in a wide range of areas including health care, banking, construction, land use planning and development, natural resources regulation, medical malpractice, securities, commercial disputes, personal injury, insurance coverage, and more. Several attorneys are also certified in alternative dispute resolution, offering parties other means for solving legal problems.

EDWARD K. PRITCHARD, SR.

THE LATE EDWARD K. PRITCHARD was the first in a family of lawyers. A 1930 graduate of the University of South Carolina School of Law, Pritchard served in the South Carolina Legislature from 1926 to 1930. Graduating first in his class, he joined Stoney & Crosland law firm, soon becoming a partner in the firm, which included Thomas P. Stoney, the mayor of Charleston.

In 1948, Edward Pritchard formed his own law practice. Considered a gifted speaker, he was president of the Charleston County Bar Association in 1957 and president of the South Carolina Bar from 1962 to 1963. "He never spoke from notes," recalls his son, attorney Edward (Boopa) K. Pritchard, Jr. Invited to address several bar associations around the country, the senior Pritchard later became active in the American Bar Association, serving as Chairman of the American Conference of Bar Presidents and becoming well known around the country. He also served as Lieutenant Governor of the Carolinas District. He was such a great persuader that he was able to talk Rachel Norwood, the nurse who had cared for his wife during several pregnancies, into taking a secretarial course and becoming his secretary. "He called me his personal, private, and confidential secretary," says Norwood. "I loved working for him." She was his right hand for 20 years, right up until his death.

Best known for his practice of criminal law, Pritchard formed Pritchard, Myers, Morrison & Bloom in 1964 with close friends, business associates, and his son Boopa, who joined the firm in 1964 after graduating from the University of South Carolina Law School. This firm existed until Pritchard's death in 1977.

"My father was well-recognized among his peers as being one of the best lawyers in Charleston, and having one of the brightest minds," notes Boopa. One of the cases he remembers being discussed around the family dinner table was a bootleg liquor conspiracy case out of Colleton County. "There were a lot of famous defendants, including a local magistrate and solicitor," says Boopa. "I remember Daddy coming home and talking about the intensity of the case—the judge held court from the crack of dawn until late at night, and even on Saturday."

Pritchard was a member, and president, of the Kiwanis Club, and was actively involved in real estate development during the latter years of his life. Boopa says he recently received the biggest compliment ever from a client's father who observed him in court. "He told me, 'I saw flashes of your daddy in you during that trial,'" he says. Pritchard's two grandsons, as well as a son-in-law, are also lawyers. In October 2003, his name was added to "Memory Hold the Door," formed by the South Carolina Bar Association to memorialize outstanding legal achievements.

TOP: *Edward K. Pritchard, Sr.* ABOVE *(left to right): Edward K. Pritchard III, Edward K. Pritchard, Jr., and Thomas B. Pritchard.*

RIESEN LAW FIRM, L.L.P.

Founded in 1975 by Frederick W. Riesen, Jr., Riesen Law Firm provides services to individual citizens of the coastal and midstate areas. Comprised of eight lawyers sharing an office in North Charleston, each maintains his or her individual practice.

The attorneys of Riesen Law Firm focus on general civil and criminal trial practice in all state and federal courts, plaintiff's personal injury, workers' compensation, admiralty, longshore, criminal defense, DUI, and federal employment law. Concentrations of the resident attorneys' practices are in plaintiff's personal injury work, claimant's state and federal workers' compensation claims, and criminal trial and appellate defense.

All the attorneys of Riesen Law Firm are active in the community and belong to and actively participate in the Association of Trial Lawyers of America, the South Carolina Trial Lawyers Association, the South Carolina Association of Criminal Defense Lawyers, and the South Carolina Claimant's Association.

Members of the firm include Frederick W. Riesen, Jr., Gary Alan Ling, E. Paul Gibson, Timothy Clay Kulp, Philip A. Berlinsky, Allison A. Stover, Jody V. McKnight, and Frederick W. Riesen, III.

ROBERTSON & HOLLINGSWORTH

Robertson & Hollingsworth was founded as a solo practice by Claron A. Robertson, III on May 1, 1988 with the capable assistance of his long-time secretary and friend, Ms. Donna Gilreath. "Rob" graduated from Duke University in 1972 and the University of Virginia School of Law in 1975. He began practicing immediately after graduation with the Charleston firm of Buist Moore Smythe & McGee, where he was a partner until resigning to begin his own firm. On June 15, 1991, the firm, which had grown to comprise several lawyers, relocated to its new quarters in the First Union (now Wachovia) Building, where today it occupies approximately 6,000 square feet of the most contemporary and technologically up-to-date facilities in Charleston.

The firm's evolution continued with the addition of several partners and associates and a change of name to Robertson & Hollingsworth on January 1, 2001. Partners as of January 1, 2005 include Rob Robertson, Dunn D. Hollingsworth, Robert Patrick Flynn, Perrin Q. Dargan, III, Theodore L. Manos, and Paul R. Rahn, as well as associates David B. Marvel, C. Tyson Nettles, and Jason A. Daigle, all of whom have demonstrated academic and professional accomplishments consistent with the highest standards of the South Carolina Bar.

The firm has developed special expertise and extensive clientele in construction, architecture, engineering, and environmental law, and advises many leading companies throughout coastal South Carolina as general counsel on a wide variety of issues, including contracts, employment matters, and regulatory compliance. The firm is listed in Martindale-Hubbell's roster of Preeminent Attorneys in the United States and in *The Best Lawyers in America.* Robertson & Hollingsworth is committed to an excellent professional practice enhanced by the exceptional opportunities and quality of life characteristic of Charleston and the Lowcountry.

LAW OFFICES OF STANLEY C. RODGERS, LLC

DESPITE LIMITED EXPOSURE TO THE law profession while growing up in New Ellenton, South Carolina, Stanley Rodgers always believed that practicing law was a noble and honorable occupation. His initial respect for, and interest in, the law profession eventually led to his entering the University of South Carolina School of Law, where he served as student works editor for the *South Carolina Law Review*. His J.D. degree from the University of South Carolina School of Law followed his B.A. degree from Harvard University, awarded in 1989.

Mr. Rodgers began his career with a large firm in Columbia. He then moved to Charleston and worked in a medium-sized firm for several years before leaving to practice with another lawyer for five years. He opened his own practice in 2002 in downtown Charleston.

Mr. Rodgers concentrates on personal injury, construction litigation, commercial litigation, real estate disputes, and insurance coverage. He says, "To me, part of what's interesting about law is that every case is different—the people are always unique, the specific facts are unique. You learn different things all the time in different areas." Mr. Rodgers enjoys focusing on a few areas rather than specializing in just one.

Outside of the law profession, Mr. Rodgers enjoys spending time with his wife, Elizabeth Krawcheck Rodgers, whom he met at the University of South Carolina School of Law, and their three young daughters, Tyler Elizabeth, Emma Blake, and Anne Ellenton. He is also an active member of Bethel United Methodist Church.

W. BROOKS STYLES

ORIGINALLY FROM ASHEVILLE, NORTH CAROLINA, W. Brooks Styles pursued his undergraduate degree from Presbyterian College in Clinton, South Carolina. In 1973 he received his J.D. degree from the University of South Carolina Law School in Columbia, South Carolina.

After finishing law school, Mr. Styles practiced in Columbia with Lewis Lewis & Robinson and, in 1978, he opened a branch of the firm in Charleston. In 1981, Mr. Styles began practicing with Burkett Wooddy Cisa & Styles.

Practicing real estate law, Mr. Styles became a sole practitioner in 1994 in his office located off Rivers Avenue in North Charleston. He was a founding member of the Dorchester County Habitat for Humanity chapter in 1993 and has served as legal counsel to the Mortgage Lenders Association of Greater Charleston since 1986. He is a member of the Charleston County Bar Association, the South Carolina Bar Association, and the American Bar Association.

Mr. Styles has two grown daughters and one grandson, and resides in Summerville, South Carolina with his wife Ellen.

RICHARDSON, PATRICK, WESTBROOK & BRICKMAN, LLC

In February 2002, attorneys Terry Richardson, Jr., Charles Patrick, Jr., Edward Westbrook, and Michael Brickman established Richardson, Patrick, Westbrook & Brickman, a practice guided by the ideal that everyone has a right to seek justice through the legal system.

After practicing law together for more than two decades, the partners of Richardson, Patrick, Westbrook & Brickman wanted to take their practice to new heights—to create a firm where differing opinions and approaches thrive, but shared legal philosophies are the foundation. Eleven partners left a former prominent practice to establish a firm focused on representing plaintiffs who have been injured as a result of corporate misconduct. The founders of Richardson, Patrick have established a legal practice where the individual client is not lost in massive litigation.

The new firm was founded in the heart of historic downtown Charleston with less than a dozen employees. It expanded to about 100 employees, including 28 attorneys, within a year. As a result of the firm's rapid growth, an additional office was established in Mt. Pleasant, which increased the firm's presence to three locations, including an office in Barnwell, South Carolina, the home of one of the founders, Terry Richardson.

Top Left: *Terry Richardson, Jr.* Top Right: *Charles Patrick, Jr.* Above Left: *Edward Westbrook.* Above Right: *Michael Brickman.*

Richardson, Patrick is committed to resolving disputes that truly matter to society. Primarily representing plaintiffs, the firm's litigation in tobacco, asbestos, product liability, and other cases has gained it national recognition. In March, 2003, it obtained a record-setting judgment against Philip Morris in Illinois for $10.1 billion in a "low tar" tobacco class-action suit.

Richardson, Patrick is perhaps best known for its ongoing legal efforts in nearly every state across the country to defend the rights of thousands of individuals harmed by exposure to asbestos. In the 1980s, when mesothelioma, a form of cancer caused by inhalation of asbestos fibers was still virtually unknown to the public, the lawyers of Richardson, Patrick were already on the front lines driving asbestos litigation against hundreds of manufacturing and construction-related companies nationwide whose employees were exposed to asbestos and harmed in the work environment. The firm continues to be a leader in this area of law, and has also played a significant role in landmark settlements against "Big Tobacco," representing individuals, government agencies, and private companies against all types of polluters.

The firm has expanded its areas of legal expertise to include a wide range of issues, including: asbestos and mesothelioma cases, consumer fraud, deceptive trade and antitrust violations, environmental harm, healthcare fraud, defective medical devices, dangerous pharmaceutical drugs, predatory lending practices, product liability, securities fraud, tobacco class actions, toxic torts, and corporate fraud.

With a focus on social justice, the attorneys at Richardson, Patrick have been instrumental in obtaining impressive verdicts and settlements on behalf of victims across the country. As plaintiff lawyers, they exude confidence in taking on the big cases and working for redress from major corporations and other defendants whose products or actions have caused undue cost or harm to people's lives. "Richardson, Patrick, Westbrook & Brickman is a vital firm with a lot of energy," says partner Charles Patrick, Jr. "We are dedicated attorneys who enjoy the pursuit of justice through litigation."

SAVAGE & SAVAGE, P.A.

Charleston defense attorney Andrew J. Savage, III.

ANDREW J. SAVAGE, III HAS BEEN A LEADING defense attorney in Charleston for over 20 years. The majority of his work at Savage & Savage involves criminal defense in both state and federal courts and the representation of health care professionals before administrative boards and commissions.

A native of Kingston, New York, Mr. Savage wanted to be a lawyer from an early age. "I had two uncles who practiced law," he explains, "and what they did fascinated me. From childhood, I had a great desire to live in the South." To this end, Mr. Savage attended the University of South Carolina School of Law after graduating from Fordham University. In 1975, he got his start as a South Carolina state prosecutor. After working just two years as an Assistant Solicitor in Columbia, he became chief trial counsel for the South Carolina Attorney General's Office.

In 1981, Mr. Savage started his own practice. In the late 1980s and early '90s, Mr. Savage successfully represented defendants in a number of high profile murder cases. He represented Roudro Gourdine, a Charleston officer charged with homicide in the death of a recently arrested young man, and 17-year-old Mary Lynn French in a death penalty trial in Colleton County where she was charged with the murder of the police chief of Cottageville. He later successfully represented the "Charleston Sniper," Cleveland Gore, and Charleston restaurateur, Sergio Franco, who was charged with the murder of his wife. Mr. Savage was one of the defense attorneys for the "Charleston Five," members of the International Longshoremen's Union charged with rioting on the Charleston docks in early 2000. Throughout his career, Mr. Savage has been known for his vigorous and creative representation of his clients.

David L. Savage joined the practice in 1990. He specializes in civil litigation in state and federal courts, including personal injury and wrongful death. Andrew and David are also joined at Savage & Savage by David W. Wolf.

Mr. Savage has been included in *The Best Lawyers in America* since 1991 in the practice area of criminal defense and has an AV rating in Martindale-Hubbell. He has also devoted his skills and experience to the greater Charleston community. He served two terms as a member of the Charleston County Council (1986-1994) and is a commentator and legal analyst for both television and radio. For more than 20 years he has represented members of the law enforcement community as counsel for the Southern States Police Benevolent Association and the Fraternal Order of Police.

Mr. Savage's goal at Savage & Savage is to continue providing excellent representation for his clients. Part of fulfilling this goal, he believes, is giving individual attention to each client. "We are never going to become a large law firm. I want to stay personally involved in all of our firm's cases. I really enjoy my contact with our clients and being able to find a satisfactory resolution to their legal problems."

Mr. Savage is also passionate about his family, which includes his wife, Cheryl, and their four children, Kimberly, Meghan, Andrew, and Heyward. The newest additions to his family are his four grandchildren, Kathryn, Jack, Michael, and Connor.

STIRLING & O'CONNELL

Founded by Ann Stirling in 1977, the firm became Stirling & O'Connell when Michael O'Connell joined in 1996 after 15 years in public defense.

BOTH OF THE PARTNERS OF Stirling & O'Connell—Ann Stirling and Michael O'Connell—have a reputation for doing good. "We have big hearts and try to exert them," offers Ann Stirling, who founded the firm in 1977. Both partners served as Public Defenders for Charleston County and their tradition of looking out for others in the community has endured during the firm's 29 years of practicing family and criminal law.

"Both Michael and I started our careers by providing quality legal services to those who are unable to afford lawyers," explains Stirling. In addition to their high quality of private representation, the firm remains committed to those ideals through active volunteer work and by representation in appointed cases. Both partners have been awarded the highest Charleston County Bar recognition for community service.

High honors, great qualifications, and a focused practice have resulted in the firm's handling some of the county's most complex and challenging family and criminal cases. "We limit ourselves to these two specific areas of law so we can provide a high quality of work," explains Stirling. The firm's support staff is experienced in the challenges that both family and criminal practice can present.

A graduate of the University of North Carolina at Chapel Hill and the University of South Carolina Law School, Stirling practices exclusively in the area of family law and has done so since shortly after she entered private practice. Stirling was the first woman to try a criminal case in Charleston and many years later was the second woman in South Carolina to be inducted into the American College of Trial Lawyers. She has been included in the family law section of *The Best Lawyers in America* every year since 1994. She is a Fellow with the American Academy of Matrimonial Lawyers and has been recertified by them in family law. She is a certified mediator and a trained arbitrator in family law. She receives the highest rating from Martindale-Hubbell, the national organization which assesses and rates attorneys.

Michael O'Connell, who joined the firm in 1996, practices both family law and criminal law. A graduate of Belmont Abbey College and the University of South Carolina School of Law, O'Connell spent 15 years as a state and federal public defender before joining Stirling. Listed since 2000 in the criminal law section of *The Best Lawyers in America*, O'Connell has taught at The Citadel, was a member of, and has served on, the faculty at the National College of Criminal Defense, and has served as Hearing Officer (Judge) for the Occupational Safety and Health Division of the South Carolina Department of Labor. He is also a certified mediator. He and Stirling have been married since 1977 and have two children. They are both active in their local church.

"We work hard at being ethical and highly competent lawyers," says Stirling. "Both of us still truly enjoy practicing law and being active in our community. We want to help people in their time of crisis."

STUCKEY LAW OFFICES, LLC

As Charleston law firms continue to increase in size and complexity Stuckey Law Offices remains a family affair, composed of James A. Stuckey, Jr., his daughter, Elizabeth Stuckey Murphy, and his son-in-law, Christopher L. Murphy. Jimmy Stuckey has practiced law in Charleston for 38 years, being brought to the city in 1967 by U.S. Senator Ernest F. Hollings to practice with him and later federal district court judge Falcon B. Hawkins. Elizabeth Stuckey and Chris Murphy joined Mr. Stuckey in 1997, following their graduation from the University of South Carolina Law School. Ms. Stuckey received her undergraduate degree from Wofford College and Mr. Murphy finished at Gettysburg College.

Mr. Stuckey is also a graduate of Wofford College and the University of South Carolina Law School, where he was a member of the South Carolina Law Review. Following graduation, he served with the Judge Advocate General Corps in Korea as chief trial counsel for the Eighth U.S. Army, and in California, where he was admitted to the California State Bar and to practice before the federal district court, and the Ninth Circuit Court of Appeals. Mr. Stuckey and state senator T. Dewey Wise formed the law firm of Stuckey & Wise in 1973. Later Mr. Stuckey formed the law firm of Stuckey & Kobrovsky with Lawrence C. Kobrovsky.

Stuckey Law Offices specializes in governmental defense and defense of civil rights litigation. Mr. Stuckey is a frequent lecturer on these topics. In 1972, Mr. Stuckey was granted the first writ of prohibition issued by the South Carolina Supreme Court in its original jurisdiction in more than 100 years in the case of *New South Life Ins Co. v. Lindsay, et. al.* His case of *Sellers v. Public Sav. Life Ins. Co.* was annotated in American Law Reports as a leading national case on the burden of proof in a drowning case.

Mr. Stuckey was one of the founders and initial directors of the Charleston County Public Defender Corporation. In 1976, he served as chairman of the Charleston County Council. A widely circulated photograph shows him, as chairman, and Elizabeth, age seven, cutting the ribbon to open the Kiawah Island resort to the public. Mr. Stuckey was the Democratic nominee for Congress in 1986. He has served as chairman of the Carolina Lowcountry Chapter of the American Red Cross and the Charleston County Democratic Party, and as president of both the Charleston Rotary Club and the Gibbes Museum of Art. Also, he served five terms on the South Carolina Bar House of Delegates.

In law school Elizabeth Stuckey Murphy was elected to the Wig and Robe honor society for "excellence and proficiency in legal studies," clerked for the chief judge of the South Carolina Court of Appeals, and received the prestigious Corpus Juris Secundum awards for the highest averages in both torts and evidence. Christopher L. Murphy focuses on criminal and civil trials, condemnation actions, and DirecTV litigation. He clerked for circuit court judge John L. Breeden, Jr. and is a certified mediator and arbitrator. Sandra S. Garvin has been Mr. Stuckey's legal secretary for 33 years.

Stuckey Law Offices enjoys the distinction of an AV rating by Martindale-Hubbell. According to the *South Carolina Lawyer*, the firm received the largest jury verdict in the state in 2004.

Stuckey Law Offices consists of James A. Stuckey, Jr., his daughter, Elizabeth Stuckey Murphy, and his son-in-law, Christopher L. Murphy.

LAW OFFICE OF MARK C. TANENBAUM

FOR THREE DECADES, MARK C. TANENBAUM HAS BEEN devoted to helping those who have been hurt by the carelessness of others. The law office of Mark C. Tanenbaum was formed in 1980. The core of the longstanding firm's practice is representing victims of negligence in product liability actions, premises liability cases, auto collisions, auto crashworthiness cases, toxic torts, bad faith insurance claims, and elder abuse and neglect cases.

"We leave no stone unturned when it comes to determining what went wrong and in trying to set it right," declares Mark Tanenbaum. "Our five-lawyer team has been successful in gaining the expertise and the means to "stand toe-to-toe with the corporate giants."

The firm has often helped engineer solutions to safety issues, bringing responsibility to the marketplace that otherwise wouldn't exist. In a recent case against a state highway department and a private paving contractor, the firm won a victory not only for its clients, but for the public as well. Faulty paving methods on an interstate highway led to more than 600 accidents, 10 deaths, and many other severe injuries. Calling on the best experts in the country, the firm determined what had gone wrong with the repaving and made substantial financial recoveries for their clients. "We also forced a change in the way the highway department repaves all interstate roads, so that these sorts of tragedies won't happen again," explains Tanenbaum. "We believe it is the duty of the plaintiff trial lawyer to help make this a better environment for all. From the beginning of my career, I saw the profession as a way to put ordinary people on an equal footing with corporate America and the government. We remain dedicated to that ideal."

After graduating from the University of South Carolina School of Law in 1973, Tanenbaum helped start the Public Defenders office for Charleston County, and the partnership of Gibbs, Gaillard, Rowell & Tanenbaum, before going out on his own in 1980. Dedicated to representing victims of negligence, his firm has won many important and influential cases, particularly in the areas of tenant rights, product liability, and personal injury. Its work in the area of tenant rights has led to additional protection for tenants in South Carolina.

Named to *The Best Lawyers of America* since 1995, Tanenbaum is a member of the Charleston County Bar Association and served as president from 2002 to 2003. He has served on the Board of Governors and on the Executive Committee of the South Carolina Trial Lawyers Association, is a Sustaining Member of the Association of Trial Lawyers of America, is a member of the Attorneys Information Exchange Group, and is President of the Charleston chapter of the American Board of Trial Advocates.

Each member of the Tanenbaum firm brings a vital strength to the table. Mia Lauren Maness, who clerked for the Honorable Weston Houck, U.S. District Court Judge of South Carolina, specializes in product liability, tort, and personal injury. Stephen A. Butaitis specializes in personal injury cases, emphasizing nursing home abuse and neglect cases. Jonathan F. Krell, who clerked for the Honorable Gerald Smoak, 14th Judicial Circuit, and Christian A. Marcum, former Clerk to the Honorable Kaye Hearn, Chief Judge, South Carolina Court of Appeals, focus on personal injury and product liability.

SWOPE LAW FIRM, P.A.

THE SWOPE LAW FIRM, FOUNDED IN 2001, IS COMPRISED of the husband-and-wife team of William and Denise Swope. The practice places strong emphasis on tailoring their services to meet the individual needs of their clients. "We are committed to providing quality legal services to our clients in the Charleston community in the areas of family and criminal law," says Denise.

Denise received her Bachelor of Arts and her J.D. degrees from the University of South Carolina. She began her career at the Solicitor's Office in Charleston in 1991 and the same year she returned to the Lowcountry to open her own practice, Law Offices of Denise Grainger Swope, Esquire, while also teaching in the Continuing Education Program at the University of South Carolina. She has also taught law courses at Charleston Southern University since 1994.

William received his B.S. degree from Vanderbilt University and his J.D. degree from the University of South Carolina Law School. He began his legal career at the Laddaga Law Firm in 1991, while also teaching in the Continuing Education Program at the University of South Carolina. In 1993, he opened his own practice, Law Offices of William Koatesworth Swope, where he remained until 1998. William has also taught at Charleston Southern University since 2000.

The Swope Law Firm believes in giving back to the Lowcountry and is therefore dedicated to staying involved in the community. Denise and William both have extensive involvement in civic organizations and have both received vast recognition for their work.

TESCHNER LAW FIRM, LLC

TESCHNER LAW FIRM, LLC PROVIDES its clients with legal services to meet their estate and business needs with tax efficiency and practicality.

Susan Teschner's business, tax, and accounting background is the cornerstone to accomplishing this goal. A graduate of NYU School of Law's joint J.D./LL.M. program, Ms. Teschner is armed with a top legal and taxation education. Her extensive C.P.A. experience prior to entering law school lends itself to working with accountants and clients to marry the practical application with her legal advice. Ms. Teschner is also an active member of the community that she serves. In 2003, she was named as one of Charleston's Forty Under 40 by the *Charleston Regional Business Journal* and has worked hard to position herself at the forefront of Charleston's legal community.

Kenneth Kolb, a graduate of the University of South Carolina School of Law and an associate of the Teschner Law Firm, supplements Ms. Teschner's practice. Mr. Kolb worked as a paralegal prior to entering law school to understand the practical application of estate planning and business law. Mr. Kolb works closely with clients to ensure that their legal documents match their desires and to implement the client's estate and business plans.

The staff of the Teschner Law Firm is also a significant component to the success of the firm. Christy Waltz has been with the firm since it opened its doors and an integral part of the firm's activities. Her attention to the needs of their clients is unparalleled. Assistants Bret Lucarelli and Irene Greene complete the Teschner Law Firm's family and provide the friendly attention that the firm believes clients deserve.

PAUL E. TINKLER

Paul Tinkler opened a solo practice in March 2001 after spending 22 pleasurable years working with Robert Wallace at Wallace & Tinkler. Since that time, Mr. Tinkler has moved from the Franke building to his current location downtown. More recently, associates Colleen Condon and Spiro Ferderigos have joined Mr. Tinkler.

Mr. Tinkler specializes in domestic litigation, medical malpractice, business litigation, and personal injury. He also spends a substantial amount of time as a mediator.

Mr. Tinkler grew up in Greenwood, South Carolina. After graduating from Erskine College and the University of South Carolina School of Law, he worked as a clerk with state circuit court judge Klyde Robinson until beginning his work with Robert Wallace. In 1985, Mr. Tinkler represented the plaintiff in *Ludwick v. This Minute of Carolina, Inc.* This created the public policy exception to the at-will employment doctrine.

Today, Mr. Tinkler serves as a member of the Charleston City Council. He is also a member of the American Association of Trial Lawyers, the South Carolina Association of Trial Lawyers, the Charleston County Bar, and the South Carolina Bar. A former South Carolina chess champion, Mr. Tinkler remains an active chess player. He has also served as an assistant Boy Scout leader. His family includes his wife, Elizabeth ("Libby"), daughter Mary, and son William.

GEOFFREY H. WAGGONER

Formerly a premedical student, attorney Geoffrey H. Waggoner maintains a lifelong interest in medical matters. The North Charleston attorney subscribes to and regularly peruses several leading medical journals, a pastime which helps him with his medical negligence and personal injury practice. "I try to keep my hand in it," says Waggoner. "Many of my cases involve serious injuries or unusual medical issues."

The son of a *New York Times* correspondent, Waggoner grew up in Europe and New Jersey. Discovering an affinity for the Southeast, he graduated from Duke University and the University of South Carolina's School of Law (1977), and settled in Charleston. As a law student in Columbia, he had been advised against starting his practice on Charleston's Broad Street, long the city's legal hub. "I was told I might not fit in with the Charleston establishment, so I struck out in what was then the wilderness—North Charleston," he says. After 28 years of practice, three daughters born in Charleston, and "four tough years" on the Charleston County School Board, however, Waggoner says he now feels "fully integrated into the Charleston legal scene."

Named in the 2003-2004 and subsequent editions of *The Best Lawyers in America,* Waggoner also worked as a criminal investigator in Newark, New Jersey, and has served as Chairman of the Board of the Charleston area CrimeStoppers. "I guess I'm part cop," laughs the plaintiff's lawyer, "It's the good guy-bad guy thing!"

BEATRICE E. WHITTEN

BEATRICE E. WHITTEN RECEIVED her B.S. degree from Baptist College of Charleston (now Charleston Southern University) in 1987 and her J.D. degree from the University of South Carolina School of Law in 1990. She worked with Justin O'Toole Lucey at Lucey & Whitten before starting her own practice in 1993. Today, Ms. Whitten continues to work as a sole practitioner, specializing in social security disability, probate, family, and mediation law.

Ms. Whitten has a great deal of experience with social security disability, working, she says, "at all phases, starting with people who haven't even applied yet going up to appeals in the federal district court." Ms. Whitten also has a reputation as being an expert in probate law, advising many clients and colleagues in this area. Before earning her law degree she worked as a clerk in the probate court for ten years. For the past 12 years, she has taught a class on probate law at Trident Technical College, where she is an adjunct professor.

As a mediator, Ms. Whitten serves two distinct roles. First, she works as a certified civil mediator, mediating family and civil disputes. Second, she is a contract mediator for the United States Postal Service. This work involves mediating equal opportunity employment disputes.

In 1990, Ms. Whitten was the recipient of the Pro Bono Service Award. She is a member of the South Carolina Bar and South Carolina Women Lawyers Associations.

S. THOMAS WORLEY, JR., ATTORNEY AT LAW

TOM WORLEY'S PRACTICE BEGAN IN 1973 IN PARTNERSHIP with the now deceased John Bradley, a 14-year veteran of the state legislature and former chairman of the Joint Delegation. There was just one other lawyer practicing in Mt. Pleasant during those early years. The decision to set up shop in the then-quiet area proved visionary. "Mt. Pleasant has really boomed, creating a large volume of real estate work here," explains Worley, who discovered an affinity for real estate law fresh out of the University of South Carolina's School of Law during his first job with a downtown law firm. "It's a great place to be." In a town that's grown to accommodate more than 200 law practices, Worley remains the longest actively practicing attorney with the oldest continuing law practice.

As well as real estate closings, Worley's general practice includes family court, probate, and general civil litigation. "I like the daily variety," says Worley. He's also done some criminal work. A highlight of his practice, in fact, occurred when he was co-appointed to represent a man charged with murder, with the state seeking the death penalty. The first trial ended in a mistrial. Before the second trial, the state dropped the death penalty demand.

A graduateof The Citadel, Worley served for 17 years as a board member for the Charleston County Department of Social Services. Active in First Baptist Church, he teaches Sunday school and enjoys time with his family.

APPENDIX

PAST PRESIDENTS OF THE CHARLESTON COUNTY BAR ASSOCIATION

1924-1925
T. W. Bacot

1925-1926
Arthur R. Young

1926-1927
Arthur R. Young

1927-1928
J.N. Nathans

1928-1929
J. N. Nathans

1929-1930
John I. Cosgrove

1930-1931
John I. Cosgrove

1931-1932
H. L. Erckmann

1932-1933
H. L. Erckmann

1933-1934
Gordon Miller

1934-1935
Gordon Miller

1935-1936
George F. vonKolnitz

1936-1937
George F. vonKolnitz

1937-1938
Sidney Rittenberg

1938-1939
Julian Mitchell, Jr.

1939-1940
George L. Buist

1940-1941
Lionel K. Legge

1941-1942
Nathaniel B. Barnwell

1942-1943
Augustine T. Smythe

1943-1944
Malcolm E. Crosland

1944-1945
Harold A. Mouzon

1945-1946
J. C. Long

1946-1947
Henry Buist, Jr.

1947-1948
Thomas P. Stoney

1948-1949
Paul M. Macmillan

1949-1950
J. D. E. Meyer

1950-1951
Frank H. Bailey

1951-1952
Arthur Rittenberg

1952-1953
Coming Ball Gibbs

1953-1954
Brantley Seymour

1954-1955
Robert McC. Figg, Jr.

1955-1956
Louis M. Shimel

1956-1957
Frederick H. Horlbeck

1957-1958
Edward K. Pritchard

1958-1959
G. L. Buist Rivers

1959-1960
Gedney M. Howe, Jr.

1960-1961
Charles W. Waring

1961-1962
T. Allen Legare, Jr.

1962-1963
Ben Scott Whaley

1963-1964
Morris D. Rosen

1964-1965
Huger Sinkler

1965-1966
J. C. Hare

1966-1967
Charles H. Gibbs

1967-1968
Laurence O. Stoney

1968-1969
William H. Grimball, Jr.

1969-1970
S. S. Seidemann

1970-1971
Augustine T. Smythe, Jr.

1971-1972
J. Kenneth Rentiers

1972-1973
Joseph R. Young

1973-1974
Irving Levkoff

1974-1975
A. Baron Holmes, III

1975-1976
Gaines W. Smith

1976-1977
E. Lloyd Wilcox

1977-1978
I. M. Goldberg

1978-1979
D. A. Brockington

1979-1980
Robert M. Hollings

1980-1981
Joseph H. McGee

1981-1982
A. Arthur Rosenblum

1982-1983
Joseph W. Cabaniss

1983-1984
Robert B. Wallace

1984-1985
Nathaniel L. Barnwell

1985-1986
Arthur Howe

1986-1987
Robert Patterson

1987-1988
Benjamin A. Moore

1988-1989
Charles Goldberg

1989-1990
Benjamin Goldberg

1990-1991
Robert Clement, Jr.

1991-1992
Capers G. Barr, III

1992-1993
Elliott T. Halio

1993-1994
Coming B. Gibbs, Jr.

1994-1995
John M. Bleecker, Jr.

1995-1996
Lee M. Robinson

1996-1997
E. Bart Daniel

1997-1998
John P. Linton

1998-1999
Frances Cantwell

1999-2000
M. Dawes Cooke, Jr.

2000-2001
Michael Moloney

2001-2001
Brady Hair

2002-2002
Douglas Pratt-Thomas

2003-2004
Mark Tanenbaum

2004-2005
Carol Ervin

2005-2006
Francis X. McCann

BIBLIOGRAPHY

Baldwin, Agnes Leland, *First Settlers of South Carolina, 1670-1680*, University of South Carolina Press, Columbia, South Carolina, 1969.

Bittker, Boris I. and Lawrence Lokken, *Federal Taxation of Income, Estates and Gifts*, Vol. I, 3rd edition, Warren, Gorham and Lamont, 2003.

Bradford, M. E., "The Prophetic Politics of Rawlings Lowndes," *Southern Partisan Magazine*, Columbia, South Carolina, Spring 1987.

Canady, Joy Paul, Jr., *Gentlemen of the Bar, Lawyers in Colonial South Carolina History*, Garland Publishing, New York, 1987.

Cote, Richard N., *Mary's World, Love, War and Family Ties in Nineteenth-Century Charleston*, Corinthian Books, Mount Pleasant, South Carolina, 2001.

Coit, Margaret, L. and John C. Calhoun, *American Portrait*, University of South Carolina Press, Columbia, South Carolina, 1950.

Cupp, Ruth Williams, *Portia Steps Up to the Bar, First Women Lawyers of South Carolina*, Ivy House Publishing, Raleigh, North Carolina, 2003.

Edgar, Walter, *South Carolina, A History*, University of South Carolina Press, Columbia, South Carolina, 1998.

Elzas, Barnett A., *A Document Relative to a Proposed Settlement of Jews in South Carolina in 1748*, S.C.P.M. Misc. v86, No. 9, Charleston Library Society, Charleston, South Carolina.

Howe, Belle, *Re: Gedney Main Howe, Jr., 1914-1981*, Privately Published, Action Printing, Adamsville, Alabama, 1985.

Hugue, L. Lynn, *Nicholas Trott:* "A Man of Law and Letters," *South Carolina Historical Magazine*, Vol. 76, No. 1, South Carolina Historical Society, Charleston, South Carolina, 1975.

Law, James H., *John and Edward Rutledge of South Carolina*, University of South Carolina Press, Columbia, South Carolina, 1997.

Lener, Gerde, *The Grimke Sisters of South Carolina, Rebels Against Slavery*, Houghton Mifflin Company, Boston, Massachusetts, 1967.

Littlejohn, C. Bruce, *Littlejohn's Half Century at the Bench and Bar*, South Carolina Bar Foundation, Columbia, South Carolina, 1987.

May, John Amasa and Joan Reynolds Faunt, *South Carolina Secedes*, The South Carolina Confederate War Centennial Commission, 1960.

McCrady, Edward, *The History of South Carolina Under the Proprietary Government, 1670-1719*, Macmillan Publishers Limited, 1897.

McNeil, Jim, *Charleston's Navy Yard*, Naval Civilian Administrators Association, Charleston, South Carolina, 1985.

Meigs, William Montgomery, *The Life of John Caldwell Calhoun*, Vol. I, The Neale Publishing Company, 1917, Reprinted by DaCapo Press, New York, 1970.

Moise, Warren, *Rebellion in the Temple of Justice: The Federal and State Courts in South Carolina During the War Between the States*, iUniverse Inc., New York, Lincoln, Shanghai, 2003.

Moore, John Hammond, *Southern Homefront, 1861-1865*, Summerhouse Press, Columbia, South Carolina, 1998.

Moore, John Hammond, *South Carolina in the 1880s, A Gazetteer*, Sandlapper Press, Inc., Orangeburg, South Carolina, 1989.

New South Associates, *Restoration Archeology At the Charleston County Courthouse Site*, Stone Mountain Georgia, Privately printed, 1993.

O'Neall, John Belton, *Biographical Sketches of the Bench and Bar of South Carolina*, Vols 1 & 2, The Reprint Company Publishers, 1975.

Pease, William H. and Jane H. Pease, *James Louis Petigru, Southern Conservative, Southern Dissenter*, University of Georgia Press, Athens and London, 1995.

Poston, Jonathan H., *The Buildings of Charleston*, University of South Carolina Press, Columbia, South Carolina, 1997.

Ramsey, David, M.D., *First Settlement in 1670 to the Year 1803*, Vol. II, Hinson Collection, Vol. 2, Charleston Library Society, Charleston, South Carolina.

Rogers, George C., Jr., *Generations of Lawyers, Attorneys of the South Carolina Bar*, South Carolina Foundation (1992).

Rosen, Robert, *A Short History of South Carolina*, Lexikos Press, (1982).

Rosen, Robert N., *The Jewish Confederates*, University of South Carolina Press, Columbia, South Carolina, 2000.

Rosen, Robert N., *Confederate Charleston*, University of South Carolina Press, Columbia, South Carolina, 1994.

Severens, Martha R. and Charles L. Wyrick, Jr., Compiled by Charles Fraser of Charleston, *Essays on the Man, His Art and His Times*, Carolina Art Association, Charleston, South Carolina, 1993.

Underwood, James Lowell and W. Lewis Burke, Jr., Editors, *At Freedom's Door, African American Founding Fathers and Lawyers in Reconstruction*, University of South Carolina Press, Columbia, South Carolina, 2000.

Wallace, David Duncan, *South Carolina, A Short History*, University of South Carolina Press, Columbia, South Carolina, 1961.

INDEX

Page numbers in italics show an illustration

D

E

F

G

INDEX TO LAW FIRM HISTORIES

ACKNOWLEDGMENTS

PATRONS

HALIO & HALIO • JOSEPH P. CERATO • MIKELL SCARBOROUGH • ROBERTSON LAW FIRM • ROBERT L. GAILLARD
BEN F. MACK • BARR UNGER & MCINTOSH • WILLIAM A. GREEN

THE PUBLISHER WOULD LIKE TO THANK the following sources for granting permission to reproduce pictures from their collections in this book:

2-3: Robin McDonald. 4-5: Kevin Curran. 6-7: Kevin Curran. 8: Library of Congress. 9: South Carolina Historical Society. 10: (above) Library of Congress; (below) South Carolina Historical Society. 11: (above) Robin McDonald; (below) South Carolina Historical Society. 12: Library of Congress. 13: South Carolina Historical Society. 14: Library of Congress. 15: Library of Congress. 16: South Carolina Historical Society. 17: South Carolina Historical Society. 18: South Carolina Historical Society. 19: South Carolina Historical Society. 20: Library of Congress. 22: (above) Library of Congress; (center) South Carolina Historical Society; (below) South Carolina Historical Society. 23: South Carolina Historical Society. 24: (above) South Carolina Historical Society; (below) Robin McDonald. 25: (above) Library of Congress; (below) South Carolina Historical Society. 26: (above) Library of Congress; (below) South Carolina Historical Society. 27: (above) South Carolina Historical Society; (below) Library of Congress. 28: (both) Library of Congress. 29: South Carolina Historical Society. 30: South Carolina Historical Society. 31: Library of Congress. 32: (both) Library of Congress. 33: Public Domain. 34: Robin McDonald. 35: Library of Congress. 36: (above) Robin McDonald; (below) South Carolina Historical Society. 37: Library of Congress. 38: (both) Library of Congress. 39: Library of Congress. 40: South Carolina Historical Society. 41: Library of Congress. 42: (both) Library of Congress. 43: Library of Congress. 44: (above) South Carolina Historical Society; (below) Library of Congress. 45: (both) South Carolina Historical Society. 46: Library of Congress. 47: (both) Library of Congress. 48: Library of Congress. 48-49: Library of Congress. 50: South Carolina Historical Society. 51: (above) South Carolina Historical Society; (below) Library of Congress. 52: South Carolina Historical Society. 54: Library of Congress. 56: Library of Congress. 57: (both) South Carolina Historical Society. 58: South Carolina Historical Society. 59: South Carolina Historical Society. 60: Library of Congress. 61: Library of Congress. 62: Library of Congress. 63: South Carolina Historical Society. 65: South Carolina Historical Society. 66: South Carolina Historical Society. 67: South Carolina Historical Society. 68: South Carolina Historical Society. 69: South Carolina Historical Society. 70: South Carolina Historical Society. 71: South Carolina Historical Society. 72: South Carolina Historical Society. 73: Portrait by Kevin Curran. 74: Courtesy Buist Moore Smythe McGee. 75: Courtesy Gaines W. Smith. 76: Ruth W. Cupp. 77: Library of Congress. 79: Courtesy Morris D. Rosen. 80: Courtesy Robert B. Wallace. 81: Courtesy Buist Moore Smythe McGee. 82: Library of Congress. 83: South Carolina Port Authority. 84: Ruth W. Cupp. 86: South Carolina Historical Society. 87: South Carolina Historical Society. 88: Courtesy J. Lawrence Duffy. 89: Courtesy Charles H. Gibbs, Jr. 90: South Caroliniana Library, University of South Carolina. 91: Courtesy Charles S. Goldberg. 92: Mike Coker. 93. Courtesy Gedney Howe, III. 95: National Weather Service. 96. (above) Courtesy Judge Richard E. Field; (below) Courtesy Buist Moore Smythe McGee. 97: Ruth W. Cupp. 98: Courtesy Thomas S. Tisdale. 99: Courtesy Buist Moore Smythe McGee. 100: Courtesy Claire Goldberg. 101: (both) National Weather Service. 103: Kevin Curran. 104: Courtesy John M. Bleecker, Jr. 105: Courtesy Morris D. Rosen. 107: (both) Ruth W. Cupp. 108: Kevin Curran. 109: Charleston School of Law. 110. Courtesy J. Brady Hair. 111. Kevin Curran. 112: (above) Courtesy Gerry Kaynard; (below) Charleston School of Law. 113: (above) Charleston School of Law; (below) Courtesy Brent's on Broad. 115: Library of Congress. 116-117: Kevin Curran.